THE FORGOTTEN

Reconstructing and Reclaiming African Spirituality in the Post-Truth Era

Teboho Pitso

SUN PRESS

First edition 2023

ISBN 978-1-991201-96-6
ISBN 978-1-991201-97-3 (e-book)
https://doi.org/10.52779/9781991201973

Set in Adobe Garamond Pro 11/13.2

Typesetting and production by African Sun Media
Cover design by African Sun Media Create

SUN PReSS is an imprint of African Sun Media. Scholarly, professional and reference works are published under this imprint in print and electronic formats.

Publications can be ordered from:
orders@africansunmedia.co.za
Takealot: bit.ly/2monsfl
Google Books: bit.ly/2k1Uilm
africansunmedia.store.it.si *(e-books)*
Amazon Kindle: amzn.to/2ktL.pkL
JSTOR: https://bit.ly/3udc057

Visit africansunmedia.co.za for more information.

―――――――――――――――――――――

"I agree with the author that: 'Time has come for the world to dance once more to the rhythms of African genius so the world could proceed to the next levels of advancement and civilisation.' The West has determined for too long what constitutes civilisation. It is refreshing to have projects like this which offer perspectives other than Western philosophical thought."

– Reverend Minister Georgina Kwanima Boateng –
Presbyterian Church of Ghana and
Columbia Theological Seminary, Georgia, USA

―――――――――――――――――――――

TABLE OF CONTENTS

DEDICATION

The book is dedicated to the melanin-rich tellurians who were spiritually privileged to traverse, tame, and mollycoddle the part of earth that is ensconced between two great oceans we are yet to name as their rightful heir. This earthly part claims a border on the Southern part of the Mediterranean Sea and is pregnant with natural resources of all kinds. It attracts envy. It is a place of plenty that shaped the African worldview and a deep sense of munificence that led to our ubuNtu cultural orientation. The envious kind sought to arrest our kindness and capture as well as stunt our superior intellectual capacity that gave the world civilisation, philosophy, and science to seize our resources for selfish, narrow interests. In attempts to vitiate our solidarity, they imposed their egocentric, highly individualistic culture and belief systems on us as well as distort history to advance their superiority complex, a smugness that blinds truthful accounts of history.

Those scholars who have over years ventured deep into archives, Egyptian stelae, cuneiform scripts and other ancient scrolls, and who painstakingly reconstructed Africa's role in human progress, in particular areas such as science, philosophy, mathematics, and spirituality, I dedicate this book to your efforts of restoring our collective dignity. Posterity will forever be grateful to all your scholarly endeavours. Here is yet another modest contribution to such a restorative project.

I also dedicate the book to my former colleague and friend, Paul Mokhoabane, whose departure to the other side left me with a void that is hard to fill. *Tsamaya ka kgotso, tsela tsoeu! Ha re nne re phure leshoetla le ha o le motsheo.*

The Kunene family in Vaalpark is commended for successful completion of mediumship development, embracing and practising African spirituality as well as contributing to the well-being of our African brothers and sisters through contributing to their re-reconceptualisation of their identities in terms of African spirituality and living their lives in terms of African precepts. *Malambole phambili!*

Mohale Pitso for the challenges ahead: *Qina Mthimkhulu, Bhungane!*

ACKNOWLEDGEMENTS

Matshidiso Qoba Mthimkhulu (aka Tshidi), my life partner, has played a major role towards maturing my spirituality and walking beside me on this pilgrimage of assisting people, in particular Africans, to reclaim and re-reconceptualise their identities through African spirituality and philosophy. Africans were stripped of their collective dignity through religious puffery about 400 years ago. It is not the superior logic of Abrahamic religions that proselytised Africans, but a combination of coercion, slavery, menticide and colonial conquests of Africa that created an enabling environment for the extirpation of African spirituality and identity, and the total elimination of African heritage that helped advance scientific thought and civilisation, and offer superior spirituality based on evidence. African spirituality is an evidence-led practice. Those who have had African spiritual awakening serve as witness accounts that lead to tacit knowing, a key episteme in African worldview.

I am also indebted to my now incorporeal fathers, Sechele Qoba Mthimkhulu, Mohale George Pitso Mthimkhulu, Makoala Abel Qoba Mthimkhulu, Pule Samuel Pitso Mthimkhulu, Molefi John Ramatsebe, Liphaphang Joseph Pitso Mthimkhulu, Ndoli Pitso Mthimkhulu, as well as Sabata Andries Mateba Mthimkhulu.

A special tribute to my mothers who have already moved on to the realm beyond the azure dome, Mateboho Ramatsebe and Mathapelo Mateba Mthimkhulu.

Malefane Lebusa is acknowledged for the book *Diboko tsa Basotho* by Fezekile Futhwa that has helped many to find their *isithakazelo/ ho thella/ thoko* and reclaim their identities and reconnect with their ancestral homes (*isibaya/ lesaka*). The contribution of Fezekile Futhwa to African spirituality and the scholarship of African Studies is immeasurable.

Tseko Qoba Mthimkhulu is acknowledged for quickly learning the African virtue of Temperance, the idea that guests of the house should leave the house having been given some kind of sustenance in true African culture. A great cook he has become. Muzikayise Qoba Mthimkhulu for embracing his spiritual gift and using it to make the world a slightly better place. Sineqiniso Mthimkhulu for choosing this spiritual path.

To the Molapo family in Kiblerpark, King Thesele, Prince Masilo, Princess Manapo, and Princesses Napo and Motebang for embracing their African identity as direct descendants of King Moshoeshoe. Ramatsebe family in Zone 14, Sebokeng, for persistence.

FOREWORD

I am grateful for the opportunity to write a brief foreword for Teboho Pitso's ground-breaking work, *The Forgotten: Reconstructing and Reclaiming African Spirituality in the Post-Truth Era*. I have always admired Pitso's work and this book is no different. I thoroughly enjoyed reading it and my first conclusion was that this book is as historical as it is timely. That is, Pitso traces the history of African spirituality and brings it to bear on our present moment in the post-truth era. This work addresses central questions around the relationship between Western colonisation and African spirituality. Pitso destabilises the longstanding myths espoused by European colonisers and missionaries. He brings Christianity back to its African origins in brilliant prose and thorough research. Most importantly, Pitso celebrates African genius in all its forms, from advances in religion to scientific discoveries.

Pitso does an excellent job of analysing the pitfalls of Western historical methods that have largely obscured and neglected the role of African thinkers and African spirituality, both in terms of Christianity and world civilisation. This book is an important work for anyone interested in the scholarly study of history and African religion. Pitso carefully dissects how false assumptions about religion in Africa have seeped into our public consciousness, which has been naturalised. The task at hand, which Pitso does so well, is challenging these myths with historical data and research that cast a new and more favourable light upon African peoples and their spirituality. For example, Pitso grapples with the term 'belief' and explores its linguistic and historical underpinnings to expose its Western leanings.

I am particularly impressed by Pitso's clarion call for Ubuntu philosophy. Ubuntu is shared across many cultures in Africa and advocates for a communal view of life. It teaches that we are all related in deep spiritual and inextricable ways. Pitso's analysis of Ubuntu philosophical history and its potential remedies for our current issues is a refreshing reminder that we have in our cultural mores the moral tools and spiritual roots to face our pressing crises. I walk away from Pitso's moving book feeling both informed and hopeful that the world will acknowledge and incorporate African philosophy and spirituality. Pitso urges us to seek justice by reconnecting with Ubuntu, which he also reconciles with Christian teachings. Weaving together African cosmology and Biblical interpretation, this book traces the complex history of Christianity in Africa. Pitso makes the powerful and convincing argument that African spirituality shaped Christianity in significant ways.

In this book, Pitso describes African spirituality as love, truth and equality. While Pitso notes the difference between the diverse cultures and traditions in Africa, he considers the underlying principles of African religiosity a reflection of shared philosophies across these myriads of traditions. I see his philosophy as an extension of John Mbiti's work *African Religions and Philosophies* (1969), which sought to paint a portrait of the central philosophies and spirituality shared among African religions. Pitso also does an outstanding job at connecting the strength of African spirituality to everyday religious practices. For example, in Chapter 5, Pitso describes how African spirituality's emphasis on fortitude guides mental strength and well-being. Throughout this book, Pitso draws upon science, religious doctrines, and history to build a complex and fascinating argument about the merits of African spiritualities. Such an argument is much needed in a time of fierce social debate regarding the teachings and role of religion in African society.

Lastly, Pitso engages with important ethical concepts such as justice through the lens of African spirituality. He argues that justice emanates from the caring community cultivated by African spirituality and the Ubuntu philosophy. His analysis of justice and spirituality sheds light on the ways in which African religious traditions embrace a diversity of thought and encourage public dialogue. In addition to historical and religious scholarly analysis, Pitso offers readers practical advice on how to understand and practise key tenets of African spirituality such as prudence. In other words, Pitso helps the readers apply his research to their spiritual journeys. I have worked in the field of African religions my entire career and am proud to see this book contribute to the field in so many important ways. Pitso makes the significant knowledge contribution of analysing the powerful yet often overlooked roots of Christianity in Africa.

Professor Jacob K. Olupona

Director of Graduate Studies
Professor of African and African American Studies
The Faculty of Arts and Sciences
Harvard Divinity School
Harvard University

Faculty Associate
Weatherhead Centre for International Affairs

WHY THIS BOOK?

Festive seasons celebrations (Western Christmas, new year based on Western winter solstice), colonial public statues including those in some schools and universities, heritage days, prescribed materials in education are never there to reflect what happened in the past or what society must really know for sure. They are also not there to trigger our memory and make our past vivid and clear. They are there to effect forgetting because forgetting as Ernest Renan suggests *"is a crucial factor in the creation of a nation"*. Forgetting is intended to invariably effect obliviousness to acts of violence, coercion and menticide that served to create a nation. The dominant power structures in society benefit from forgetting, because forgetting attempts to eliminate all forms of remembrance that could trigger challenges to national metanarratives that sustain such power. Memory is therefore subversive in nature because it poses a struggle against power and mass deception. It is rare that suffering and humiliation of a defeated sector in society gets commemorated in ways that deserve solemn reflection on the traumatic experiences of our ancestral past instead official commemorations become ubiquitous as tools of forgetting, celebrations of our own mental capture. Commemorations are intended to manipulate our perceptions of the past and relegate them to the cesspool of the periphery to enforce forgetting. Social memory becomes reduced to unworthy surface images that protect past mistakes so they can validate dominant power and its inherent racial, gender as well as economic inequality. The right to dig deep into the past and tell our own stories represents the inalienable right to restoration of our dignity and sense of self-worth. We cannot become active participants in our own humiliation and in subversion of our interests. Participating actively to official commemorations achieves that feat. This book is a start, a struggle against *"abuse of memory"* and against forgetting. *Hetla mo Africa!* Look back and re-conquer your pain, make it visible, transparent and reclaim your captured soul as the alternative is too ghastly to contemplate. What is **forgotten** can be retrieved. What was stolen such as land can be reclaimed. Our social memory is key, hence this book. It seeks to reconstruct, reclaim, restore and retrieve our true self from the scrapheap of history where our collective memory was deliberately sent to die and decompose to preserve a version of a nation the metanarratives dictate.

RECLAMATION PROJECT

Introduction

The project focuses on uncovering lies and myths that sustain the colonial and European supremacist agendas and restores Africa's role in originating civilisation, science, mathematics, philosophy, spirituality, and Christianity. It forms part of questioning the deification of Global North episteme as a universal theory, the intent of which is to marginalise Southern theorisation and other legitimate alternatives. The project thus contributes to Southern theorisation that draws theory from multiple practices and lived experiences of those from the austral geographic location (Global South) whose understanding of time is secular. Such theorisation challenges the embedded Global North perspective as a universal theory and further denounces the imperialist gaze on contemporary science as the sole spectacle and arbiter of its significance in society. The Global South episteme, whose sources are indigenous practices, collective knowing, and collective experiences, has all the right to claim its stake in hallowed spaces of knowledge production.

The project is thus both a retrieval effort and a critique of coloniality (epistemic disobedience) from which its intellectual prowess derives. Scientific social thought has to be, by dint of intellectual prowess, multi-perspectival so other epistemes, in particular those marginalised over time, can claim their stake in the saliences of a global society whose driving force is productive complexity and Society 5.0 precepts of multiple perspectives, connectivity, green economy and virtual interconnectedness as sources of all productivity, including in knowledge generation.

THE DEONTOLOGICAL JUSTIFICATION OF AFRICAN SPIRITUALITY

1. **Intrinsic Morality:** African spirituality is based on ubuNtu philosophy that posits that the **intent** to do good and serve the greater good is the ultimate arbiter of all human action and behaviour. There is no greater responsibility than to strive for equality and the fairer redistribution of resources collectively accumulated.

2. **Ethics of Care:** The insatiable need to share and care for one another as one humanity deriving from Ntu (oneness of humanity) is at the heart of African spirituality, hence the need to be attentive and responsive to the needs of others based on one's requisite competence and capabilities. The responsibility to refer those in need to the competent others depending on the type of need represents the highest level of honour.

3. **Human Action:** Courses of action undertaken based on moral intent should lead to outcomes that benefit the greater good.

4. **Human Dignity:** All people have an inherent sacred value that draws from one's identity, culture and heritage. It is impugnment of the worst kind to attempt to persuade others to reconceptualise their own identities in terms of one's own identity, to compel them to live according to the precepts of one's culture, and to manipulate people into celebrating one's heritage. There is no honour in any form of mental capture.

OTHERED SELF

'Othered self' is when an African or Global South citizen becomes an active agent of imperial voice and helps to voluntarily spread imperialism, foreign belief systems, and European supremacist agendas. At this point, an African or Global South citizen is completely captured mentally and the Western ideology of supremacy is at its most powerful. The imperial voice manipulates Africans or Global South citizens into embracing colonial mindsets, and embedded in this capture are notions of self-hate, self-depreciation, and a sense of worthlessness that renders one helpless and defeated. In this scenario, 'self' has entirely reconceptualised itself in terms of foreign ideas, beliefs and cultures, to a point of feeling shame to express its own identity, belief and culture.

Yet, vestiges of Africanness or indigenous knowledge are not entirely extirpated and come in various distorted forms because who fights oneself without consequences? In the deep of the night, glaring emptiness in a captured African or Global South citizen persists and gnaws at one's sense of true self. African or Global South voices whisper incessantly in the dark, signalling their searing deprivation and abandonment in the contemporary medley of all cultures. The shrill sound of empowerment beckons from the wilderness to fill the mindset bereft of African or Global South cognitive content, a perennial *infra dignitatem*. This way, the unctuous attempt to be validated and loved by imperial powers diminishes and one's African or Global South dignity is restored. In this sense, the world gains multiple perspectives that enrich our lives and our collective march to a multi-perspectival approach to complex problem-solving as a truly global democratic theorisation becomes real. Domination of the world, the legacy of white supremacy, becomes an abominable affront and an ignominy of our unsavoury past best left in the scrapheap of our undesirable history where only the demented seek hope.

DECOLONISING MY SOUL: MY JOURNEY TO RECLAIM AFRICAN SPIRITUALITY

Wangui wa Kamonji (The Elephant @theelephantinfo)

"At 11pm on Thursday, 20th October 2011, I turn the last page of *Coconut* by Kopano Matlwa, and I know I am not going to church again [...] having been a staunch Catholic.

"After seven years of being on the journey [...] I have begun to wonder about the silence around African spirituality, and its persistent labelling as sorcery or devil worship. As a researcher of the environment, I see the connection of these silences and the colonial enterprise which forced forgetting of an all-alive Earth, the ancestors and other un-embodied beings like nature spirits and rendered the earth as a space for domination.

"The questions that propelled me were in the silences. Whereas Christianity, Islam and Hinduism and even Buddhism, had some form and reality for me, I wondered what African religion was, I was never told about it or came across it […] while I was studying in the United States."

Wangui's newly gained perspective and moment of clarity lead to gleaning a New Learning Paradigm.

New Learning Paradigm

1. Gain a new perspective and epiphany – Moment of clarity / realisation of greater truth.

2. Immersion into research.

3. Identify, understand, and make transparent the big unknown (make the public aware of the inherent contradictions this new perspective reveals).

4. Develop a model / paradigm that makes the unknown known.

5. Build a prototype and showcase for critical public scrutiny.

6. Change practice / behaviour.

CONTESTED NAMING OF OUR CONTINENT

Perennial debates exist as to the exact name for our continent and multiple versions of its naming remain contested and mainly unresolved, particularly when writing about our ancient continent, pre-Roman, and colonial conquest. While these variations exist on the naming of our continent, for the purpose of this book, this continent shall be known as Africa as drawn from Kemetic theory.

Pre-Roman and Colonial Conquest Theory

Our ancient, virgin territory was known as Corphye, Ortigia, Lybia, or Ethiopia (*Aethiopia*). These names were used prior to the European settlement in our continent. These names no longer refer to a continent. Rather, some of them today refer to countries in our continent.

Kemetic Theory

The most common name associated with our ancient continent is Alkebulan. It is considered as the only name of indigenous origin and refers to the 'Garden of Eden' or 'Mother of Mankind'. Egyptians are said to have called themselves "*Afru-I-eka*" meaning our birthplace, womb, or motherland. This is the most plausible explanation of how Africa got its name given that Egyptians, pioneers of ancient civilisations, science, medicine, engineering, would most probably have a name for their environment. Furthermore, this Egyptian naming of our continent occurred prior to Roman and European invasion of our continent. This is the reason for and context of its use in this book.

Roman Theory

Our continent, in terms of this school of thought, was named by Romans but there are, at least, two contestable namings. First, Romans are said to have named it after the people they encountered in the Carnage area known as Berber, *Afri*, *Afarak* or "*Afri terra*", hence 'land of *Afri*' or *Afarak* became 'Africa'. Second, it was said to be named after the Roman concept "*Apphrike*" or "*Aprike*", meaning 'not cold' or 'sunny' but referred mostly to Tunisia, Algeria, Libya, and Egypt. There was also a land found south of the Sahara about 2 000 years ago and was called *Aethiopia* (Greek origin) to describe the entire continent.

Africus Theory

Africus is a Yemenite chieftain who attacked and invaded the northern part of our continent in the second millennium and named it after himself. Africus had a deep desire for immortality, hence he named our continent "*Afrikyah*" after himself.

Phoenician Theory

The name, in this perspective, derives from two Phoenician concepts "*frigi*" and "*pharika*", meaning 'corns and fruits', developing into the 'land of corns and fruits' – Africa.

Alkebulan Theory

This is said to be the original name of our continent that was used mainly by Carthagenians (Tunisia) and Ethiopians. It means Garden of Eden, motherland, or womb.

Source:

Iliffe, J. (2007). *Africans: The history of a continent*, 2nd Edition. Cambridge: Cambridge University Press. https://doi.org/10.1017/CBO9780511800375

RESEARCH METHODOLOGY

This book is based on the **Desk Case-Study** research approach. Therefore, huge swathes of materials, documents, books, articles, and stored research on African spirituality were elicited from the Internet and served as the basis of curating knowledge for this book. This candidate research approach is beneficial, because the researcher gets exposed to huge data quantities and multiple perspectives that moderate solipsistic, populist, and polemic tendencies that can otherwise derail the scholarly and scientific approach to this kind of work. In addition, the **experiences and viewpoints** of those individuals that have re-reconceptualised their identities in terms of African culture and spirituality were solicited, and evidence adduced from them is spread throughout the book. **Video-based and audio clip evidence** of those that have undergone the spirit mediumship development have also been used as evidence to support claims in this book.

Immersive research was conducted in Zavora, situated in the northeast of Maputo in the District of Inharime, the province of Inhambane (Mozambique). It is a pristine, virgin territory where electrification is reduced to less than 1% and people still rely mostly on agriculture and traditional modes of irking out a living to provide an epitome of African life. It was a crucial research site given that it depicts African societies and their practices of ubuNtu values and African culture. The roads are mostly impassable by ordinary cars, and 4x4-bakkies are essential ways of accessing these remote places. This has minimised the impact of colonialism on the lived experiences of these villagers, thus retaining its original African culture and spirituality. The greatest benefit of immersive research in this study was to allow me as a researcher to capture the behaviours, cultural practices, emotions and cognitive perceptions of individuals functioning within the collective context and at the very moment when such phenomena occurred. It was the most liberating moment when I was finally accepted as an insider after numerous visits. The benefits of acceptance as an insider are that you get invited to rituals that only members of a community attend, including sensitive ones that involve medicinal use, spirit mediumship, ancient initiation rites of circumcision, as well as rites of passage for the young boys and girls coming into adulthood.

Sources:

McCaston, K. (1998). *Tips for collecting, reviewing and analyzing secondary data*. Atlanta: CARE.
MacDonald, E. & Wilson, H. (2011). *Immersive market research*. Warc Best Practice.

QUOTABLE QUOTES

"Yet, no person can go into the good night of the past and successfully retrieve the truth. We venture deep into the past only by legends and fallible historical methods of inquiry, the outcome of which can best be described as the most probable, while truth is almost unattainable. The past somehow holds the truth to ransom and creates opportunities for unscrupulous predators to set their lure and snares in order to capture the gullible and intellectually lazy for narrow gains" (Chapter 1, page 35 of this volume).

"In our darkest hours, in our deepest despairs, through our sorrows, in our trials and tribulations, our turbulences, in our deepest pain, through unbearable storms and our greatest weaknesses (*phalo e eme le lesemelo*), the African elders counsel: *Hae, hae, hata mabala, khumbul' ekhaya, nenda nyumbani* (go home and reconnect with your spirit and source of power)" (Chapter 3, page 85 of this volume).

"There is a good reason nobody studies history, it just teaches you too much" (Noam Chomsky, 2022).

"The most potent weapon in the hands of the oppressor is the mind of the oppressed" (Biko, 1987:68).

"Alternative ways of thinking about the world certainly persist. But they are readily marginalised as African discussions of indigenous knowledge have shown – intellectually discredited, dropped from the curricula of schools and universities, or ripped off by corporations pursuing intellectual property rights" (Odora-Hoppers & Richards, 2011:84).

EXPANDED VIEW OF REALITY

New Pathways for Exploring Highly Democratic Theorisation

- It has to be inclusive of all sorts of theorisations gleaned on a planetary scale to democratise the knowledge production space. Rigorous justifiability and perspicacity must still be at the heart of this endeavour as well as broadened checks and balances.

- Global North theorists, researchers, and scholars as well as those still harbouring primitive supremacist ideas ought to sober into understanding that the entire human race does produce theory and new knowledge.

- Substantial dialogue with theories, ideas, and methods of data collection from the Global South must take precedence to mainstream such discourses in research and scholarship. This will be a major restoration and reclamation project that could lead to epistemic justice.

- A greater awareness and realisation that a multi-perspectival universal body of knowledge can exist. This should remain the ultimate goal of research and scholarship.

- Science and scholarship ought to embed viewpoints, perspectives, and problems from across the entire globe.

- Knowledge ought to be considered complex and multi-perspectival and should be drawn from multiple places and disciplines.

- Extirpate a warped reality drawn narrowly from the Global North.

- Mainstream the grounding and justification of knowledge generated from other experiences.

- Abandon the colonial and postcolonial science where data collection and application occur in the Global South and theorisation in the Global North.

♦ Self-understanding of global society has to incorporate all knowledge forms.

Source:

Connell, R. (2007). *Southern theory: The global dynamics of knowledge in social science.* New York, NY: Routledge. https://doi.org/10.22459/AHR.44.2008.04

REFRAMING: HOW AFRICA SHAPED CHRISTIANITY

Fact 1:

The model of a European university was shaped within African Christianity and lead to the establishment of the second university in the world, University of Bologna in Italy (1088 CE). The first university in the world was founded by a woman, Fatima Al-Fihri, in Morocco, Africa and named the University of Al-qarawiynn (895 CE).

Fact 2:

The historical and spiritual exegesis of Christianity matured in Africa before being exported to Europe.

Fact 3:

African thinkers developed the very core of ancient Christian dogma.

Fact 4:

Ancient ecumenical decision-making followed African conciliar patterns.

Fact 5:

Western forms of Christian formations were shaped through Africa's monastic discipline.

Fact 6:

Ancient neoplatonic philosophy was developed in Africa and exported to Europe.

Fact 7:

Ancient literary and dialectical competencies that helped shape Christianity were developed and refined in Africa.

Source:

Oden, T.C. (2007). *How Africa shaped the Christian mind: Rediscovering the African seedbed of Western Christianity.* Downers Grove, IL: IVP Books.

AFRICAN NEW YEAR

Part of the forgotten heritage of Africa is the celebration of the African New Year. The many colonised Africans just blindly follow the Gregorian calendar and Western celebrations of their year-end on 31 December and their new year on 1 January. These celebrations occur during the Western winter season, which starts on 1 December and lasts until 31 March. The African New Year marks the end of winter on 31 July and the onset of Spring on 1 August. Spring is named *Selemo* to mark the beginning of a new year. The seasons are divided into Spring (1 August – 31 October), Summer (1 November – 31 January), Autumn (1 February – 30 April), and Winter (1 May – 31 July). This calendar is guided by the reading of stars and moon patterns since time immemorial.

Basotho particularly follow a cluster of seven stars that appears during the New Year when winter makes way for spring. These clusters of stars are called *Selemela* (*Pleiades*) from whence the season of *Selemo* was named and guide Basotho each year about the type of crops to be planted. Basotho architecture and mathematical knowledge is also used in the *ditema* (*litema*) writing system as the capturer of ancestral messages and draws influence from *Selemo*. *Ditema* is a mural art system consisting of decorative and symbolic geometric patterns that were generated inside and outside homesteads through engraving, painting, relieve mouldings, and mosaic. Basotho ethno-astronomy celebrates stars such as *Motjhotjhonono* (comet), *Tosa* (Jupiter), *Mphatlalatsane* (Venus when appearing from the East, morning star – *mphatlalatsane naledi ya meso*), *Sefalabohoho* (Venus when appearing on the west, sunset star), *molalatladi* (milky way, where lightning is said to rest), and others. Basotho had no access to telescopes but knew about Jupiter and its surrounding moons (*Tosa le madinyane a yona*) which could not be seen with the naked eye. My paternal grandfather, Mohale Pitso (1917-1975), used to teach these stars to me and their significance to African daily lives and spirituality when I was around 5 years old.

There are other Africans who celebrate Spring on 1 September. This is based on the Lunar Year, which consists of three seasons of four months each, hence 1 September represents the onset of a New Year and the new season also called *Selemo, Isilemo, Shirimo, Chirimo* and *Kilimia*. This view has its roots in archeo-astronomy. The seasons are divided into the **ploughing period** (1 September – 31 December), **harvesting period** (1 January – 30 April), and **winter period** (1 May – 31 August). The Zulu nation follows this Lunar Year, hence celebrating the New Year on 1 September. Spring, whether celebrated in August or September, marks the period of clearing mother earth, planting and growing fresh produce, as well as conducting rituals of rain-making to ensure that the season of fecundity is secured. This explains the **indispensability of land for Africans as an embodiment of their belief system.**

Source:

Zulu, Z. (2019). The Basotho origin of mathematics – Public Lecture.

READ HERE FIRST

In and around North Africa as well as regions circulating Euphrates River (present-day Iraq) around 5000 and 3000 BCE (before common era), a new concept developed. It included advanced city-states, monuments in the form of North African pyramids, specialised workforces, establishment of public institutions, and the freeing of the human hand in wealth accumulation using technologies to create human conveniences. This concept came about because of a complex diversity of peoples living around one another, using different languages, and setting up distinctive institutions that served civil duties and religious interests (Danesi & Perron, 1999).

This was the onset of civilisation in the entire human race. Yes, Africa gave the world advanced civilisation – a complex social order consisting of super-tribes with a strong signifying order (value-creating system) that gave birth to the concept of super-culture, which went beyond the narrowness of tribal, cultural, and religious propensities. Southern Africa waited until around 1200-1300 CE (common era) to set up a city-state called Maphungubwe in and around the Limpopo valleys. Political power as a societal concept became pervasive in this Maphungubwe society, leading to the classification of people into leaders and commoners, making for the earlier formations of elite politics that resulted in the creation of an economic oligarchy. This state of affairs created conditions for societies to be covertly ruled by the few super-rich individuals who buy and control political power. An oligarchy is a minority of super-rich individuals in society who, in ancient times, took control of trade deals between countries and was enabled by a prevailing political power that marked the onset of ideology, a set of opinions or beliefs about how society should function. The oligarchic ideology attempts to justify the privileges and power of the super-rich elites as enabled by a prevailing political power.

As science, ideology seeks to understand power formations in society. My essential focus is on the formation of super-cultures through a signifying order, and argues that ancient Africa was at the centre of normalising political power and its class ideology through advanced civilisations. It should thus be the one trailblazing in shifting societal power away from political ideologies to a universal cultural heuristics, hence my interest in super-culture and its signifying order. African culture is based on shared resources, the cycle of ubuNtu and communality, all of which banish poverty, unfair resource accumulation and distribution as well as a strong empathy. These African cultural values are described in detail in Pitso's book, *Privileged: Identity, History, Culture and Heritage in the Age of Deep Learning* (2020). The values described in this and many other books, as well as articles on African culture, provide the basis of contribution to a universal cultural heuristics.

A universal cultural heuristics is a kind of a super super-culture that orders human and property relations in ways that lead to greater equality, evenly spread societal resources, and the supremacy of dignity for all. This is only possible when poverty is completely eliminated from the face of the earth, because it is a creation of those selfish, loveless humans who naively thought that avarice is a virtue and abandoned humane and ubuNtu values. **These modern savages must be defeated in our lifetime**. A universal super super-culture is a collective of various cultures and spiritual beliefs that signify values of love, equality, collective dignity, fairer redistribution of societal resources, and restorative justice of a legal, social, economic, and epistemic kind. It is in this sense that an African spirituality had to be reconstructed to lead a crusade against political ideologies and lobby for a universal cultural heuristics as the fundamental, centripetal force that drives the functioning of society. A universal cultural heuristics should order human and property relations in a fairer way and direct humans into the centre of ubuNtu ethos and similar values from other belief systems. It is in this space that an African spirituality integrated with other beliefs can play a major role in shifting societal power paradigms from ideology to culture. African spirituality accompanied by beliefs that share similar values has to lead a meaning-making societal process that creates a universal cultural heuristics and signifies only values that serve the greater good and entrench collective dignity.

It is this essence and rationale for creating a universal cultural heuristics that drive this book. Africa must once again take the lead as it did in ancient times in ordering society towards equality, love and collective dignity through a universal cultural heuristics. There are various ways ancient Africa shaped the world we live in, other than just privileging it with advanced civilisations setting it as better suited to move the world to a better, higher societal design. In the words of Ivan van Sertima (1983), a university professor of note on African contributions to the advancements of the world:

> The nerve of the world has been deadened for centuries to the vibrations of African genius.

The time has come for the world to dance once more to the rhythms of African genius so it can proceed to the next levels of advancement and civilisation. We firmly believe that a shift from political ideologies to a universal cultural heuristics would help move the world forward by getting rid of modern leeches in the form of economic oligarchs whose power is enabled by capitalist political ideology.

We now cite a few examples of such ancient African contributions to world advancement and why Africa should once again lead advancement efforts towards a just world. Africa, particularly the northern part, contributed immensely to the development of astronomy, starting from systematic observations of the night skies, careful discernment, and the accurate plotting of the stars' movements (Strathern, 2001). North Africa contributed a year-long calendar consisting of twelve parts, now called months, and surmised that a year consisted of 365 and a quarter days. In Kenya, particularly Mali, its Dogon people had detailed astronomical observations, and to this day, Dogon cultural ceremonies remain directly linked to different space events discerned through vast astronomical knowledge they amassed since around

3000 BCE. Ancient Dogon people already knew about Saturn's ring, Jupiter's four moons, and the spiral structures of the Milky Ways. In Africa, science had always been linked to spirituality and culture.

Mathematics, in particular geometry, arithmetic, and mensuration, took shape in North Africa. Ancient Nigeria developed the Yoruba Numeric system and so did Zaire. The entire ancient African societies developed sophisticated tools of metallurgy that resulted in steam engines, metal chisels, and other metal equipment, particularly in regions such as ancient Rwanda, Tanzania, and Uganda. Architecture and engineering throve in North Africa while medicinal advances were made in North Africa and what are now modern Nigeria and Southern Africa. Africa set sail to explore places like North America and Europe long before Europeans tried that feat. Hence, Spain and Portugal (Iberian Peninsula) were under the rule of Africans for many centuries since 756 CE. Under this territorial rule, Spain and Portugal (known as al-Andalus African colony) became the heartbeat of economic and cultural progress enabled by advanced education, science and art. Notable further readings on African contributions to the modern world include *History of Black Scientists, The Lost Sciences of Africa, The Black Pioneers of Science and Innovation, Black Women in Science, The Lost Legacy, Blacks in Science: Ancient and Modern, Great Achievements in Science and Technology in Ancient Africa, Black People Invented Everything,* and *Revealing the African Presence in Renaissance Europe.*

This time we need to teach the world humanness and the grand spirit of sharing through contributing to a universal cultural heuristics. This means reversing the devastation of menticide which compelled most Africans to reconceptualise their identity in terms of foreign belief systems such as Abrahamic religions and lose, in the process, a sense of dignity, self-respect, and confidence in their own African spirituality as the key to their success and access to ultimate reality. Our main concern about Abrahamic religions is their paradigm of operation that is a torturous, mind-numbing tedium of routine-based ceremonial rituals and rites (Loftus, 2010) that reduce humans to terminally incurious and mentally captured beings. The possibilities of thinking outside Abrahamic religious doctrines and their dogmatic nature are almost non-existent and those exploring ideas beyond these doctrines are considered heretical.

Another most debilitating characteristic of Abrahamic religions is its commitment to reduce human capability to render humans helpless so a super-hero could save them. Furthermore, they extirpate any sense of self-worth, identity, and confidence in one's ability to resolve one's problems including spiritual ones. The cornerstone of African spirituality, its very plinth, is captured succinctly by the aphorism "*know thyself*" which was freely plagiarised from North Africa by Greek philosophers and some Abrahamic religions. Many people are **strangers** in their own existence because they lack the deeper and most fundamental understanding that the knowledge of self is the surest path to developing an understanding of one's spiritual being and purpose in life. It follows logically that any efforts that seek to proselytise one away from one's belief system and culture can succeed only if one lacks a basic knowledge of oneself – who you are and why you are here on earth. Embedded in the concept of "*know thyself*" is an understanding that one is spiritually assigned a role to make the world a slightly better place as well as preserve the identity and heritage of one's ancestral home. One's first responsibility therefore is to search and find one's inner kingdom, that which defines you and gives meaning to your life. In the words of Mark Twain, an American author:

> The two most important days in your life are the day you were born and the day you find out why. (Seybold, 2016)

Mark Twain must have been inspired by this African aphorism of "know thyself", which accentuates the need for each one of us to discover our mission and life purpose as we use that understanding to make the world a slightly better place. The state of inner kingdom, once achieved, eliminates inner turmoil, maintains balance, and makes one pursue one's life in terms of truth, justice, and serving the greater good. A similar Kemet quote on "*know thyself*" is:

> To face a real daemon, you must first look inwards and conquer your own darkness. (Marques, n.d.)

This African view of life suggests that humanity's entire problems stem from those who are strangers in their own lives, the source of all darkness. This means to attain inner kingdom, one has to identify, confront, and defeat strangers that live within. It is these inner strangers that make us vulnerable and gullible to religious and ideological puffery. Finding inner kingdom begins with confronting the **strangers of meta-ignorance, agnotology, sadomasochism, and mimesis**. One needs to look at tools and techniques used by those seeking to control and manage one to their advantage. They primarily manage the flow of information, what one must believe and reject. The most glaring, egregious, and obvious method of thought control is to make one reject one's own belief system, suppress one's cultural identity, and reconceptualise one's identity around their beliefs and cultures. Thought control agents then create inner strangers, as discussed below, and stunt our inner kingdom in ways that destroy our creative genius:

Stranger 1 (meta-ignorance): *Ignorant of one's ignorance*, not knowing that you do not know (TROPE 1: *Don't know that you don't know*) and not knowing what you do not know (TROPE 2: *Don't know what you don't know*). Many people conduct their lives and premise their beliefs based on what others considered as significant other – professors, teachers, pastors, kin and kith – have brainwashed them into believing. At this point, one fails oneself because one denies oneself the opportunity to search for knowledge, evaluate it, and determine whether it should direct one's life as one opens up for the possibility that new knowledge could extirpate deeply-held beliefs. Many people stuck in beliefs and religious brainwashing fail to recognise that they know very little about the belief or religion, therefore they are not aware that they do not know and that their belief or religion is itself a lie or something based on plagiarised myths and ancient knowing.

The most dangerous aspect of this stranger of ignorance is the failure to gain insights and the level of awareness necessary to discern aspects of a belief or religion that one can confidently defend rationally, logically, and with credible evidence. This is the condition one has to meet to reach a stage of being aware of one's level of ignorance. At least, at this level, one is aware of what one knows and what one does not know, a crucial part of gaining wisdom and unshackling oneself from bonds of ignorance. A person's scope of ignorance is known, at this stage, and can be adequately measured or estimated leading to a crucial *moment of clarity*: **knowing what you do not know**. This is not easy to achieve as it requires sustained effort and energy to *research* and critically learn. For fanatics and fundamentalists in belief systems or religion, including its dogmatic scholars, this stage of clarity is almost impossible to achieve, because it involves questioning deeply entrenched versions of 'truth' or what passes as truth values in a particular belief or religion.

The capability (capacity + resources) to function in Society 5.0 (super-society), which is highly data-driven, should intensify from 2025 and is globally interconnected, therefore assuming a multi-perspectival approach to any form of productivity, including knowledge production (Degushi, Hirai, Matsuoka, Nakano et al., 2020). Those stuck in an ancient mentality at all levels, including religion, would find them-selves entirely irrelevant and nonentities in Society 5.0 and go extinct. The huge resources, particularly physical infrastructure – big, intimidating buildings creating decorum of being real, although serving a deceptive purpose that support these religious enterprises –, would soon become decrepit and irrelevant as a super-society goes online and virtual. A super-society allows for high-level democratisation in all areas of society and thus enables a universal cultural heuristics (representation and manifestation of all belief systems). Another empowering level that leads to gain in inner kingdom is knowing the knowledge or knowing you are yet to gain. Gaining *new perspectives* is the central tenet of super-society and represents a key feature of a **new learning paradigm** necessary to function properly in super-society. People in super-society normalise *confronting and making transparent the big unknowns* drawn from the "*real world*" and *made transparent* mainly via advanced computing. Society 5.0 is a big attempt on building an alternative super-society that functions on a global scale and in real time, as efforts are made to eliminate the Global North legacy of domination.

One needs two things to defeat the stranger of meta-ignorance and gain control of one's inner kingdom. First, one has to reach a stage where one is fully aware that one lacks the knowledge and knowing about one's belief or religion (aware of one's ignorance). This level of awareness significantly reduces one's state of active partici-pation in one's folly. It is the height of absolute folly when one is unaware that one wallows in ignorance. Such people become so committed and dedicated to their cause of folly that it represents the only reality that they even consider as ultimate, therefore they defend it vehemently and naively. An Arabic quote captures these people succinctly:

> He who knows not and knows not that he knows not is a fool; shun him.
> (Arabian, n.d.)

The Arabian aphorism suggests that one shuns such people because they will never escape **the grip of folly**. However, in his 1876 *Praise of Folly* book, Desederius Erasmus rebukes the intelligentsia for opposing folly because of their own hypocrisy that hides their own real folly (*bêtise*), as captured succinctly below:

> And yet farther, I may safely urge, that all this [folly] is no more than the same with what is done by several seemingly great and wise men, who with a new-fashioned modesty employ some paltry orator or scribbling poet, whom they bribe to flatter them with some high-flown character, that shall consist of mere lies and shams yet persons thus extolled shall bristle up, and, peacock-like, bespread their plumes, while the impudent parasite magnifies the poor wretch to the skies and proposes him as the complete pattern of all virtue. (Erasmus, [1876] 2012:4)

Erasmus counsels that in this spectre of folly, we must never exclude the captured intellectuals, dogmatic scholars, white supremacist intelligentsia, and parochial theologians for their grip of folly is sophisticated, contains pretence of perspicacity and the decorum of respectability. These are, according to Erasmus ([1876] 2012), the modern *satyr*, brutish in their analyses and reviews but suffer *satyriasis* – high testosterone and male aggression, which hides male inadequacies and advance male as well as epistemic domination in the world. These presumably highly educated people are the same as ordinary people and never really take time to examine the truthfulness of their own convictions or ignore it completely and rather become ripe for gullibility and learned helplessness. Learned helplessness is an idea that orientates people into believing that they lack the capability to resolve their own issues and rather require some kind of divine intervention.

Second, these people do not take the time to decide on things they know for sure and things they do not know for sure. Wisdom comes with knowing the knowledge one does not know because it creates opportunities to seek and learn that knowledge. These wise people know what they do not know and therefore are capable of freeing themselves from ignorance and folly. There are, however, many who do not know what they do not know. These kinds of people get treated like children because they possess the naivety of a child. This level of treatment functions in terms of obedience and punishment as well as living up to the expectations and roles assigned by a belief system or religion.

Under these circumstances, finding an inner kingdom is an impossibility, because it involves being fully in charge of one's life, taking full responsibility for one's actions, and having capabilities to resolve one's own problems or knowing how to go about resolving them. In African spirituality, the search for one's inner kingdom is the first step towards empowering one to function within a cycle of ubuNtu and working towards the greater good. This search for inner kingdom begins with a strong level of awareness of things one does not know and an awareness of one's ignorance, knowing that one does not know and knowing what one does not know.

Inner kingdom is a light that banishes inner darkness and leads to sacred spaces. Sacred spaces are spiritually evocative milieux that are infused with divine, immanent presence as reflected in our conduct, action, and behaviours towards self and otherness (other humans and nature). These sacred spaces connect us to divine realities that pulverise our fears and ignorance. Sacred spaces banish the fear of death, for death has no sting once access to divine knowledge is attained. Access to knowledge and knowing is the surest path to one's inner kingdom, but one has to **confront one's ignorance** to create awareness of what one knows and what one does not know. This is no easy matter as it is a huge mindset shift and requires more than just cognitive dissonance. The motivation to change one's attitude towards one's belief is an enormous task even so when such a belief has been imposed on a person over years. A whole book has to be committed on how people successfully change their beliefs and it has to begin with attitudinal change, unsettling entrenched ways of thinking, which is outside the scope of this book.

Stranger 2 (agnotology): *Conditioned ignorance.* Agnotology is the art of deliberately inducing ignorance either for purposes of cultural, political or religious capture or for marketing puffery often by using inaccurate, distorted or misleading data. To clarify the main difference between conditioned ignorance and meta-ignorance, it is important to make a distinction between a theory of absence and that of presence in the production of ignorance. Ignorance has great benefit in highly democratic societies because it helps sustain skewed power relations and effort is committed to producing as well as maintaining it. When it is produced to particular ideological ends (gain in power), ignorance is about presence. It is about generating and sustaining its presence because it benefits those in power. A typical example is post-truth. The knowledge is available, knowable, and accessible, but it is undesirable that others should have access to it, often for reasons that serve narrow political, cultural, economic, or religious interests. This is called restricted knowledge or information. Knowledge can be restricted, because it could result in political instability, compromise a crime investigation, or lead to societal instability resulting in what could be termed justifiable restrictions. However, only constitutionally sanctioned restrictions are allowable if such a constitution enshrines human rights and the right to access to information.

Another situation where knowledge is available but restricted involves esoteric knowledge. The restriction comes about, because the knowledge produced is of such a technical nature and employs such highly obscure nomenclature that only a few experts in that research field have access to it. The ignorance is the result of inaccessibility to the highly technical nature of the language but that knowledge is knowable and accessible albeit to a particular community of practice. It is exclusionary on grounds of its technicality but accessible through gains in such knowledge. In this case, ignorance refers to a deliberate act of eschewing illumination brought about by gain in this esoteric knowledge and facing darkness of ignoring this kind of knowledge.

Distorted knowledge as a form of ignorance refers to a deliberate act of losing truth and "*abandoning oneself to error*". There is, in this case, a deliberate intent to obscure the truth, manipulate knowledge, and pursue an erroneous presentation of half-truths to achieve a deceptive end (that benefits only the perpetrators) of the distortions. Elements of presence are there in distorted knowledge, because aspects of the truth are still present in such distortions and can be discerned with dedicated effort, which traces systematic deviations from the truth. For instance, history shows that science, mathematics, philosophy, and advanced civilisations started in Africa, yet a Eurocentric model of enlightenment distorts this reality by totally eliminating the African contributions to these human advances and propagates a lie that it all started in Greece.

Conditioned ignorance numbs our thinking and intellect so that most of us can abandon the project of enriching our minds with the right knowledge. It makes the task of searching for appropriate knowledge and the truthfulness of claims so daunting that many of us live our lives in perpetual ignorance to the benefit of political, cultural, economic, and religious power. Hence, efforts are made to condition people into believing that knowledge shared by the powerful is sufficient for most people to survive the exigencies and vagaries of this world. People then consider what politicians, priests, adverts, and scientists pontificate is often considered inerrant and beyond questioning. In this conditioned state of ignorance, people become prisoners of their own folly that greatly benefit political, commercial, ideological, and religious interests. It is thus so important that knowledge is managed in ways that benefit these interests. This is called induced bias.

Ignorance based on absence include knowledge-not-yet-known but could be known in the future, forgotten knowledge that existed before but got extirpated either through deliberate efforts such as menticide, propaganda, puffery, and distortions as well as cognitively inaccessible knowledge falling under the unknown category. This knowledge is not possible to access via current knowledge production methodologies and paradigms. It requires that we make a huge leap forward beyond our current tools of knowledge production. This type of ignorance is conditioned because we have not been able to go beyond the limitations that scientific endeavours and instruments impose on us. It is deliberately induced to sustain the scientific enterprise and maintenance of its power, therefore science becomes ideological, searching for ultimate power rather than continually refining and constantly challenging its own biases and conjectures.

Conditioned ignorance has been used over centuries in Africa to perpetuate lies of a political, cultural and religious nature. There is knowledge of Africa and its belief systems that have been kept away from us to perpetuate white supremacy and African backwardness. Abrahamic religions, in particular Christianity and Islam, have mastered the art of conditioned ignorance at two levels.

First, they declare knowledge of their religion as inerrant and beyond dispute. This way, it numbs proselytes and seasoned followers into ignominious obedience and use of fear to scare people out of their intellect and common sense. Fear egregiously disturbs logical thinking.

Second, by using extirpation to eliminate competing belief systems and making people abandon their own beliefs and cultures so they reconceptualise their entire lives around these foreign religions. This is the worst kind of conditioned ignorance. For those seeking inner kingdom, conditioned ignorance is not an option. It is highly sophisticated and astutely generated to place one in the mental lane the powerful have created. **One becomes a modern slave serving invisible and invincible masters.**

Stranger 3 (sadomasochism): *Learned helplessness* is the conditioned active participation in and enjoyment of activities that are essentially painful and tedious, in particular those relating to behavioural patterns that lead to the collapse of one's complex and creative problem-solving capabilities. It stems from a conditioned belief inculcated through a social process that one is incapable of resolving problems or challenges without the assistance of an assigned Messiah, some kind of superhero whose fame and potency derive from sadistic violence, like the crucifixion. This behaviour or human condition leads to maladaptive responses to things humans can solve for themselves once the disempowering propaganda is defeated. The painful condition of helplessness is self-inflicted as it is a voluntary exercise of conditioning, and many seem to derive pleasure from it. Learned helplessness thrives on *deferred controllability*, the deliberate choice to defer one's power and control to another person with the hope that one's problems will be resolved.

Furthermore, it is based on *numbed cognitive intelligence*, a condition of mind that has been manipulated and brainwashed into believing only that which the mind subscribes to unconditionally and destroys one's ability to solve complex problems. Any form of dissonance, in particular the cognitive type, is resolved through rejecting data or evidence that threatens the existing state of belief. *Behaviours* associated with learned helplessness include failure to learn adaptive responses to difficult problems and creative problem-solving. This behaviour stunts people into believing that they cannot solve problems even when potential solutions are right in their faces. To have a thorough understanding of learned helplessness and its strong association with pain, particularly if it is self-inflicted, it is important to develop a deeper understanding of sadomasochism. The deeper understanding of this sadomasochism concept would also help us critically appraise Christian religion.

Christianity's entire logical infrastructure is premised on sadomasochism, the gory, blood-sputtering suffering of one man, real or mythical, whose only leverage is the gore and macabre, as his teachings are not unique in Africa, because they define who we are as Africans. Given his time in Africa during his formative years, we can reasonably infer that we taught him these lessons. The analysis will show that people's responses to pain, in particular their empathetic feel of it, actually open them up for vulnerability and possible mental capture.

A good starting point to understand sadomasochism and how it creates learned helplessness upon which intellectual predators of this world leech to control and manipulate others, is to understand selfhood as a key component of finding inner kingdom. It also assists in dealing with these inner strangers that stunt the achievement of an inner kingdom. **Selfhood** refers to a **state of conceptualising one's identity in terms of one's culture and heritage.** This makes one distinct from others who belong to a different culture and whose heritage is materially different from one's own. An appropriately developed selfhood is one of the prerequisites for achieving inner kingdom. Selfhood thus has a higher level of self-awareness (Baumeister, 1988) and self-affirmation. Selfhood is developed to pursue the quest for well-being and general happiness (a state of *eudemonia*). Well-being and *eudemonia* are states in which humans function optimally and achieve physical and mental health. Selfhood therefore seeks to banish suffering rather than celebrate or even deify it. Selfhood is about being in charge and in control instead of helpless, which is a self-defeating behaviour that sabotage our right to be happy and well. Selfhood, once attained, substantially increases one's self-esteem and the potential to self-actualise. A self-actualising person, meaning one who has gained their inner kingdom, shows the following characteristics as gleaned from Kaufman (2018) and Ratner (2018):

◆ A strong sense of purpose and substantially increased self-awareness especially regarding one's identity, culture, history, and heritage.

◆ Readiness to be self-persuaded by irrefutable evidence and incontestable facts.

◆ Free from prejudice and discrimination in particular refraining from considering one's beliefs and understandings as the only show in town.

◆ Ability to solve complex problems in a creative way and within a multi-perspectival framework.

◆ Ability to meet the demands of fairness and work towards a socially just society.

Sadomasochism seeks to ensure that people do not reach a state of high self-esteem and self-actualisation. It appeals to base behaviours of pain and suffering as it offers a temporary and powerful escape from self-awareness and efforts to attain self-actualisation. It provides fertile grounds for modern barbarians to misdirect people into empathetic feelings that glorify pain and suffering, thus resulting in abandoning one's sense of awareness and pursuit of self-actualisation. Those who do not quest for self-actualisation are easy to manipulate into reconceptualising their identities in terms of the ideas of those that seek to manipulate them. Furthermore, it is easy to render them helpless through indoctrination and menticide thus creating conditions for mental capture. This mental capture enables these modern slaves to become active and willing participants in their own mental bondage and humiliation that celebrate pain and ignominy as symbols of sacrifice for incorporeal rewards such as access to heaven which defies logic.

Those who get persuaded to abandon self-awareness, selfhood, complex problem-solving, and attainment of self-actualisation for a temporary escape from the exigencies of mundane life and the false expectation that a superhero will solve their problems merely by mouthing his name suffer from self-acquired mental illness, a delusion that bothers on schizophrenia. Schizophrenia, in its essence, is about a fragmented mind that blurs the line between reality and imagination. This is the worst form of self-induced helplessness and self-inflicted ill-health. Escape from self-awareness derives mostly from recreational activities and religion is very much part of the deal. In the study of sadomasochism among women and men, it was determined that the effects of power on arousal by sadistic thoughts are quite significant and stronger among women than men (Lammers & Imhof, 2015). In other words, emotional cruelty, pain inflicted on others to derive satisfaction or gain power, can be used manipulatively through the fear or preoccupation with the gory to control others. This explains why more women than men tend to attend religious gatherings whose narrative of the gory and macabre appeal to women's base emotions as research indicates.

In no way does this suggest that women tend to exhibit emotional cruelty. Rather, it indicates their susceptibility to narratives that are premised on the gory and macabre, as is the case with the Jesus story. Christianity is fully aware of this intrinsic weakness, hence the cross symbol is made visible to society to reinforce this narrative of suffering and pain as the basis of convincing people that some Jewish guy, through suffering and sacrificing his life, saved the world despite zero evidence to support that claim. **Zero**. There are no reasonable grounds to support the view that this guy died for our sins. The writings in the *Christian Delusion* book edited by John Loftus go into greater effort to pulverise the theory that is premised purely on the gory and macabre. Such brilliant deception based on conditioned ignorance feeds Christian myths and ensures its continued anachronistic existence in a society faced with irrefutable facts and evidence.

Stranger 4 (mimesis): *Unknown known.* To develop a deeper understanding of mimetic disposition of humans, it is important to understand first that humans are essentially equal and have a thorough understanding of the value of such a virtue. Second, that inequality comes about as a result of humans' desire to possess what others have for their own private use via any means necessary. It is this fundamental sense of material possession for private use and its concomitant social status that compel humans to accept and live under conditions of inequality and poverty. To eliminate such tendencies towards avarice and greed, society must remove a positive social status assigned to these selfish, avaricious, self-centred idiots because their incessant desire for more money increases instability and dire deprivation among the majority of people which results in societal ills. For avarice to thrive in society and offer false justification for oligarchic tendencies, the majority of people not only envy these selfish idiots but harbour the belief that they too can emulate and attain similar status of avarice. This is what gives avarice a good press in society. The truth is that most, if not all, of these oligarchs had to cut corners to amass such huge resources for themselves as Honoré de Balzac, the French novelist, suggests:

> The secret of a great success for which you are at a loss to account is a crime that has never been found out, because it was properly executed. (Radcliffe, 2017)

Known to the oligarch and the avaricious idiot is this truth about how they accumulated wealth and, unknown to the majority of people in society, the system of wealth accumulation is already skewed towards the oligarchy and it is almost impossible to penetrate those spaces of avarice and greed. Efforts to emulate or copy the avaricious idiots are futile as only the few that are prepared to compromise basic human conduct can survive this merciless underworld. This mimetic or imitative tendencies of people believing they can achieve similar avaricious heights as the oligarchy give credence to greed and hold back efforts of achieving equality in society.

Given that these inner strangers vitiate our inner kingdom (the apex of human existence), it is important to suggest some possible ways of eliminating or managing them out of our human systems, whether emotional or psychological. **Inner kingdom is about being in charge, not helpless.** Inner kingdom is closely associated with the psychoanalysis concept of healthy narcissism. Healthy narcissism refers to a solid sense that a person possesses once they have gained high self-esteem and strong self-worth, making it possible for such a person to align self with the greater good. This way, people with a strong and healthy narcissism are more capable of resisting alien influences and mental invasions from political, economic, and religious sorts. Mental invasion occurs at the four levels described as strangers: meta-ignorance, agnotology, sadomasochism, and mimesis. Once these strangers are allowed to cultivate a state of helplessness then the mind becomes ripe for thought control and intellectual capture by displacing healthy narcissism, high self-esteem, and self-actualisation. A person in possession of healthy narcissism, high self-esteem, and self-actualisation tends to use these capabilities as a proactive, protective shield whose purpose is to preserve selfhood against insidiously encroaching alien stimuli that could endanger it through unwelcome invasion. It is important to note that strangeness of itself is good for a person because it creates conditions for creative and innovative problem-solving. It is strangeness with intent to invade and capture our intellect that is contested and must be defeated to gain inner kingdom, a key enabler of functioning within the cycle of ubuNtu. Mental invaders and prisoners, especially the religious type, tend to use cheap labels such as heresy to pulverise our own sense of worth and create conditions for mental capture.

'Heresy' is a label coined to discourage intellectual engagement with the content and context of Abrahamic religions, in particular some contradictions and fictitious stories drawn from other cultures that pass as inerrant, God-justified truths. Humans, in these Abrahamic belief systems, are deprived of their innate intellectual abilities and capabilities of provocative mental stimulations that have progressed humanity into Society 5.0, noted for its combination of artificial and human intelligences in co-creation of value (Pitso, 2020). This state of religious affairs is sad because humanity is deprived of creative genius that could emerge from followers of these Abrahamic religions. Indeed, they have been some exceptions who attempted to take these religions out of their Dante's *selva oscura* (dark), intellectual miasma.

However, the most egregious acts of extirpation from Eurocentric myths of white supremacy and Abrahamic religions were their almost successful attempt to eliminate African spirituality from the face of the earth. While this obnoxious attempt on the elimination of African spirituality was nearly successful riding on colonial power, the resilience of Africans and their deep desire to reconnect with their own spirituality has ensured the continued survival of this powerful African spirituality. Its power resides in the effort and resources invested by myopic Europeans and their invasive religions in attempting to extirpate it. There is such power in African spirituality that the colonialists refuse to return our land in some parts of Africa, an embodiment of our spirituality, because they know that our genius would be restored once we reclaim our land. It is this African genius that helped the West to crawl out of their 900 years of the Dark Ages. Furthermore, African spirituality is one of the few belief systems that intertwine science and spirituality (Strathern, 2001). This means that Africans operating within this African belief system were allowed mentally stimulating environments that provoked their curiosity, intrigued their intellect to search for truth through scientifically led approaches and leading to an evidence-led spiritual practice. African spirituality is thus based on a human empowering and benevolent paradigm of operation. It defines one's sense of humanness in terms of the humanness of others. I am human because others are human too. It is in this sense that African spirituality rejects outright the existence of poverty and inequality as both are in direct violation of the fundamental virtue of African spirituality (Temperance) upon which other virtues of Fortitude, Prudence, and Justice depend.

The exercise of Temperance depends largely on the equality of land and property ownership and any deviations to this inalienable human right is heresy and blasphemy to the real owner of land – the Supreme Being. In Africa, ownership of land belongs to those who came before us, those walking this earth now and those who are yet to visit this world. The longer it takes to redistribute land in a fairer way, the greater the ignominy to those gone before us and the greater the disadvantage to those who are yet to walk this earth. Generational disadvantage and injustice are the worst kind of crime because they deprive future generations of their inalienable right to live decently and truthfully. It appears that Africa has succeeded in liberating the West and move it out of the barbarism of the Dark Ages, but relics of that unsavoury period in the life of Westerners, in particular psychological effects of that soul-searing period, remain in their psyche. The hardships of this dark period seared into their psyche and emotionally drained their sense of calm humanness that, unfortunately, appears as an albatross on the neck of their current and future generations. This extreme deprivation compelled a violent reaction to their condition that they used effectively to take away the resources of generous Africans by force and other resource-rich countries. Philosophies of humanness and ubuNtu would never impact the psyche of most Europeans, because their 900 years deprivation period keep them in a constant state of fear of deprivation.

Africa needs once more to liberate Europe from this collective dark fear and make Europe, as well as its diaspora, embrace humanness and ubuNtu as the plinth upon which to live a truthful life. A truthful life knows no fear, shares munificently, and seeks true love with all humanity. Time to bury the vestiges of that dark European period from whence ancient Africa saved the West. Humans are not designed to survive only but have a role to collectively create a society ruled by justice and leave a legacy of love and collective dignity. Avarice and resource chasing are so animalistic as to be utterly abhorrent. There is no honour in concentrating resources to a few individuals when that occurs at the expense of depriving others of base dignity deriving from the centrifugal force of deprivation and poverty. Individualised resource accumulation is an abominable relic of 900 years of European Dark Ages and needs to be eliminated, once again, by African humane philosophy and science-led spirituality.

Europe, once more, needs us to save it from this darkness of avarice and rapacity. Yes, Africa liberated the West from their 900 years of darkness, ignorance, and barbarism. Indeed, Europe was once a dark continent at the time when Africa was shaping scientific thought, civilisation, and advanced spirituality. This dark period in Europe experienced very little scientific advancements and cultural growth. European apologists passing as scholars have made every attempt to either reject this period of darkness as ever existing or pretended that it is wholly exaggerated, because that would pulverise white supremacy and eliminate the perpetuation of the 'deadening' of African genius. African genius existed way before the West emerged from its darkness despite some denialists' efforts. Fortunately, their own scholar of Italian origin, Francesco Petrarca (later, Petrarch) named this period between the 5th and 14th century in Europe as 'the Dark Ages' to describe the savagery, gladiatorial wars, uncivilised barbarism, and lack of scientific progress in Europe during that period.

At this very time of European darkness, Africans and Arabs were developing advanced civilisations based on science, technology, and science-led spirituality. The West's attempts to distort history are spurious and without substance especially as they relate to non-European contributions to human progress. These distortions of a historical trajectory of Europe as having started in Greece violates the highest virtue of truthful living from which the four cardinal virtues – Temperance, Fortitude, Prudence, and Justice – drawn from Kemet spirituality derive. We live truthfully when we are brutally honest about issues of life, seek equality in all aspects of our lives, and show love to all humans and nature as encapsulated in these cardinal virtues. The Kemetic Mystery System from North Africa also known as Kemet (black land) was noted for its combination of science and spiritual learning, which compelled many Europeans to come to Kemet regions to grow their knowledge base, in particular European scholars such as Hippocrates, Thales, Pythagoras, Socrates, Plato, and many others. These scholars of European origin were taught in the curriculum that included the esotericism and superiority of African spirituality and science as well as its practical applications.

The Kemetic education lasted for 40 years and none of the Greek thinkers could last that long, except for Pythagoras, who continued to study Kemet for 23 years. This helped him learn the North African theorem he named after himself and the many North African myths and legends that helped him shape stories of Christian religion (Strathern, 2001). Thales of Miletus, his mentor, encouraged Pythagoras to continue his mathematics learning in Egypt. Kemet learning did not separate education from spirituality and on the advice of Porphyry, a Lebanese, Pythagoras practised African culture, customs, and beliefs in Italy such that the strong influence of Africa on Italian culture cannot be ignored (O'Connor & Robertson, 2012). It is therefore not difficult to surmise that Christian stories that were shaped by Pythagoras claim their origins from Africa. One Greek philosopher, who acknowledged and appreciated the Kemetic education he received in North Africa, is Aristotle (c. 350 BCE) as quoted in the book by George Joseph called *The Crest of the Peacock: Non-European Roots of Mathematics* (2011:6):

> Egypt is a cradle of Mathematics, that is, the country of origin for Greek Mathematics.

Aristotle's teacher, Eudoxus, was a highly regarded mathematician who taught mathematics in Greece and studied mathematics in Egypt (Joseph, 2011). It is important, at this point, to trace the creation of the white supremacist myths that philosophy, mathematics, scientific thought, and civilisation started in Greece, including the establishment of the first university in the world. We know it is not the University of Bologna in Italy in 1088 CE, but rather in 859 CE in Africa and established by a woman, Fatima Al Fihri, as a spiritual and educational institution of higher learning. There is also an ongoing debate on whether the Nalanda institution in India established around 400 CE qualifies as a university – and in that case it would become the first university in the world. However, while established in India, it appears to have been attended mostly by Buddhists, thus making it a Buddhist institution focused narrowly on spiritual matters. Therefore, disputes on whether it qualified as a university is not relevant for the scope of the book plus it is an entirely different institution today from the one being operated as a university.

We know for certain that the University of Karaouiyn (also known as Al-Qarawiyyin University) in Africa was a true university, which catered for both spirituality and education because, at the time, scientific thought was considered an integral to spirituality. This university continues to operate in Morocco to this day. Europe used their skills of violence honed over 900 years to violently take control of political power in Africa more than 400 years ago. It set out to entrench its highly individualised ideology of white supremacy, which sought to ignore or extirpate non-European contributions to human advancement, in particular Africa, to allow the perpetuation of myths of a dark continent.

The truth is Africa has never experienced a dark age, while Europe has encountered such a dark age for 900 years. The historical Eurocentric model of perpetuating the myth of white supremacy was based on what Joseph (2011:5) calls "*The Classical Eurocentric Trajectory*" to which I add "Tragedy" (see Diagram A). The tragedy of white supremacy myth is that it has left Europeans still believing the myth in a space of perpetual untruthful living, the most wicked of all living. The beauty about truth is that it can never be hidden forever in the carapace of lies, and those that seek to hide from it often find out that the solace of a lie lacks permanence and cannot be sustained forever. In this tragic Eurocentric trajectory of epistemic development, Greece is the epicentre of civilisation, philosophy, mathematics, engineering and superior religious belief systems. According to this trajectory, after 900 years of the Dark Ages, Europe discovered Greek learning and civilisation, which progressed Europe, as the inheritor and custodian of this Greek learning. Europe then proceeded to the Renaissance period after which modern Europe came into being (Joseph, 2011). There is no trace of ancient non-European contributions to epistemic development, philosophy, and civilisation in this classical Eurocentric trajectory or, to be precise, tragedy. This egregious attempt on the side of Europe to distort history, in no way demeans the 19th-century to present-day contributions of Europe to science, technology, engineering, philosophy, and modern civilisation.

However, it all started in ancient Africa. Indeed, respect for African science and civilisation did exist in pre-19th-century Europe (Bernal, 1987) until Europe fathomed out white supremacist ideology in the form of a Eurocentric model that erroneously placed Greece as the cradle and source of all knowledge of science and civilisation. This Eurocentric model made every attempt to decimate, devalue, and distort the origins of science, mathematics, technology, and civilisation, thus denying Africa its rightful place in history. Efforts to reconstruct African spirituality have to be understood within the framework of reclaiming African legacy in science, civilisation, and spirituality, which Europeans attempted to extirpate from history and the face of the earth.

In the modified Diagram A below, Joseph (2011) demonstrates how mathematics knowledge developed and finally reached Europe via Greece. Mathematics started in Egypt, particularly regions surrounding Northern Africa and Mesopotamia including Yoruba Numerals in West Africa which were discovered around the 17th century. These mathematical developments in West Africa can be traced to the early formations of Oyo Kingdom around 1000 CE. Europe was hardly in the picture of advances in mathematics, science, philosophy, and spirituality during these ancient times. African influence during the European Renaissance, in particular its art, is quite visible and was heavily implicated in its artistic calibration. In Diagram A, Joseph (2011) is at pains to demonstrate how European culture benefitted from knowledge and cultural advances drawn from Egyptian and Mesopotamian cultures and advances in knowledge. The model debunks the myth that human civilisation and philosophy started off in ancient Greece. It provides evidence that the ancient Hellenistic culture and knowledge base derive from Egypt and Mesopotamia as it occurred in various European epochs ranging from the Dark Ages, Renaissance through to the enlightenment era when Europe finally embraced knowledge and civilisations from Egypt and Mesopotamia.

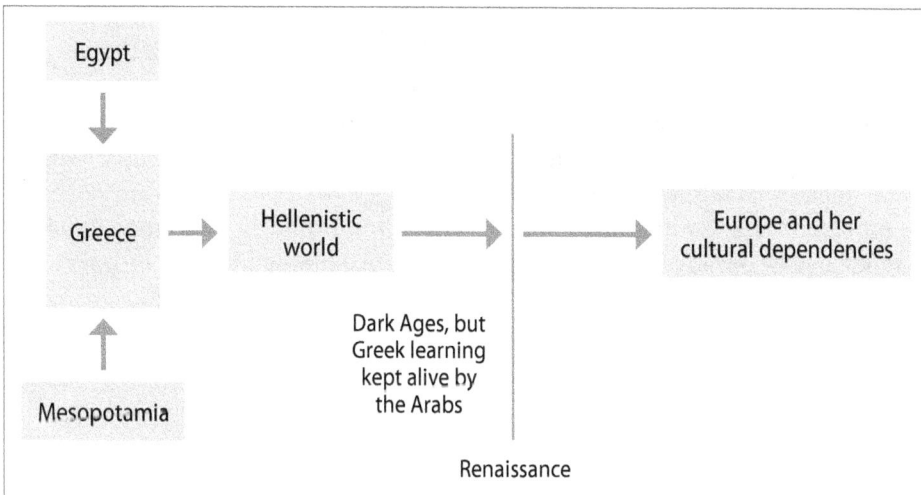

Diagram A   Modified Eurocentric Trajectory Model (Joseph, 2011:6)

While many scholars have written about African spirituality and philosophy, efforts to reconstruct a comprehensive African spirituality have not been made in any meaningful way. This is a modest contribution towards such a reconstruction of African spirituality and I hope that other scholars will attempt further refinement. It is important that we leave a working blueprint of African spirituality that mostly was conveyed via oral traditions and rarely was committed to word, particularly in other parts of Africa where advanced civilisations made presence about more than 150 years ago. African spirituality is immanent, that is, it is integral to our everyday life, conduct, and behaviour towards others and nature. Our culture, environment, and society are crucial aspects of expressing our spirituality as Africans. When any of these aspects are affected negatively then our spirituality and sense of worth are compromised. There is no honour in mental capture, because it is a violation of our basic, innate right and the stunting of the greatest gift of all – creativity – bestowed on us by the Supreme Being as the crown of human and humane existence from which African spirituality derives.

To have a thorough understanding of the positive link between creativity and African spirituality, it is important to understand the three components of self-worth, the crucial basis for self-esteem, self-actualisation, and healthy narcissism which define inner kingdom, the building block of African spirituality. Self-worth consists of competence, confidence and connectedness (three Cs). Competence, in African spirituality, is about first developing capabilities of knowledge and knowing, as well as their application in real-life situations to create conditions where all people live a life of quality, and resource accumulation is done in a sustainable way. Furthermore, knowledge and knowing must banish meta-ignorance, agnotology, sadomasochism, and mimesis so that we can be in charge of our inner kingdom that connects us with otherness (humans and nature). Both knowledge and knowing must enable us to discern what we know, thus the limits of our understandings and awareness about what we do not know. Knowledge and knowing also help us develop critical thinking, creative problem-solving, and deep analytical abilities that help us discern mental capture tactics and persuasions with the intent to sway us away from our beliefs, cultures and identities, thus compromising our sense of self-worth. Those who condemn their own cultures and heritage have the lowest of self-worth and are looked down on by others as nothing more than prisoners who willingly incarcerated their own minds and are proud of their own state of intellectual capture. There is no honour in abandoning that which defines one from birth and embracing what is foreign and anti-self, particularly because it is an outcome of a dishonest representation of one's culture and heritage. Knowledge and knowing set one free from these bondages and intellectual captures as they increase your sense of self-worth.

> Seek ye knowledge and knowing of self then find ye inner kingdom. (Kemetic teachings)

The second crucial aspect of self-worth is confidence. Confidence is a strong belief and trust in one's abilities and powers to define oneself and deal with the challenges of this world on one's terms without foreign influences. Once one's power derives from reliance on foreign influences then one's sense of worth diminishes significantly and one's confidence vitiates considerably.

> Without self-confidence we are as babes in the cradle. (Woolf, [1929] 1935:4)

Self-confidence comes from recognising our own strengths and ability to resolve our problems without some divine intervention. In my final year as a primary school learner, I read a book about a young man called David who had to escape a concentration camp during World War II to link up with his parents in Denmark. It was a long, torturous journey full of dangers and David survived because he believed in his own strengths and wits, not in some superhero or divine intervention. In fact, his survival and triumph depended on rejecting divine intervention and oozing with high self-confidence as evidenced in the following quote from the book *I am David* by Anne Holm (1963:20):

> God of the green pastures and running waters, please don't help me; I want to do it by myself so that You'll know that I found something I can do for You.

This prayer is all empowering and a true reflection of one in charge of his inner kingdom. A true thought warrior whose weapons of choice are reason and logic. This book, *I am David*, also taught me that greedy people can never be happy and their reliance on violence and cruelty demonstrate their failure to apply logical and just solutions to problems facing humanity. This means they lack self-confidence. Self-confidence is about possessing an inner strength derived from acquired skills, values of one's own culture, and heritage that one uses to make humanity better beyond philanthropy, a quilt-driven, fame-seeking selfishness masquerading as altruism. When things got really bad for David, his Eurocentric cultural knowledge of individualism and self-reliance put him through the most difficult and complex situations as evidenced by creating an empowering prayer and not one that renders him helpless. In creating an empowering prayer for himself, young David went through a process of critiquing what he could remember about religion ranging from Judaism to Catholicism. **He eschewed Jewish prayer because it was meant for Jews, as Catholics focused on a woman called Mary which David found inappropriate**. A young Danish boy could decide for himself and create his own prayer. He sought not to be captured mentally and physically. Such self-confidence is critical in protecting one's freedom and human dignity.

In the African worldview, self-confidence derives not from individualism, as is the case in this book, but from connectedness. Religion and ideologies of avarice pose a threat, not only to African spirituality, but to European culture of individualism and self-reliance. This calls for a collective struggle to get rid of these things that stunt human progress towards a society free from poverty, free from religious lies, that is, one that thrives on equality, a universal cultural heuristics, and collective dignity as key components of self-confidence. In a quote that succinctly captures a lack of self-confidence, David, in this very book, makes this observation:

> Angelo was a grown man, and here was one thing he was quite free to decide for himself, and yet he was ready to let others make up his mind for him ... that could only be stupidity. (Holm, 1963:119)

Angelo was quite happy to remain a child in a cradle. There are many of these false cradles that provide illusions of being protected and safe, yet they thrive on turning adults into forever children, meek sheep and gullible people similar to a nincompoop.

In c. 1600, a legal definition of a nincompoop was that of a mentally incapable person, who is unable to manage own affairs and cannot decide freely without fear or coercion. **The cradle of religion is the worst kind of tool that produces these kinds of credulous people**. It kills every inch of self-worth and reduces humans to the status of zombies, the living dead. The living dead are the reanimated creatures that have been reduced to a big moving mass of captured nincompoops incapable of rational thought and lacking the ability to manage their own inner kingdom. This is typical of those that pray to foreign gods and consider another nation as the chosen one (God's favourites), the apex of blasphemy. **How can God have favourites? That is a human attribute and to reduce God to that level is blasphemous**. Africans of all nations have been susceptible to efforts of turning them into the living dead. It is this collective capture and mass deception this book seeks to challenge and free us from the bondage of centuries-old lies.

The third of the components that define self-worth is connectedness. In African spirituality, connectedness is about conducting one's life within the cycle of ubuNtu. The cycle of ubuNtu is about the recognition of oneness of the human race itself and with nature, belongingness to a cycle of humaneness, equality, love, and collective dignity as well as belongingness to nature, a key source of our sustenance. It is also about the solidarity of the entire human race where a break in a chain of the human cycle of ubuNtu affects us all and requires collective effort to restore the cycle.

Cycle of ubuNtu = human solidarity (human oneness + human-nature oneness)

These issues find expression in the entire book. In Chapter 1, I describe in detail how history and its scientific methods can be used to distort truth and uphold centuries-old lies, but I also implore history scholars to protect their scientific credibility and integrity by discerning these sustained lies and biases so as to get rid of them. History, as a scholarly endeavour, is open to these manipulations by the very matter of its subject of interest which is quite difficult to prove with highly credible evidence unless original texts or scrolls are available. I also attempt to understand the concept of be*lief* because its one root is a lie, a deliberate intent to misrepresent or distort facts or truth for purposes of deception or gain in undeserved power over others using menticide and manipulations to silence truth or facts. Its other etymologically derived root from Middle English is *lief*, meaning a wish. A wish is a cognitive content deriving from surmise (informed conjecture) or absolute conviction that something is true despite lack of evidence to support such a claim. Most of the time, such absolute convictions lead to dogmatism and fanaticism, entirely undesirable aspects of human conduct given their perspectival narrowness and potential to lead to violence. It is this perspectival narrowness that led to the marginalisation and poor representation of African spirituality, despite the fact that its ubuNtu philosophy should be practised all over the world to create general happiness, equality and collective dignity.

In chapters 2 and 3, African spirituality comes forward for sharp analysis. Chapters 4 to 7 deal with the four virtues that form African spirituality. Chapter 8 is a practical process of becoming a spirit medium. Chapter 9 deals with the epistemic comprehension of spirituality. In Chapter 10, efforts of narrativising and canonising African spirituality are attempted. Chapter 11 focuses on the unfinished business of these complex issues.

_____

1

Introduction

To develop a deeper understanding of African spirituality and why it is so marginalised in the world and suffers bad press even in certain parts of Africa where it originates, we need to understand how history, as a scholarly area of knowledge production, works. History is often given the decorum of being scientific and its facts are often portrayed as beyond dispute and therefore worthy of being believable and accepted purely on the grounds of history's fallible methods of inquiry and logical disputations. Yet, no person can go into the good night of the past and successfully retrieve the truth. We venture deep into the past only by legends and fallible historical methods of inquiry, the outcome of which can best be described as the **most probable**, while truth is almost unattainable. The past somehow holds the truth to ransom and creates opportunities for unscrupulous predators to set their lure and snares to capture the gullible and intellectually lazy for narrow gains. Truth has no respect for those who serve the gods of narrowness and bigotry.

The focus of this book is on historical methods of inquiry and how legends got elevated to realms of facts through politics and religion's carefully crafted menticide projects leading to the marginalisation of African spirituality. Menticide is an effective mindset-altering psychological warfare weapon that changes beliefs, values, and the history of a people, and robs it of its heritage often for economic gain and mental control. Menticide destroys the human spirit in particular the African spirituality through mental torture, coercion, and systematic pressure nicely masqueraded as religion. This is a peculiar kind of crime that has been allowed to persist without punishment and somehow got justified by passing such propaganda as a historical fact. It is a crime so well executed that it is almost impossible to decipher and correct.

The historical methods of inquiry into our past fall within the broad canvass of the interpretive research paradigm and involve hypotheses about meanings and their derivation from their context backed by authenticated original scripts. Interpretive research paradigms fall within the ambit of informed subjectivity meaning objectivity is unattainable, hence evidence gets built over time. Controversies around interpretive methodologies emanate from the agentic power between the researcher and the researched with the researched biased to assume active agency in the research that involve them. Naturalistic inquiries tend to frown upon bias in whatever form.

Its efforts are towards hypotheses of regularities that lead to uncovered universal laws that are presumed, most of the time, to be free from bias (objective). Yet, interpretive inquiries tend to accept that a certain bias is part of the inquiry as long as the inquiry leads to higher levels of interpretation and credible meanings that can be trusted to account for the real action that took place in a social, economic or political context, or surmise the probable from evidence adduced from fallible methods of inquiry. This means that interpretive inquiries frown at subjective puffery because it represents the lowest levels of interpretation along the lines of corridor gibberish. Historical meanings are expected to derive from higher levels of interpretation drawn from established methods of inquiry, hence there is a strong sense that such meanings have an aura of science because they are adduced through some scientific endeavours and methodological rigour.

The intended message in portraying history as scientific is to deify meanings derived from it and hide its true potential as open to manipulation and alteration to serve a particular agenda – in most cases, a supremacist agenda. For history to retain the decorum of science, it has to set mechanisms in place to eliminate the tendencies of the supremacist agenda that encroaches insidiously into its hallowed scholarly spaces.

History is also an outcome of war that maps out human relations in ways that reflects the winners and the defeated with the historical narratives of the conquerors taking a leading role in shaping our understanding of our historical past. The history of the defeated often takes a backseat when key historical epochs of a society are documented, narrated and celebrated. For example, the devastating effects of the Roman Empire's wars in Africa have led many to believe that Greeks have monopoly over wisdom, philosophy, knowledge and science, yet all these intellectual products were produced right here in Africa as earlier stated, and either got stolen or learned by the Greeks as proceeds of war. The myth that Greeks gave us philosophy and other forms of knowledge are defeated only by a strong sense of reconstructing history more accurately as George James did in 1954 in his book, *The Stolen Legacy*. This is a must-read for all self-respecting Africans and those who care to know the truth or more credible accounts of our past. *The Stolen Legacy* remains largely on the margins of global discourses that drive the myth of supremacist propaganda that drives the narrative of Africa as a 'dark continent'.

The supremacist propaganda subsists on imposed standards of 'truth' derived almost exclusively from Eurocentric notions of 'truth' that are considered unproblematic, incontestable and universal. This very problematic view of history compels that historical facts cannot be frozen into posterity but must rather be treated as informed conjectures that are open to constant scrutiny, so that future generations can continue to dig for the truth rather than just become gullible and helpless consumers of what others choose to call the 'truth'. There is nothing truthful about unquestioned 'truth', for truth must withstand the highest forms of prodding and probing, not collapse during the simplest of inquiry or systematic testing.

Historical facts get generated via various methods such as critical analysis of a historical text to determine whether the narrative can be construed as something that happened, studying the geographical space, human interactions, possible anachronistic appearances, and the probability that such an occurrence could have happened in real life. This exercise includes testing for internal and external consistency of a narrative, that is, whether aspects of a story are correlating well and can be approximated to real accounts of events that took place in the past (internal consistency), including whether the time order of events can be trusted (external consistency). These reliabi-lity tests are intended to verify if historical facts can be established from a historical text or whether narratives that cannot be backed by original texts or archaeological materials, as is the case with most Biblical narratives, can be trusted and taken as true accounts of what happened in the past. Otherwise, the *"circuitous slippage"* between truth and alternative truths or facts and alternative facts can easily infiltrate our rational, scientific spaces and eviscerate history of its scientific decorum leading to some half-truths and **chants of charlatans** dancing to the rhythm of grotesque **mediocrity** and stirring **mendaciloquence** (artful lying).

For instance, in the study of the Gospels of the New Testament, Richard Carrie ran these reliability tests and other tests to determine whether these Jesus narratives can pass the muster of being called historical facts, and published his findings in the 2012 book, *Proving History*, which showed that all the narratives in the Gospels are myths drawn from ancient legends, in particular those of Egyptian Kemet Mystery and Zoroastrianism. I must insist that there is nothing wrong with these Jesus narratives being considered as myths mainly because these narratives can be examined allegorically within the framework of the probable conditions of uncertainty, as there are no original ancient texts to support and corroborate these biblical narratives. We learn a great deal of lessons and derive lots of wisdom from myths and legends. They have a place in our knowledge base as doxastic logic and gain even greater significance when considered this way as they hinge beliefs on solid human grounds as one of many beliefs or myth genres that enrich our existence. Myths may not be true encounters of what literally happened in the past but contain 'truths' that develop certain understandings about, particularly, unseen spiritual forces that we believe shape and enrich our lives and our notions of morality. It is not clear why Christian fundamentalists want to insist that these narratives are historical narratives, as their potency does not wane with loss of a historical perspective.

What it does to Jesus narratives as captured in the synoptic gospels is to rid these narratives of a supremacist agenda and the desire to dominate other equally legitimate belief systems through use of menticide and manipulation of history. Jesus, the mythi-cal, serves to provide a perspective on questions humanity generationally grapple with all the time such as attempting to offer explanations on natural occurrences such as creation, origins of religious rituals, preserving some historical events, and trying to understand our experiences in relation to both the mundane and afterlife. Similar perspectives derive from other belief systems and humanity is better served by these multiple perspectives in an era of productive complexity noted for thriving on multiplicity of perspectives (Pitso, 2021). The riding of the Jesus story on historical scholarship defies logical validity and can only be sustained through manipulation, falsehood, or flawed attempts to let these narratives pass the test of what is most probable by means that are generally deceitful. When methods of textual criticism and palaeography are used to authenticate ancient texts such as Jesus narratives as expounded in the synoptic gospels, the only possible outcome is what is most probable, that is, what could be construed to have happened so that truth is out of reach when history is the basis of analysis and questing. This means that the truthfulness of the Jesus story cannot be established within a historical perspective and its fallible methods of inquiry. It is thus not clear why scholars of Jesus studies insist on using history to justify the Jesus story as a true account of His life. There is only one plausible explanation for this position.

The Christian fundamentalists, the church, and Christian historians seek gatekeeping of their version of 'truth' rather than the actual universal truth that is incontestable in any meaningful respects. Those who seek truth cannot frown on its methods of rigour, but Christian exponents have become social elites or upper middle class alongside political elites and are experts on manipulating and strategically managing a social contract in any society to ensure their inclusion and perpetuation alongside political and economic power. Persuasion and indoctrination are weapons of choice for these skilled workers who alter intentions and emotions of others to gain greater control of them on a massive scale and ride on the crest of a populist wave, the outcome of which is grandiose power and mass deception that benefit the narrowness of elites.

The problem with such power is that it leads to delusions on a massive scale of grandeur and grandiose which leave both the perpetrator and victims with a mental ill-health. This is the only extraordinary situation where the ill do not seek help but rather continue unabated to create a mental pandemic that is not easily detected because it is part of the extant social contract that feeds a dominant political and economic power. Social contracts are supposedly negotiated agreements about how the public sphere and institutional infrastructures can be optimised to serve the greater good yet self-serving demented souls tend to distort it to serve their narrow, ephemeral interests. When societal anxiety increases exponentially because ideals of a social contract are being compromised by avaricious narrowness, societal truth claims emanating from a social contract become transparent and public awareness increases on the source of their public anxiety, gatekeepers of elites generate alternative truth claims that position greedy, demented elites as saviours of masses. Gatekeepers of elites often include historians, scientists, politicians, economists, and church leadership. In a milieu of discursive obsession with alternative truths, lying, dishonesty, and alternative facts, public distrust substantially increases and the potential for anarchy threatens the existing societal stability, those with presumed public credibility serve as the crucial buffer against the corrupt elite and get rewarded by proceeds of a crime or nefarious benefits. In developing buffer strategies and projecting their presumed credibility, these real hyenas tend to use history and science as central to their fight-back strategies, hence opening history and science to manipulation and achieving their narrow outcomes.

History and science have to defend their turf against these forces of darkness lest history becomes implicit in the commission of such atrocities and, in the long run, risks its credibility as a legitimate area of science and scholarship. Another key aspect of historical methods is how the most probable is arrived at. For instance, in trying to understand the veracity of an empty tomb, there is an absolute need to develop a thorough understanding of the Roman Empire's method or practice of crucifixion as historically conceptualised. Crucifixion was intended to humiliate and strip victims of basic dignity and decency to have a deterrence effect on those seeking to challenge the status quo or harbour similar forbidden ideologies or thoughts. Crucifixion is the ultimate ignominious way of dying reserved only for those who hold different, subversive ideas to those of a dominant political or religious power of the time.

To determine whether Jesus's preaching could have been construed as subversive by the Roman Empire, it is important to reconstruct his message. The main message of Jesus is love and peace as opposed to war and violence. Indeed, considering the Gospel of Thomas which is highly allegorical and esoteric to hide the true teachings of Jesus which might have been considered as subversive and heretical to the church's version of religious narratives, the real message would not have been uncovered or deciphered. This Gospel of Thomas was also suppressed and hidden from public scrutiny until its discovery later on. Jesus's message was not a subversive matter during His time and cannot be considered as reasonable grounds for the crucifixion of Jesus, whether as historical or mythical person. The real reason for the crucifixion of Jesus is the claim He made as Messiah of Jews and the call for peace. Surely, the Roman Empire would have no problem with such a message that calls for stability and maintenance of the *status quo* where it reigns. Politically, Jesus's message should have involved acts of sedition, that is, cause insurrection or have the potential to cause it against established political authority to earn the wrath of the established political authority. This was not the case. There is, however, a second message that relates more to the freedom of Jews as encapsulated in the concept of Messiah. In Jewish understanding, there was an expectation that God would defeat their enemies and install a Jewish kingdom with a future king and in return Jews would build God a synagogue. In Hebrew, Messiah simply means a future king.

It is also important to note that the concept of Messiah had always been there in other belief systems such as in the Egyptian Mystery System and is likely to have been adopted from these ancient African beliefs. Those opposed to Jesus and His message were the Jewish elders who felt offended when Jesus considered Himself a Messiah, thereby taking away their story of a new Jewish kingdom and inaugurating Himself as their Messiah under conquest conditions. It subverted the Jewish dream and vision of a free Jewish country. It is this self-positioning of Jesus as Messiah that was considered as subversive of the Jewish effort for a free country and heretical to their belief. It was deeply offensive from the perspectives of Jewish church leaders as it stood in opposition to the promise of building a Jewish God's kingdom on earth, hence they demanded that he be crucified so he could be humiliated as a lesson to those who might harbour similar thoughts.

The Jewish elders could have opted for other methods of punishing Jesus for heresy, but crucifixion had a strong deterrence effect. Crucifixion was a three-stage torture process intended to maximise the impact of ignominy and serve a strong deterrence purpose. Step one was to publicly carry the cross and walk to one's crucifixion place under excruciating circumstances. A crucifixion cross during the reign of the Roman Empire was estimated at 300 pounds (approximately 136 kg), which was quite heavy and the distance Jesus covered was more than half a kilometre although he was helped by an African, Simon from Cyrene (Northern Africa), to carry the cross. In His moment of weakness, Jesus was rescued by an African who helped Him carry the burden of the cross, a replay of Jesus's earlier rescue when his parents sought refuge in Africa to spare Jesus's young life threatened by Herod. **Yes, Africa saved Jesus twice in his most vulnerable moments. The evidence is right inside the Bible whether this is construed as a legend or as true accounts.** That Jesus needed to be assisted to carry His cross was part one of the humiliation project. If He portrayed Himself as powerful, failure to carry the cross substantially weakened that claim.

Part two involved the actual nailing on the cross so that all witnesses could viscerally feel the pain as a way of deterring others with similar thoughts. Step three was to leave the body on the cross so vultures and other birds of prey could eat it away, thus denying Jesus the ultimate dignity of being buried. How likely, therefore, is it that the Jewish leaders or Roman emperors could have acceded to the request to bury Jesus after consultation with the political authority of the time, which was approached by Joseph of Arimathea, who donated his tomb to Jesus. Crucified people had no graves or tombs, because the intention was to wipe them from the history of a nation so their ideas could die with them. This was the essential purpose of a crucifixion. A burial restores the dignity of a person as it perpetuates him into posterity and would have defeated the very purpose of crucifixion.

Another issue that was deliberately left vague in the narrative of Jesus's crucifixion is the social status of Joseph of Arimathea within the Jewish community. It is extremely significant in determining the plausibility of his request to bury Jesus, which meant subverting one of the apex ignominious stages of crucifixion. It is highly improbable that such a stage of ignominy could have been sidestepped that easily, especially because Jewish elders wanted to deter future messianic charlatans. Thus, it is highly improbable that Jesus's body could have ended up in a tomb. During the reign of the Roman Empire, it was highly unlikely that people of less significance could approach the church elders or Emperor, especially of the stature of Pontius Pilate, with such a request. It is only the Jewish elders who could try such a feat, but it would then mean defeating their own purpose as they are the ones that demanded that Jesus be crucified.

I am providing here an example of how a method of historical and logical disputation can be applied to reach the most probable scenario of the past and pass the test of logical validity. Given that there is no ancient scrolls or texts that account for Jesus's story in the first 20 years after crucifixion, it can only be concluded that most of His story draws from the imagination of His narrators, hence they differ materially on their account of Jesus's story. As a legend, the irrationality that distorts the crucifixion process is acceptable as the message is more important than the plausibility of a narrative itself. There are many such instances, such as Jesus is God. There is no evidence that supports this view, except in John's Gospel. It is highly unlikely that Matthew, Luke and Mark could have deliberately ignored such a crucial aspect of Jesus's story. In fact, in Mark 10:17-28, Jesus is at pains to explain that he is a fallible human being and that "good" should only be attributed to a force higher than Him called God.

This faulty notion that Jesus is God serves to show how facts can be distorted and manipulated to drive a supremacist or church agenda of menticide, which is the worst kind of atrocity to be visited upon fellow humans. There are many such efforts of distortion in the synoptic gospels and without a backup of original scripts the synoptic gospels are reduced to myth and legend. As indicated earlier, there is nothing wrong with that as the underlying lessons remain potent and salient as one of many such "truths" available to humanity as it constructs its moral fibre, especially in the complex, cosmopolitan global society. These "truths" need to rid themselves of the supremacist and menticide agendas as both vitiate their potency. This way, Christianity is stripped of its supremacist agenda and conditions are created in which all belief systems of the world, including African spirituality, could potentially contribute to the moral fibre of our complex society. It is clear that ancient African spirituality is even more susceptible to manipulation and falsehood as the result of many wars and colonial conquests that were waged against our ancestors and a sustained period of misinformation and distorted history.

It is also significant to note that Jesus, mythical or real, was not a Christian and knew nothing about this movement that purports to act on His behalf. He might have pleaded with His disciples to spread His teachings even at a legend level, but did not envisage that this could be done in ways that strip the very African people, who supported Him in His moments of vulnerability, of their dignity, culture, history and identity. Jesus, mythical or real, must have died a proud Jew and would never engage in acts that decimate others' identity and cultures. It is immaterial whether His story is a legend or true encounter of history that Richard Carrie has already proved as a myth in *Proving History* (2012). The bottom line is: in all His teachings in basic Theology guides, He never condemned other cultures. How could He, when His own teachings derive from African spirituality, whether through authorship or oral tradition.

These issues shall be expounded in later sections of this book. Science can serve the purpose of illuminating falsehood and protecting people against possible manipulation driven through altered history or manufactured facts. Science achieves this feat via its strict protocols of reliability and validity as well as its constant search for the truth that leads to reliable knowledge.

It is in this sense that all forms of knowledge are considered, postpositivist era, as informed conjectures worthy of being constantly verified and supported by evidence, hence the plinth of science is the replicability, verifiability, and trustworthiness of its results. The work of science and its production methods must pass the muster of being repeatable under the same conditions, producing the same results, and being open to further scrutiny and verification. There is however an element of science that is dangerous and reduces reality to the unreal and can be used effectively to conceal reality thus opening science to manipulation and serving nefarious agendas. This idea that science ultimately seeks to reduce reality to formulae, that is, to mathematical models that make us understand our lived reality according to the ten numbers of the numeric system, leads to a warped reality. This way, science becomes extremely reductionist as the process of creating facts and knowledge is based on the condensation of what passes reliability and validity tests as it displaces whatever failed to succeed on these tests. Many scholars would argue that alternative methods of creating facts and knowledge via text exists but are still subjected to tests of trustworthiness which includes credibility, transferability, dependability, and confirmability tests. This means that the process of condensation and displacement, the very source of reductionism, remains very much intact but mitigated in these areas of scientific endeavour with rich data sources.

I am not entirely opposed to scientific study as a social scientist, but in areas such as history, displacement could mean epistemic injustice and marginalisation of other ways of knowing. Many historians and scientists would argue that this aspect of science should be attributed to what counts as pseudo-scientific racial hierarchies of knowledge that serve supremacist agendas. However, it is European historians who sustained the perception and lie that Africa, in particular sub-Saharan Africa, had no history and consisted mostly of primitive people who were ignorant of ways of science and credible knowledge (Parker & Rathbone, 2007). Given this reality, African history only received scholarly attention around the late 19th century and deep into the 20th century. Determining how to study Africa's past involved decisions on topics and whether the entire continent's past could be studied or divided into sub-regions. In all these choices, African spirituality was given a wide berth, mainly because it would disrupt another supremacist project of menticide introduced by the Celtic churches around the late 19th century intended to extirpate all our cultures, sense of pride in our heritage, and our human solidarity. This explains why African spirituality has been side-lined for so long, including Zoroastrianism from Iranian, the oldest religions in the world on which Abrahamic religions such as Judaism, Christianity, and Islam relied so much in their formation.

Mental suicide, from which the concept 'menticide' originates, has been used as an effective subversive tool that destroyed our own beliefs and cultures. We can thus not allow science, including its justificatory warrant in the form of history, to warp our reality and wipe out our rich legacy just because of its impressive checks and balances. The worst lies are those that pass the muster of scientific rigour and there are many such instances in history and philosophy as expounded earlier in the book and shall be further explicated in subsequent sections and chapters of this book. Indeed, many scholars would argue that we make a clear distinction between science and pseudoscience and I fully agree but science too has its limitations. So many people are astonishingly gullible that any wishful thinking masquerading as 'scientific' would appeal to them and sway their beliefs and understandings. It may not matter how improbable the wishful thinking is, its masquerade would sustain the potency of the narrative and its presumed truthfulness.

There are many scholars of Christianity, better described as apologists, who drive the narrative that Christian stories are true accounts of what happened in the past even though they possess no original ancient texts to corroborate their claims and make them gain scientific merit. There is also a deliberate omission of other beliefs that precede Christianity and have strong similarities with the Christian belief system. Let us take Zoroastrianism as an example of how certain knowledge forms can be displaced and wiped from the memory of a global society by acts that are essentially political and under the guise of science. The grounds for totally wiping out other beliefs from history is mainly because they vitiate dominant narratives that history has deified through political projects. In the table on dominant beliefs (Table 1.1), we juxtapose and contrast these ancient belief systems to better inform ourselves prior to determining reasons for the marginalisation of some religions and the promotion of others. This is also intended to dispel the myth of inerrancy embedded in most of these belief systems, illuminating them as nothing more than just ancient narratives of various nations containing myths, legends, ethics, and ethos.

It is also intended to question the blasphemous suggestion that Jews are a chosen nation, which reduces God to a biased deity with ambrosia of primal emotions that sway to one nation at the expense of other equally deserving nations. **I know of no greater blasphemy.** This notion of a chosen nation, while it served Jews well in the past, cannot be allowed to continue without challenge and the spurious grounds of anti Semitism when this issue is raised are no more than an intellectual diversion and a logical dodge, both of which have run their course and have no place in our global, complex society. In no way is disputing the chosen nation theory an aspersion to Judaism or its cultural variants as these must be celebrated without hindrance within the framework that allows all ancient narratives to have their space and right to exist in our global, cosmopolitan society. Greater cultural diversity serves humanity better where all cultures, including African culture, are appreciated, celebrated, and given space to grow without subversive tendencies designed to marginalise other cultures and give space for the dominance of the others. I fully support efforts that result in the total elimination of any prejudice, bias, subversion, and discrimination of any sort in our global, cosmopolitan society, including matters of belief. Grand equality is the ultimate goal of humanity and restores our collective dignity as well as an unalienable right of beliefs to exist and shape all humanity's morality. Any nation seeking exclusive rights to God's favour is not worthy of such a privilege and will find it hard to escape the stigma of being bias and prejudiced against other equally deserving nations. Such a nation also lacks humility and a strong sense of inclusiveness and solidarity as well as the pursuit of a socially just world. It can also not escape the stigma of being a political project designed to privilege certain groupings and subjugating the others. **There is no honour in subversion or dominance of other beliefs or nations.**

In Table 1.1 (below) on dominant belief systems, a summary of the ancient beliefs is attempted. Beliefs stem from our deep desire to understand and relate to the unseen forces that we assume shape and enrich our existence. Organised beliefs stem from the Kemet traditions of acknowledging the unseen forces that make a presence in our lives and influence our decisions, conduct, and values from whence the concept 'amen' used by most Abrahamic religions originates. 'Amen' is an acknowledgement of the presence and invitation of an unseen force that is greater than us to our lives and our existence, the purpose of which is to enrich our lives and guarantee the safe passage of our souls to eternal bliss. Each of these beliefs provides a perspective on this unseen force that makes a presence in our lives. Some beliefs separate such an unseen force from our daily lives, hence the concept of transcendence – an experience beyond our mundane, material lives. All Abrahamic religions fall into this category. African belief systems consider the divine as manifest in our material world, that is, the unseen force is reflected in our conduct and interactions with fellow humans and nature. Hence, we refer to immanence, this idea that God is seen in our daily deeds and material world. In African spirituality, we observe behaviour, one's conduct and deeds towards others and treatment of nature for signs of internal psychology, that is, the beliefs, values, and intentions that guide individual decision-making especially towards serving the greater good. Hence, African spirituality is considered as a progenitor of science because of its emphasis on observation and lived experiences as sources of determining the physical, psychological, and spiritual health of people.

Our next focus is on a brief elucidation of ancient beliefs so we can figure out why African spirituality remains side-lined and why humanity is poorer for it. In a powerful essay that appears in the 2010 *Christian Delusion* book edited by John Loftus, Edward Babinski explains how Christian scholars sought to extirpate the presence of other ancient belief systems to perpetuate the myth that Christianity and its

Bible were the only original religion and text that can be considered inerrant and the only spiritual voice that represents the will of God. This myth persisted and was stronger around the middle of the 19th century. However, numerous archaeological discoveries and linguistic breakthroughs from the 18th century to this day provide irrefutable evidence that:

◆ Ancient Egyptian texts committed to hieroglyphic writings contain religious, or more precisely, African spirituality concepts that precede the Hebrew Torah and Christian Bible.

◆ Zoroastrianism, alongside African spirituality, is one of the oldest religions that came before Abrahamic religions.

◆ Abrahamic religions' scriptures, rituals, and view of the cosmos mirrored those of ancient African spirituality and Zoroastrianism, which necessitated the need to invest time and resources in extirpating these ancient religions that preceded Abrahamic religions so that a myth could be perpetuated that Abrahamic religions are the only legitimate voice of God. Riding on this myth was also the idea that Israelites/Jews were a chosen nation favoured by God, which is absolute nonsense. There is absolutely no evidence to support this despicable claim. It is also so blasphemous as to warrant no further attention. It is egregiously obnoxious and unworthy of a scholarly gaze.

Furthermore, modern scholarship (Tobin, 2010) has provided evidence that the Bible:

◆ Contains multiple inconsistencies and contradictions that make it difficult to rely on it when seeking divine truths.

◆ Has no factual basis that is supported by archaeological discoveries and research. Pseudo-archaeology is shamelessly trying though.

◆ Is a smorgasbord of fairy tale, myths, legends, and stolen legacies from other belief systems. It has no story of itself as most are plagiarised.

◆ Subsists on failed prophecies and irrationality of miracle narratives that bear no reasonable analogy to present-day reality and can best be described as outcomes of hallucinations and feats of phantasmagoria.

◆ Thrives on forgeries, plagiarism from other belief systems, and persistent efforts to undermine and extirpate other belief systems, in particular, those from which it stole a lot.

◆ Cannot be the inerrant word of God. This is particularly important to accentuate, because this represents the highest level of sacrilegious impiety, that such a deeply flawed and cobbled up web of deceit could so be linked with divine matters.

As Tobin (2010:181) so elegantly argues:

> Given all this, the Bible cannot be considered an inspired God-breathed docu-ment. Rather it seems to be written by superstitious people who were creating God in their own image [...] therefore Christianity is not a reasoned faith. It cannot stand up for critical scrutiny.

The fundamental problem with Christianity is that it never questioned itself. It never quarrelled with itself, hence its inability to stand for critical scrutiny and test the superiority of its own logic. We are rational beings and only superior logic should appeal to us even in matters of religion or spirituality. This explains why African spirituality has been closely linked with science since ancient times. It has to be conspicuously self-critical and hold the humility that it is one of many belief systems in the world so that only its superior logic will ensure its survival. It is not about undermining or, at worse, extirpating other belief systems, rather it is about its superior logic and evidence-led practice. All belief systems including African spirituality and Christianity need to, by dint of common sense, are underpinned by reason and logic because they are human phenomena. Reason leads to sanity, a state of calmness that allows one to be convinced by evidence, logic, and facts. Where none exists, processes of making the absence of evidence, logic, and facts present in our lives have to be engaged. Using such methods must always lead to objectivity or informed conjecture we can question and quarrel with on a regular basis until the truth is approximated, not necessarily achieved as that take even longer time. We can only lay the foundation upon which others would continue the quest for truth.

Imagine if Christianity quarrelled with itself years back and stopped attempting to extirpate African spirituality, what could have been achieved by way of reasoned logic for both of these belief systems. They ought to be intelligible, hence we talk of spiri-tual intelligence, the capabilities to develop creative genius, superior logic and one's complex problem-solving abilities using, in addition to traditional cognitive proces-ses, potentialities we can only describe as divine and beyond our ordinary compre-hension. This way, people need to confront, challenge, and defeat animalistic instinct for it seeks automated responses and behaviours that lead to monotony – the tedious, repetitive, and dumb. Most belief systems require such behaviours to thrive but this is inhuman and inhumane as it declares us less human and more animalistic. Without intelligence, we are just instinctive animals. In other words, instincts seek to destroy our free will, choice, and reason. If African spirituality seeks such then it is not my belief system because it becomes inherently malevolent and anti-African. African spirituality is based on Prudence virtue and rationality is guided by standards of prudence.

In Table 1.1, the main ancient belief systems are described, showing their historical epochs to demonstrate that Abrahamic religions, including Christianity, are fairly younger than Zoroastrianism and African spirituality.

Table 1.1   The dominant ancient beliefs of the world

Belief	Zoroastrianism	Judaism	Christianity	Islam	African spirituality
Age	+4 000 years	-4 000 years	+2 000 years	+1 400 years	+4 000 years, even far earlier
Salvation/ Soteriology (save from what, how?)	Concept not relevant, no need for salvation just believe in Zarathustra and in heaven, fight evil	Sin, arrival of Messiah	Sin, accepting Jesus	Evil, infidel, accepting Muhammad (PBUH) teachings	Concept unknown but similar to mortal coil needs encapsulated in Temperance virtue, complete eradication of poverty, save humanity from hunger as expression of divinity/ubuNtu.
Embodiment	Zarathustra	Messiah	Jesus	Muhammad	Land and its responsible use and sharing.
Book	Avesta	Torah	Bible	Quran	None but draws from certain aspects of Egyptian Mystery System and oral accounts.
Worship	Not prescriptive	Prayer	Prayer	Prayer	Not practised, for reverence
Vertical communication	Via Zarathustra and rituals	Via Messiah and rituals	Via Jesus and rituals	Via Muhammad and rituals	Via ancestors as intermediaries and rituals using natural resources
Afterlife and source	Heaven and hell, good deeds	Heaven or hell, believe in Messiah and obeying ten commandments	Heaven or hell, believe in Jesus and obeying ten commandments	Heaven or hell, believe in Muhammad and acts of altruism	Join Community of Saints (ancestral home/ isibaya) based on moral action which is a precondition for assuming the role of a spiritual conduit and serve as intermediary
Deity	Monotheism	Monotheism	Monotheism	Monotheism	Monotheism
Rituals	Sacred fires, purification	Purification, circumcision, rites of passage, prayer	Baptism, Eucharist, Confirmation, prayer	Faith profession, alms, fasting, pilgrimage, prayer	Various traditional feasts for celebration, cleansing, and rites of passage
Teachings	Goal: conquer evil through messianism, judgement after death, heaven and hell, Cosmic Order superior to earthly chaos.	Goal: defeat evil, messianism, judgement after death, heaven and hell, free will, ten commandments	Goal: defeat evil, messianism, judgement after death, heaven and hell, ten commandments	Based on the five pillars under rituals: profession of faith, alms, fasting, pilgrimage, and prayer	*Temperance + Fortitude + Prudence + Justice =* ubuNtu (oneness of humans and nature)

Zoroastrianism

This belief system is based on the concept of one God (monotheism although some scholars consider it as dualistic, thus polytheistic), who is called Ahura Mazda and credited with creating all things in the world (origins of the creation story). He is considered compassionate, omniscient, omnipotent, loving and just.

Zoroastrianism claims its existence as from the 2nd millennium BCE, meaning before historical dating or periodising was referenced with the birth of Jesus Christ. It is the oldest religion that gave most of humanity the concept of God as the creator of the universe. The embodiment of this belief system is Zarathustra, who is considered as the Messiah that performed miracles and considered Himself "the truth, the light and the word". He was born on 25 December and witnesses followed the star to where He was born and gave gifts. Zarathustra had twelve disciples and is set to have risen from death and ascended to heaven. Baptism is one of the main rituals performed in this belief system. Its main symbol is the cross that gets to be worshipped on Sundays. For a deeper understanding of this belief system, refer to the book *The Spirit of Zoroastrianism* (2012) by Prods Oktor Skjaevro.

Judaism

Judaism very much pivots around monotheism with the promised Messiah at the heart of its belief system. The foundation of Judaism is a historical grand narrative that entails values and ethics that pertain to the development of Jews as a nation of Israel and as captured in the Torah. It also pivots around Moses as a liberator and also the promised Messiah who will ensure total liberation of the Israeli nation. Another useful book in understanding Judaism is the Talmud, containing descriptions of the ceremonial and civil laws of the Jews as well as their legends. There are two versions, the Babylonian and Jerusalem Talmud, both containing teachings for the growth and development of Jews. These teachings revolve around concepts of heaven and hell, defeat of mortal suffering, and purification. The Torah is based on the five books of Moses plus prophets, other writings, Talmud, and Shulchan Aruch get adapted to contexts where Jews live and form the basis of law and ethos that drive Jewish life. Baptism, circumcision, and rites of passage form part of its rituals.

Judaism is not a static, rigid belief system. Rather, it is quite an eclectic system consisting of a number of movements that reflect nuances and differences in the interpretation of the meaning of Judaism to suit certain lifestyles. Traditional orthodox Judaism has tended to keep the rigid interpretations and ancient meanings of what constitutes the Judaism belief system. It considers these traditional practices and mores as unquestionable and unproblematic as well as free from political influence.

However, movements that challenged this orthodox rigidity in Judaism had a strong political and social influence and adapted Judaism to their circumstances and contexts.

These movements started off around the late 19th century in Germany with the Reformist Judaism as influenced by Germany's new liberal politics. This point confirms the strong confluencing between religion and politics both of which yearn power and the need to control and direct people to a particular agenda driven by a specific grand narrative. Moses Mendelssohn writings are credited with the genesis of the Judaism movements that refused to accept orthodox Judaism as is and rather studied as well as selected content that made sense to their contemporary lives. Mondecai Kaplan continued in this vein of studying and adapting Judaism to their contexts and reality around the middle of the 20th century while struggling with concepts of Jews as a chosen nation and transcendence. This Reconstructionist movement differs from other reformist movements in that it relied heavily on a scientific approach to understanding and adapting Judaism to modern societies.

In the early 1970s, Rabbi Sherwin Wine, most probably influenced by African spirituality, shifted Judaism from a vertical relationship where concerns apply only to humans and their relationships with God as facilitated via prayer and rituals. He accentuated and cultivated an ethic and conduct that signified otherness, that is, other humans and respectful treatment of nature. Rabbi Wine had strong relations with Tunisian Sociologist, Robert Memmi, and both set up a society that drove ideals of human dignity rather than concerns with transcendent matters. You can sense strong social justice and ubuNtu principles in this humanist Judaism with a strong immanence character.

Christianity

Starting off as a small Judaism sect, Christianity benefitted from the political and war successes of the Roman Empire and later as part of an elaborate colonial political project in Africa. There is a legend that Mark, one of the disciples of Jesus, was the first to introduce Christianity to northern Africa and this is highly contestable. Firstly because there were highly organised African empires in the 1st and 2nd centuries who could not accept that a culturally disruptive discourse takes precedence over well-established traditions and cultures. Secondly, with its intention to inaugurate Jesus as king, Christianity would not easily find favour in African empires that pivoted around kingship.

Thirdly, Mark lacked credibility in Africa as a foreigner with limited resources to mount such a huge shift in a cultural paradigm. Furthermore, there was little benefit for African empires to embrace Christianity. For instance, it is stated that the Ethiopian emperor adopted Christianity as a way of fending off the threats of the Roman Empire. Similarly, Moshoeshoe of the Basotho nation also used it as a buffer against the encroachment of coloniality in his kingdom and threats of land grabs. This sounds like a plausible explanation in lieu of one that involves Mark. There was no way Mark could just walk into an African empire based on kingship rule and make Christianity interesting to the emperor. This was the 1st century and strangers were treated with extreme caution and suspicion. There is no evidence either way that Mark met up with the Ethiopian emperor. The only plausible explanation is that of the Roman Empire conquering parts of Africa and installing its own political power and the religion Constantine adopted in the 7th century as the religion of the conqueror.

The real spread of Christianity occurred under a political clout, unlike Islam that rode on economic trading in its formative years in Africa, although later it also used politics for its spread. In the interior of Africa, Christianity was brought by the Portuguese and Dutch as an education and colonial project via missionaries, but they were met with great resistance and again was used by Kings like Moshoeshoe in Lesotho to stave off the colonial project as earlier stated. This element of Christianity that of being susceptible to exploitation to achieve political and economic goals, persists unabated to this day. It remains a political project.

This Christian exploitative element forms a critical part of its business model that underpins most churches and leads to its usefulness as a political and economic tool. It is spiritually subversive and blasphemous, because all these manipulative endeavours are done in the name of the Supreme Being.

What then is Christianity?

It is a monotheistic belief system that is based on the notion that people are born in sin and need to accept Jesus as their saviour to access the kingdom of Heaven. It is a sub-set of Judaism with noticeable differences. It embraces the idea that the Messiah is already on earth in the form of Jesus and has already met the condition of suffering or sadistic violence for his followers so they can be cleansed of their sin and gain the reward of securing a seat in heaven. It is unapologetically a cultural narrative of the history of the Jews and Jesus including their teachings that set Jews as a chosen nation, a claim that is disputed in this book.

Purification via baptism is central to their rituals and the cross is a symbol of Christianity that represents salvation, redemption, and reward of heavenly bliss. The Bible, of which the first five books, the Pentateuch or Torah, form the basis of laws and teachings that guide Christian life, remains its bloodline. Christians also draw wisdom from psalms and the sketchy biographical life of Jesus as captured in the synoptic gospels. Its spread in Africa relied heavily on the subversive techniques of menticide and the ascendancy of coloniality. Rituals include prayer, regular church attendance, confirmation, and Eucharist. Like most cultural projects, Christianity has versions that depend on situatedness on the political spectrum.

Conservatives believing firmly in the inerrancy of the Bible occupying one extreme of its dichotomy, moderates who are also called revisionists because they seek to make Christianity relevant to contemporary life occupy the middle and Reconstructionists, who seek to give Christianity a humanist flair and focus on otherness (humans and nature) and matters of social and economic justice sit on the other extreme. These various permutations of Christianity, and they are many, provide evidence that the Bible is open to multiple interpretations and distortions thus its inerrancy vitiates on the face of this evidence.

As a cobbled-up document, the Bible is no more than any literary device driving a particular 'historical' narrative designed to persuade people to abandon their cultures and embrace a culture of another ordinary nation. The embracing of the cultures of other people entails loss. Loss in identity. Loss in culture. Loss in heritage. Loss in solidarity. Loss on land which is central to African spirituality. Every loss is accompanied by a distressing reaction, a sense of grief, negative emotions, and a strong miasma of hopelessness. Africans' loss of land and a strong cultural subversion means that we remain in generational grief and distress that lead us to seek solace in ways that are generally unsavoury. Church, alcohol, and sports remain our main coping strategies in the face of a total onslaught on our land, nerves, state of sanity, and *compos mentis*. The day Christianity becomes central to reclaiming African land and seeking a socially just world is the day it will begin a *mea culpa* journey towards corrective action and redemption from its 'sin' (wrongs) of contributing to the deprivation of one nation of its identity, culture, resources, and heritage. Christianity itself as a colonial project is responsible for the devastation in human relations and remains impervious to the celebration of cultural diversity. Things could have been different if Christianity eschewed politics and cultural capture via menticide and use of other subversive techniques.

The Christian message of love, redemption, salvation, and promise of a better tomorrow is quite appealing on its own and resonates with ubuNtu. The fact that Jews, Moses and Jesus, spent their formative years in North Africa, the hub of knowledge and civilisation, means that the African culture of ubuNtu and serving public good would have influenced their worldview and spiritual outlook. While evidence of their presence in Africa is recorded in the Torah, Talmud, and Bible, there is a concerted effort to conceal the impact of African influence on Moses, Jesus, and Jewish and Christian culture. This smacks of intellectual dishonesty. Spanish archaeologists have recently discovered the depictions of Jesus in an Ancient Egyptian tomb providing evidence of His presence in North Africa either as a legendary or historical figure. The reason this discovery did not hawk headline news is because this depiction shows Jesus raising His hand in a way that symbolises worship of some African deity. Furthermore, this depiction of Jesus occurred in the Egyptian city of Oxyrhynchus about 100 miles south of Cairo known for worshipping the Egyptian god of the afterlife, Osiris.

The thought of Jesus worshipping an African god was too ghastly to contemplate or consider because the whole Christian project would collapse, as it is currently constituted mainly as a supremacist project. I see nothing wrong with Jesus worshipping

Osiris as it was an important part of growing up for Jesus and dealing with the complexities of life at a particular point in His life and within a particular historical juncture. The supremacist project would definitely collapse, because it is based on the faulty logic that Africans are inferior and have contributed very little to civilisation, philosophy, and religion. Evidence paints a completely different picture. North Africa, in particular Egypt, provides a setting for most of the Jewish historical narratives as captured in the Old Testament including the formative years of Moses and Jesus. So, key embodiments of Judaism and Christian religion in Moses and their formative years' worldview were shaped through ancient African history and culture. Egypt also provided a safe haven for Jesus to grow and learn unhindered after His parents ran away from their unstable native land. Shortly after the demise of Jesus, a Coptic Christian religion started off in Egypt with a strong ancient African history and culture making it one of the first phases of Christianity which also made transparent the African influence on Christianity.

Let us end by demonstrating how Christian tenets existed long before Jesus and Christianity. All Abrahamic religions – Judaism, Christianity, and Islam – have a strong Ancient Egyptian belief system influence which is set to have started in c.3000 BCE and shaped Egyptian society and its scientific as well as philosophical outlook. The Egyptian belief system pivots around five concepts. First, it places faith in the **resurrection** after death as well as the existence of paradise and hell. Second, the Egyptian belief system makes use of the **cross** (*ankh*) that carries the message of eternity and life after death, while early Christians made use of the fish symbol (*Ichthys*) and only adopted the cross around the 4th century because of its powerful symbolism of transcendence. The oldest creed of the Egyptian belief system is the **Holy Trinity** of God Osiris, Goddess Iris, and their son Horus whom Iris bore without engaging in any sexual encounters with Osiris, hence the concept of the **virgin birth**. The Egyptian belief system also involved a **celibate** life that the Roman Catholic church later adopted as a religious order. Resurrection, the cross symbol, a Holy Trinity, virgin birth, and a celibate religious order represent the core of the ancient Egyptian belief system that existed many years before Judaism, Christianity, and Islam.

Zoroastrianism was also vital in shaping Abrahamic religions and their grand narratives. There was thus a valid reason why ancient African spirituality and Zoroastrianism belief systems were marginalised and attempts were made to extirpate them. They weaken the supremacist agenda of Christianity, Judaism, Islam, and coloniality as political projects. Zoroastrianism and African spirituality belief systems also share notions of serving the greater good, rejecting a pessimistic and dualistic reality as they both subsist on a holistic, optimistic view of reality.

In essence, Zoroastrianism and African spirituality denounce the **apocalyptic thought** that forms the essence of Abrahamic religions. Apocalyptic thought frames Abrahamic religions' ideas that the world is in a perpetual struggle between good and evil with God gaining prominence in all that is good and evil is associated with demonic and bad things. Apocalyptic thought is thus characterised by dualism, pessimism, vindication, and imminence. Those that serve good and challenge evil in their lives will be vindicated and rewarded with a place in heaven. Therefore, their salvation rests on defeating evil and demonic forces. The idea that the kingdom of God is near (imminence) and non-believers will be doomed features strongly in their sermons. Viewed in this apocalyptic perspective, Abrahamic religions locate the power of God as independent from our daily lives and lived experiences and rather believe there is a place somewhere called heaven, hence its strong adherence to transcendence. In contrast, African spirituality is more immanent, believing that our daily lives and lived experiences with fellow beings and nature reveal the power and nature of God. God, in African spirituality, dwells within us and in our endeavours to serve the greater good (ubuNtu) and preserve nature. The apocalyptic thought can be traced from the books of Joel, Zechariah, and from Isaiah 24-37, but a classic detailed description of apocalyptic perspective can be found in the book of Daniel.

All these narratives about revelation and the end of time can be traced from the 6th century BCE, that is, the pre-exilic period during which the Jews were undergoing extreme hardships and were making a covenant with God regarding building His kingdom and the temple dedicated to worshipping Him in return for God's mercy and protection. Exposure to extreme hardship especially one that involves oppression, lack of socioeconomic opportunities, and slavery compel our brains to look for mitigation of these strenuous circumstances. Some of the ways of forming mitigation is to develop a belief in something that gives hope such as religious attendance, frequency of prayer, and the belief that things will be better in the afterlife as those who caused harm on others will be punished. There is, however, no evidence that the frequency of religious attendance and prayer mitigates socio-economic hardships (Bradshaw & Ellison, 2010), yet people persist on this path because it does provide some hope, even if it is false.

In this sense, apocalyptic thought can be strongly associated with those who are economically and socially deprived, disinherited, and dispossessed. Given that their reality is unbearable and painful, it follows that these people would have a pessimistic view of the present and would easily find solace in an alternative reality that offers hope for a better tomorrow or afterlife. It also follows that the immediacy of pain and hardship would compel a view that the end of time is nigh. There is also a legitimate point that those who created this pain and hardship are seen as evil and demonic as those who are recipients of pain and hardship occupy a special place in the afterlife. These are circumstances and realities of people that are mature for exploitation by unscrupulous agents that purport to represent the best interests of the poor – the poor socio-economically, the poor spiritually but often materially rich or well-off as well as those who are greedy and wish to mitigate their guilt of living off ill-gotten resources.

These groups of people provide a huge market for agents of apocalyptic thought which resulted in the scholarly attention on religion and economic theory. Defined economically, beliefs are considered as cultural systems, that is, they have a bearing on human behaviours particularly relating to work and wealth. Apocalyptic thought does not seek to end poverty. Rather, it sees poverty as a ticket to a good afterlife along the lines of the blessed are the poor. **This is absolute nonsense.** Poverty is not the absence of wealth, rather it is the subversion of justice and entrenchment of a human system designed to concentrate wealth to the few elites in society and condemn the rest to penury. Poverty has nothing to do with divine matters. It is malevolent (a deviation from the cycle of ubuNtu) and visited upon fellow humans by savage human systems designed by modern barbarians passing as civilised humans, *snakes in suits*. My greatest gripe with Abrahamic religions is their view of poverty as essentially a virtue. There is no honour in poverty and avaricious wealth when they lead to human suffering. **I know of no greater dark malevolence**. On the other side of poverty lies **justice**, not wealth. Pursuance of justice from the African spirituality perspective leads to the total elimination of poverty at all levels as shall be expounded later – physical, psychological, sociological, economic, and ultimately spiritual.

For Abrahamic religions, including Christianity, to salvage whatever credibility it has left after the irreparable harm it visited upon African spirituality and culture, here is an agenda of atonement – contribution to the total elimination of poverty by working towards justice and the return of land to its indigenous owners. Land represents the embodiment of our African spirituality and our source of our version of soteria (connectedness), although in our worldview there is no such concept as 'salvation', hence the closest to salvation is reconnectedness with our ubuNtu values, in particular the Temperance virtue. Our essence is restorative and corrective, hence restorative justice. Our protection from harm or dire situations emanates from our land. You take our land, you take our physical, psychological, and spiritual safety. You render us hopeless, helpless, and disconnected from our essence, our being. If Christianity is for us, help us reclaim our land and pay for the sins of menticide that enabled our land dispossession and forged a belief in an imaginary heavenly place while colonisers yearn for our rich African resources. There is no greater malevolence than to put in place a religion that glorifies poverty, while it is a beneficiary of the most egregious system of skewed resource accumulation and distribution.

Islam

Muhammad (PBUH) is considered the embodiment of this monotheistic belief system. Six beliefs are at the core of Islam – belief in one unique, omniscient God called Allah, angels, holy books (Torah, Bible, Quran), prophets, Muhammad as the last prophet, and judgement day. The inerrancy of the Holy Quran drives this belief system and the status of Muhammad as the last of the seven prophets is well established.

Believers must submit to the five pillars that define this belief system:

1. **Confession of faith** to God and Muhammad as the messenger of God. As a ritual, it involves whispering it to newly born children and to the dead.

2. **Prayer** must be conducted five times everyday in the direction of Mecca.

3. **Fasting** entails deprivation of food, drink and sex for a certain period as a purification ritual.

4. **Alms** involves embracing material wealth and playing a role in assisting the less privileged. This is the source of sustaining inequality and defending the status quo that entrenches poverty. This is the worst kind of oppression, because in giving alms to the poor, they are literally sentenced to that condition and live a lie that makes it difficult to fight injustices of this world. **All forms of charity are evil**. They appeal to and draw from the savage, primal Darwinian instinct of altruism, which is essentially selfish. We become charitable because it serves our ego at various levels. First, it reduces our **guilt** in becoming complicit in sustaining an unjust system because we are its direct beneficiaries. Second, it builds our **reputation** and enhances our **status** in society. Third, it can serve as a **future investment** as you would expect to receive some favours from the beneficiaries of your alms in the future. As a temporary respite while fully engaged in efforts designed to set up a just system, I can live with it.

5. **Pilgrimage** involves visiting Mecca, the sacred shrine of Islam, at least once in a lifetime.

Islam grew rapidly in North Africa in places such as Egypt and Sudan, mainly as part of an economic project around the 11th century. Given that Christianity had already claimed the political clout in Africa, Islam found itself unable to access African land, so crucial in African spirituality and the main means of persuading Africans to embrace another belief system. This made it difficult for Islam to assert itself, especially in the interior of Africa, as Christianity as a political project had already asserted its influence and power. This struggle for influence in the interior of Africa continues to this day as Africans remain a nation besieged on all fronts, spiritually, politically, culturally, economically and socially.

Around the 16th century, Islam attempted to take control of the eastern coast of Africa in areas such as Mozambique, using maritime trade but lost to Christianity. This defeat to Christianity meant that the Saharan maritime trade that Muslims controlled over centuries, as it attempted to assert its own belief system, gave the advantage to Christianity and its spread in Africa. This issue points to the fact that trade or political clout was central to the project of converting Africans to any of these beliefs, leading one to conclude that subversive means including persuasion were effective tools of convincing Africans of the superiority of the gods of these belief systems. The African god was less important and had no place in these lofty beliefs, and therein lies blasphemy. That we worshipped one true God (monotheism) and all our African ways of doing are true and legitimate weakened as political power and influence over Africans and their resources trumped all other considerations.

It had not occurred to Muslims and Christians that by manipulating their deity into their human affairs in service of mundane needs (economic and political) was in itself an act of blasphemy and irreverence as most involved war, killings, and dehumanisation of fellow beings including depriving them of their God-given resources, cultures, and identities. Dehumanisation and deprivation of resources for those that have rights over these resources represent the worst of the malevolent acts there are in the world but to want to use God or a deity as a justificatory warrant must go down as one of the worst acts of infidelity to one's beliefs and deity.

Another great crime, sin, or infidelity is when subversive techniques are used to eviscerate another nation of its identity, culture, and heritage by erasing its historical past, legacy, and contributions to building modern society in areas of knowledge, philosophy, science, and spirituality. This leaves such a nation in a perpetual state of inferiority and belief that its own African nation is unworthy. However, the *coup de grace* has to be the stripping of this African nation's embodiment of spirituality and sacred shrine in the form of land. Land is to Africans as Mecca is to Muslims, it defines us physically, emotionally, philosophically, and spiritually. Land is our sacred shrine and embodiment of our spirituality. When you take land from Africans, you literally destroy their belief system and livelihood as shall be expounded in later chapters. While the right of Muslims and Christians to hold their belief system sacrosanct is appreciated and should be upheld in the highest esteem, that right must be extended to the African belief system in the service of cultural diversity in an increasingly cosmopolitan global society.

One of the main reasons for that cultural diversity is because all these belief systems share one common deity (monotheism).

Resilience of African Spirituality: A Brief

The African belief system is based on sharing resources in ways that ensure all people have enough for sustenance. It rejects avarice and individual greed. Surely, this is how we should live in this world and all God-based belief systems ought to embrace this African position for the opposite is blasphemy and gross injustice. Any system designed to advantage one grouping in ways that disadvantage the others is a cruel human system that has nothing to do with a deity. This explains why justice is so central to African spirituality. A subversive agenda of these Abrahamic religions driven by economic interests and politics needs to be excoriated so their real essences and true reverence to a deity are revealed outside these supremacist agendas. People of other cultures should join either of them because of the power of their message, not because subversive techniques of menticide, persuasion, manipulation, or brainwashing were used. The basic intent of these beliefs should not be a supremacist agenda, but should rather revolve around spiritual fulfilment. In a culturally diverse society, diverse cultures need to be celebrated and accorded the same status as people choose what comforts them spiritually and that they can commit freely, not for material gain or political protection. African spirituality will be elaborated on in the next chapters. It is important to note that just a century ago, Christianity and Islam constituted less than a quarter of the population of Africa and the vast majority of Africans believed and practised African spirituality (Pew Forum Research, 2010). Christianity and Islam represented a small, insignificant minority whose messages were unappealing to most Africans until their land was stolen, representing the essence of their African spirituality, and poverty and deprivation in this African nation began (Dasré & Hertrich, 2020). Despite concerted efforts of Christians and Islam, African beliefs and practices persist to this day as the most resilient belief system that relies on the superiority of their logic and does not undermine other belief systems to survive, as that is unAfrican. The report attests to this truth of a resilient African spirituality (Stencel, 2010:33):

> The continued influence of traditional African religion [sic] is also evident in some aspects of daily life.

Anatomy of Belief

Belief is that which we hold with absolute conviction, that which we give the highest esteem and absolute trust to without fail. It anchors our thoughts and actions, that is, it underpins all our human behaviours. yet we know little about it despite substantial scholarly work that has been done to develop its better understanding. This scholarly work involves those who see belief as central in holding us back and vitiating our freedom, an anachronistic relic that has no place in our highly advanced societies. This perspective considers beliefs as derived from primitiveness and ancient ideas that have no place in our cosmopolitan, complex societies that are shaped by credible scientific knowledge. Another view entails belief as the greatest thing that ever happened to humankind, for without it mankind is lost and life becomes meaningless. But what is a belief other than what I just explained and how did it come to be so central in our lives that we either fight against it or embrace it? Kneale (2014:11) considers belief as *"mankind's greatest imaginative project"* that resulted in other inventions such as religion and formal education. Kneale (2014) acknowledges that belief has served humanity well in some cases especially in literature, art, and architecture. This view is based on defining belief in terms of cognitive content that is held as true. However, belief is also understood as some vague idea upon which people bestow their trust. This particular belief is the dangerous kind because it feeds on ignorance and perpetuates human stupidity, intellectual lassitude, and learned helplessness. It is also one that subsists on fear and open people up to gullibility and manipulation. It is clear that humanity benefits from a belief that has a strong cognitive content yet humans lack the will and time to exert the effort required to achieve a belief with a strong cognitive content.

But why is it important to be a theist, one who believes in a force far superior than oneself?

Almost 80% of the world's population believes in some kind of supernatural concept (Mercier, Kramer & Shariff, 2018). There was a time when humans did not believe in anything supernatural and things worked just fine. The human propensity towards belief compels for its deeper understanding, especially in this knowledge-based global society that is driven by productive complexity.

Productive complexity places emphasis on a multi-perspectival approach to complex problem-solving, leading to the need to create milieux in which all belief systems contribute to a universal cultural heuristics noted for consensus rather than coercion or dominance of one or few belief systems. This is one of the major reasons why African spirituality had to be reconstructed and reclaimed so as to assume its rightful place in mainstream belief systems and contribute to universal cultural heuristics.

Without belabouring the point, the current global society and its economic setup create a strong sense of alienation and destruction of solidarity with its highly individualised approach to wealth creation, leading to the entrapment of people into a cesspool of either deprived mortal coil needs or avarice. The creation of virtual social media platforms in the 21st century society has created aloof, spiritually disconnected beings that assume the status of an avatar in lieu of humans as traditionally understood. In my own 2020 book, *Privileged: Identity, History, Culture and Heritage in the Age of Deep Learning*, I make the point that humanity seeks perfection and immortality by making humanity its own project-in-progress that employs capabilities of technological heuristics to turn itself into a god (*homo deus*). Under these conditions, humanity rejects ancient notions of a belief and religious mumbo jumbo. It seeks only its hedonistic understanding as a highly elevated species that has defeated any notions that position it as weak and imperfect.

The ultimate ethical question and goal in humanity's quest for perfection is the pursuit of activities that lead to *eudemonia*, that is, human prosperity and flourishing. There is no place for beliefs especially ancient beliefs that place humanity as weak and helpless. Belief, in this hedonistic perspective, is an enemy of humanity and is premised on learned helplessness and intellectual laziness. Learned helplessness creates the illusion that people are incapable of overcoming their predestined trap and that some superhero or belief in some religious mumbo jumbo hero would extricate people from their predicament. This is obviously absolute nonsense as human capabilities are quite infinite especially in resolving matters that concern them. We have not yet appreciated the scale of our human capabilities and potential to resolve our own problems and challenges.

We have, however, been made to believe that we are hopelessly trapped by the original sin. In this cesspool of hopelessness, people wallow without hope and belief offers some solace, reassurance of a better tomorrow, and temporary respite from these modern-day challenges and hardships. This situation has led to a farrago of multiple sub-beliefs even within the same belief system. For instance, take the many versions of Christianity and Judaism. Beliefs and their practices developing out of our human need for meaning, purpose, and transcendence, that is, the need to perpetuate beyond our mortal coil, share common constructs with hedonistic understandings of life as both seeking eternal happiness although the *locus* of that happiness differs. A belief can thus be understood as a representation and a function of cultural history that connects us and link us to posthumous reality or state of earthly nirvana. Understood this way, belief can be a useful tool of advancing the cultural history of one nation in a generally cosmopolitan society with diverse and eclectic cultures. Once it assumes that posture then belief becomes ideological for it seeks to map out human power relations in a particular way. To defeat an ideology-driven belief, one has to become a culturally informed cognitive agent because such beliefs pursue dominance of one culture over the other. Do not be fooled by the use of the concept of religion. It only means being bound together by a common conviction and serves to hide and obfuscate the reality that a historical culture of one nation dominates a particular society or psyche of those an ideology-based belief seeks to subjugate to define property relations in a specific way.

Religion, at its most subversive, is about making people believe in the history and culture of another nation often involving the abdication of one's own history and culture. It is impossible not to also lose one's sense of pride, dignity, and respect in the successful project of menticide. Menticide, a total onslaught on one's mental state, seeks to render one impotent to confront the world on one's own terms and perpetually keeps one in an inferior mental state unless cognitive dissonance is applied and a huge mindset shift occurs. Beliefs derive salience from cognitive, emotional, and compassionate empathy. It is from this human quality of empathy that ideology-based beliefs draw sustenance. Cognitive empathy suggests that one is persuaded to take the perspective of the persuader but not without some intellectual engagement that has a rejection option. Emotional empathy is about deep inward feelings that a person undergoes when seeing another person experiencing similar inward feelings. Compassionate empathy is similar to emotional empathy with the addition of an action to deal with the feeling, often of a discomforting nature. These three types of empathy are strong sources of menticide and manipulation and will receive further attention in the next sections of this book.

This strong link between a belief and empathy suggests that the process of believing is quite an emotional one and reversing a belief involves alterations of these deep emotions. There are thus grounds to appreciate why people suspend their cognitive faculty when dealing with matters of belief even in cases that involve gains in perspective. Many scholars have not come to an understanding of how a belief can so easily eat reason, evidence, facts, and logic for lunch, to paraphrase Peter Drucker. First, belief serves as a distinct marker of cultural identity in such a way as to distinguish one from others. This cultural distinction is also an expression of important social relationships and provides a strong sense of being bound together by a common mission, leading to strong networks of solidarity and a sense of security. Cultural identities are often cultivated via empathy, hence their obdurate resistance to reason, logic, and evidence. Empathy, in this sense, has to be understood in relation to a power structure embedded in belief systems that helps to institutionalise beliefs. Understood this way, empathy entails a state of awareness about another person's emotions deriving from some kind of hardship, sadness, or pain leading to emotional sharing. When defined within a power structure or institution, empathy leads to a state of vulnerability and possibly gullibility for power structures that almost always seek to insert unequal human relations in any interrelationships. In its most positive outlook, empathy drives the notion of perceiving and feeling the emotions of others from a neutral point of view. In its vitiating sense, it can be used to persuade people not only to be aware of others' sufferings but to adopt an active concern for the conditions of the other, leading to a state of vulnerability and possible gullibility. It is this latter kind of empathy closely associated with sympathy that is dangerous in a belief system and opens people up to manipulation and exploitation.

Religions that use subversive techniques to convert people of another culture to the religion's preferred culture tend to master the art of this kind of empathy. The relationship between belief and empathy understood within a power structure provides the basic infrastructure for mental enslavement. This is the reason why cognitive empathy is so important as it carries with it the neutrality and intellectual tools necessary to identify half-truths and subversive techniques that seek to instil blind faith in a belief system. Once hooked into it, a belief also serves the purpose of being an "*organising centre*" for our lives so that a change in belief is quite a disruptive process that leads to anxiety, uncertainty, and instability in our lives. For people that are already experiencing hardships, disrupting entrenched beliefs can be quite traumatising and can be seen as an added burden to their hardship and a loss of sense of security and networks of survival, however faulty they might be. Hence, people prefer the comforting lies of their beliefs over the truth about their beliefs because of the perceived security and reassurance that tomorrow will be better even when that is a pie in the sky, to torture a cliché.

Belief, as culturally understood as in this book, carries some assumed truth-value and can easily pass as knowledge especially among those who unconditionally accept it. As a deified construct within a particular grouping, its truthfulness is considered incontestable, inerrant, and unproblematic as it is also learned as absolute knowledge. Once given this status, belief is at its most dangerous to a point where its exponents and victims can kill for it.

The Nature of a Belief System

Belief, in its conceptual essence, is about absence, a condition of lacking the necessities fundamental to a phenomenon to be considered as present in a situation or reality. The conditions that eliminate the presence of belief are irrefutable facts, evidence, and reasoned logic. These decimate the necessity for belief in any context and so belief ceases to exist. However, traces of facts, evidence, or reasoned logic can manifest even in cases where a belief is strong. This makes it possible for a belief to pose as factual, evidence-led, or logical making it quite difficult to discern its pretences.

A belief system, it can rightfully be argued, began when humans discovered that the human quality of empathy can be exploited to impose a particular social order that embeds certain power structures and order humans to behave in ways that benefit those in power. A belief system thus has to meet certain conditions:

♦ It is created and can thus be destroyed by facts, evidence, and reasoned logic.

♦ It represents a rigid cognitive stance as it shuns alternative cognitive positions, in particular those premised on rationality. Prior to gaining facts, evidence, and reasoned logic, it is a prerequisite for those seeking the truth to have a tentative belief that facts, evidence, or reasoned logic can subsequently pulverise it but until then such an informed conjecture becomes the basis of tentative, assumed truth. Such a belief remains tentative because efforts are made to gain irrefutable facts, evidence, and reasoned logic. When no effort is made to gain these three conditionalities then belief replaces them, gaining their posture, semblance of respectability, and masquerades as an equal to these conditionalities. Belief in this pretentious condition is the dangerous type that helps capture and control unsuspecting human minds.

♦ It involves power and deferment to it that leads to subjugation or absolute sub mission.

♦ It has a structure and infrastructure that sustains or collapses it.

♦ There has to be a straightforward and simple vision that is sold and shared, often premised on learned helplessness. Learned helplessness is this notion that develops in humans that weakens their cognitive ability to resolve their own problems as stated earlier. It does not always start with the person but develops from external agency which persuades a person to abandon self-sufficiency, self-determination, and own agentic power in complex problem-solving in preference of external power of some divine hero or intervention as earlier stated.

♦ It has to regulate behaviour and influence decision-making.

♦ It has to have distinct symbols of identification, recognition, and pride, leading to some emotional attachment.

- It can be rational where cognitive content is high and can be entirely irrational as in situations where vague ideas underpin it. Irrationality is its worst form.

- It has threshold concepts that shape cultures and behaviours. Concepts and symbols of a belief system provide explanatory exes for clarifying the universal reality of a specific belief system and offer explanatory routes that generate myths that serve as the superstructure of a belief system.

- All belief systems underpin a kind of 'society' consisting of a material structure (economics – production, distribution, and consumption), ideological infra-structure (dominant and enduring ideas about how society should function) as well as mythical and utopic infrastructure. The mythical addresses our origin and its justificatory warrant. The utopic deals with ultimate reality and our final goal or destination – eternal bliss or earthly nirvana.

There are many kinds of belief systems but we'll restrict this book to political and religious belief systems. These belief systems are characterised as expounded in Osterholm (2010):

1. A stronger and more affective component, that is, they have a stronger connection to situations and experiences that have strong emotional content. As stated earlier, this emotional attachment builds strong bonds of solidarity and networks of survival that make it difficult to break and free believers from such system bondage.

2. Episodic nature meaning they create a strong awareness of space ownership and time placement where experiences and situations are commonly created to sustain a cluster of wishes and aspirations that can be defended and protected at whatever cost necessary.

3. Clusters of beliefs, that is, a smorgasbord of wishes and aspirations considered sufficiently sacrosanct to warrant their defence and unquestioned loyalty.

4. Quasi-logical principles meaning these belief systems subsist on arguments that are similar but weaker than true rational and logical arguments still have an effect on the intended audience. Often these arguments cannot survive the muster of rigour and scholarly scrutiny.

Belief systems emanate from our primeval collective effort to avoid pain and function under conditions of absolute certainty and predictability. It was a quest for safety and security in a hostile and dangerous primitive life that enabled belief systems. Humanity sought comfort and a better life, hence its gravitation towards beliefs and other humans saw this as an opportunity to develop a system that could cater for this insatiable human need for safety. There was a strong opportunistic element in the development of belief systems as they are a human-created organisational structure designed to exploit the insecurities of people and make lofty promises of a better tomorrow where peace, love, and absolute safety are guaranteed. This is some kind of selling a pie in the sky.

The real intention of a belief system, however, is **control and regulation of human behaviour** in ways that privilege certain clusters of understanding that map human relations in particular ways either to service narrowness or the greater good. A belief system has a strong human relations component that accentuates certain connections, convictions, and preferences that an internal power structure generates, sustains, and entrenches among believers through establishing specific belief situations that make belief systems episodic. Belief situations are noted for four basic tenets that map human relationships in particular ways. First, relations among humans can be mediated through **blind faith** or credulity where the truthfulness of established propositions and ideas about a belief or clusters of belief is accepted without question purely on grounds of the presumed authority of those in power. This approach to human relations tends to generate fanaticism among believers and tends to reduce adult believers to the status of a gullible child. At a moral level, human relations are prosecuted in terms of reward and punishment, that is, at the lowest rung of moral and ethical conduct. This is the most dehumanising and ignominious conduct that can ever be visited upon an adult.

Second, humans can experience some kind of **doubt** where the belief or clusters of belief do not resonate with the experiences and knowledge that the believer is exposed to. This doubt compels in the believer the need to question the truthfulness of the belief proposition. In psychology, this phenomenon is called cognitive dissonance, the inconsistencies that exist between belief propositions and exposure to new knowledge or new experiences. Believers tend to react to dissonance in various ways and four can easily be identified: avoidance of a discrepancy, reconciliation of the experience or knowledge that creates the inconsistencies with the belief proposition often including some level of dishonesty, distortion of the experience or knowledge to fit the belief proposition, and rejection of a belief proposition and assertion of the experience or knowledge that caused the discrepancy.

Third, human relationships within a particular belief situation can contain a strong contradiction where the belief content or set of propositions of a belief system has no observable effect on the behaviour or actions of the believer (hypocrisy). Fourth, a belief situation can create human relationships where there is absolute commitment to a belief system followed through by behaviour and action. The difference between this belief situation and blind faith is that the believer has evaluated the merit of a belief system (and often compared it with other competing belief systems) and came to a conclusion to rally their life around the chosen belief system. These commitments manifest in membership, loyalty, and interactions that reveal total adherence to a doctrine, precepts of ethical conduct, rituals, myths, and legends of that particular belief system. Doctrines contain messages and belief content, including myths and legends as rituals encompass prescriptive actions and ceremonies performed that are uniquely associated with a belief including worship or paying homage to belief's embodiment. Ethical conduct prescribes and proscribes certain behavioural expectations drawn from the belief doctrines.

History of Silencing the African Belief System

The African belief system was transmitted orally and despite its commitment to writing, originating in northern Africa, the interior of Africa had not been exposed to this benefit. It is only in the last 170 years that the oral transmission of values and cultures was done through the written word in the African interior, but even then it was Christian religion in the form of a Bible that was committed to word in almost all indigenous languages. The motivating factor for teaching Africans in the interior to read and write was to drive the Christian message and displace African spirituality. This was a major means of silencing African spirituality in the late 1700s with the arrival of the Portuguese in the interior of Africa, missionaries in Xhosaland around 1793 and in Lesotho in 1833. There was also a concerted effort not to document earlier interior African history, its highly developed civilisation such as Maphungubwe that existed in the Iron Age between the 11th and 13th centuries that represented one of the first states in southern Africa. It remains mainly marginalised.

This was the greatest challenge in reconstructing African spirituality from the perspective of its interior inhabitants. Interior Africa has no written ancient scripts of note that historians could refer to and authentic its veracity. The historical methods have to meet four conditions to merit credibility. First, there has to be an ancient written text that could be subjected to verification and critical analysis. An ancient original text is a crucial piece of evidence necessary in historical methods and interior Africa lacks a lot on this score. Although, the North African developments in writing, science, and philosophy helped capture the essence of African spirituality that is similar across the continent, it remains marginalised in mainstream discourses. The essence of African spirituality was committed to Egyptian stelae and writings thus serving as the original text for African spirituality. That way, a point of written reference for African spirituality exists although Christian religion and colonialism sought to extirpate such existence of African spirituality to perpetuate the myth of white supremacy.

Second, there has to be a concerted effort to understand what the author meant at the time. The credibility of the source has to be beyond reproach and the narrative in the text has to fit into existing historical accounts. African spirituality in the interior of Africa falls on the first sword as it has no written text that accounts for it before the common era (BCE), that is, the historical period before the assumed birth of Jesus which was shrewdly used as the determinant of historical periods to embed Christianity in Western civilisation's historical accounts. Ancient African spirituality in the interior can thus not meet the muster and rigour of historical scholarship. This opened African spirituality up to marginalisation and made Africans in the interior ripe for spiritual takeover. The Christian missionaries and Islamic fundamentalists took full advantage of the situation and embedded Christianity and Islam among Africans as African spirituality took a backseat in the cacophony of belief systems.

Another determining factor, as a third factor, was the African philosophy of ubuNtu that was essentially munificent because Africans lived in abundance, profusion, and fecundity. There was no room for avarice as there was enough for everyone and the principles of collectivism and humanness meant that poverty was never part of African lives. The other contributing factor was immanence, the notion that the divine manifests in the material world in the form of our human conduct towards one another and our relationship with nature. Our relationship to otherness is at the heart of African spirituality so that wrong deeds towards fellow beings and unbridled exploitation of nature are considered as heretical and blasphemous. The concept of ubuNtu meant that our humanness and kindness to one another, even to total strangers, reflected our spirituality but opened us up for spiritual and political takeover. Our attitude to take only that which meets our sustenance demands from nature meant that sustainability was at the heart of our spirituality. It is this spiritual theory of Africans that was marginalised and attempts were made to extirpate it through colonial conquests and spiritual takeover in the form of Christianity and Islam.

Another contributing, the fourth factor was ownership of land as, according to African spirituality, land belongs to those who walked it before, those that are still living on it, and those who still have to walk it. In essence, land belongs to a deity who created it and no human should lay permanent claim on its ownership as per our African spirituality. These were ripe conditions for the colonial and Christian/Islam projects to take over Africa by using subversive techniques as shall be expounded in the next sub-sections. The last contributing factor relates to the interpretation of biblical texts. It is important to note that emphasis on the **literal, historical interpretation** of the Bible was deliberate and had the persuasion intent. The biblical texts were presented as axioms, that is, as truths that required no further justifications or further research.

In securing the inerrancy of these biblical texts, the project of menticide and cultural conquests would stand a good chance of being successfully implemented. This type of interpretation of the Bible focuses only on the past and given that interior Africa's past was sketchy, it provided an opportunity to fill a historical void through assumed axioms of biblical texts. This is a typical manipulation technique preferred by those hell-bent on conquering Africans or any other nation. The other equally legitimate interpretations of the Bible were under-accentuated and let us find out why. The second level interpretation of the Bible is called **allegorical analysis** that attempts to link Bible stories (past events) with our current reality (the present) in ways that lead to two further analyses of these stories.

Allegorical analysis of the Bible creates space for multiple meanings of biblical text, that is, allows these texts to be interpreted in relation to our daily lives and lived experiences. This was obviously a problem to a colonial project because it meant that issues of social and economic injustice as well as slavery and segregation would have no place in our modern societies and aspects of the Bible that justify these ills of society would have to be expunged – Genesis 38, 1 Samuel 18, Ephesians 6, just to mention a few. Without expunged, problematic aspects of a Bible as sampled above, it would weaken the idea that the Bible is inerrant plus the supremacist agenda of the colonial project would fall on its sword.

The third analysis drawn from the second is the **tropological** or **moral interpretation** that provides grounds for how humans should live among themselves and in relation to nature. This moral interpretation of the Bible resonates with ubuNtu and raises questions around social and economic justice that stood in contrast with Western civilisation with its individualistic approach to human affairs and the capitalist economic setup with an inherent unfettered exploitation of nature in the service of highly individualistic oligarchs with their signature rapacious avarice. This level of analysis was undesirable in Western civilisation because it would place social justice discourses at the heart of church teachings thus position churches as institutions that oppose capitalism and individual avarice, hence its general under-emphasis in church teachings and doctrines.

The last level of interpretation, the **analogical** that deals with incorporeal (afterlife) issues of ultimate reality has tended to accentuate transcendence in lieu of immanence.

Immanence argues that truth and accountability as central tenets of divine judgement can be exercised through rational thinking and can be gleaned from our behaviour towards fellow beings and nature. In immanent interpretations of afterlife, notions of hell or heaven do not exist as human behaviour can be corrected in this world through restorative justice and reconnectedness with the ubuNtu values. African spirituality does not recognise a cruel and punishing deity that is ready to take His own creation to a wicked evil creature for eternal suffering and pain because these people violated some commandments. This is considered blasphemous and a poor view of a deity. It was also part of a menticide project shrewdly designed to undermine African spirituality by attempting to link it with a cult, idolatry, or ancestral worship, which were absolute rubbish.

African spirituality does not recognise worship of a superhero as ancestors are considered as junior spirits that serve as conduits and intermediaries between the living and Ultimate Reality. African spirituality is not a cult or practise idolatry. A cult is a belief system premised on the notion of worshipping a particular person or object which is entirely foreign in African spirituality. Idolatry entails worshipping something or someone other than the Supreme Being and African spirituality does not have the concept of worship, so these were deliberate distortions by Christian missionaries and their dishonesty in misrepresenting African spirituality goes even against their own commandment of not bearing false witness against one's neighbour. Scholars such as Mbiti (1977) have done their bit to accurately describe African spirituality and challenge the menticide and mendacities perpetuated by Christian missionaries. It is the *ménage à trois* of Christianity, Islam and colonialism that really marginalised African spirituality, a threesome polyamorous affair that sought to access and rape our natural resources and entirely extirpate our Africanist ways of knowing and doing to weaken our solidarity and collectivism.

Another foreign concept in African spirituality is that of a prayer, a form of bribing or attempting to manipulate the Supreme Being into considering and protecting only our interests in lieu of the entire human race. I know of no egregious profanity than this one directed at the highest sacred authority in our lives. The highest and ultimate authority has set out inexorable laws of nature that govern our lives and to expect the ultimate authority to bend these laws to suit you because of only a prayer is blasphemous.

African spirituality breaks reality into three aspects – the human world, the physical world of fauna and flora, and the spiritual world consisting of junior spirits and the Supreme Being. Our philosophy posits that our success as humans depends on intricately bringing these three worlds together on occasions when this has become necessary. The necessity is often the result of some ceremonies such as thanksgiving, wedlock, bereavement, or mediumship inauguration. During all these special occasions, specific rituals are performed which share a commonality – the intersection of the three worlds: human, physical and spiritual.

The commonality is that humans use the physical (plants and animals considered as lesser vital forces that fortify greater vital forces called humans) to link us up with the spiritual world. In other words, a point of sacred connectedness between humans, the physical, and spiritual must be achieved for our spiritual messages to receive some attention in the ultimate reality of spirituality. Access and attainment of the lesser vital forces involve exertion of effort and energy so that without effort expectations of success are outright ridiculous. It is therefore absolute nonsense to suggest that Africans commit sacrifices through animal slaughtering to appease ancestors. This is rubbish. The sacred intent is to combine the three worlds and create a strong sense of interconnectedness. Ancestors are not blood-sucking bats who visit all sorts of ills to a family once blood is not spilled. This is the worst misrepresentation of African spirituality perpetuated by those seeking to undermine our belief system. It is deeply offensive and based on egregious lies. Care is taken when animal slaughtering forms part of a ritual that needs to be performed often for *isibaya* (belonging to ancestral home) crucial in making vertical communication protocols possible. The union of two people in marriage also involves exchange of livestock to solidify the matrimony. The celebration of our new year on the first of each August, which our own governments in Africa fails to declare as a holiday. I **nevertheless, never go to work on this sacred Africa day** and owe no one an apology. Not a single politician in Africa dare to stand up and say, "**happy new year to all Africans**". I guess the state of mental capture runs deep.

This *Selemo sa Basotho* links strongly with the positioning of the sun as it gives way to a rotation to a new season in Africa, a season of fecundity. This is also in preparation for *mokete wa lewa* (harvest thanksgiving ritual), the time of the ripe first-fruits part of which must be given to a king or queen acting on behalf of *Tlatlamatjholo* (African deity) as appreciation for fecundity and season of plenty. It is veneration for a season of plenty and surviving the winter. These days, we share them among ourselves, while in other areas of Africa it is still performed in its purity. It is clear that our astronomical understanding of our galaxies has a direct bearing on our ritual practices such as celebrating our new year on 1 August each year (Snedegar, 1998).

The link between spirituality and science has always been very strong until coloniality attempted to extirpate our sense of spiritual-science nexus being failing, in the process, quite dismally. We continue to practise our way of life unhindered despite all this negativity and attempted extirpation. The season itself lasting three months (August, September and October) is known as *selemo*, meaning the onset of a new year. It is time to work the land and ensure success for all. We find something for ourselves that our deity can be proud of and reward us accordingly. We do not believe in getting things for free or easy. Such a mindset was created by colonisers and missionaries to create an impression of a lazy, consumptive society yet evidence shows that we have always been a hardworking and indefatigable nation, hence prayer was never at the centre of our spiritual practice because we believe firmly that we need to do things for ourselves – *vuka osenzele* so the Supreme Being can be proud of us. This explains why the land issue in all parts of Africa must be expedited.

Prayer without effort is considered, in African spirituality, the worst kind of profanity. It is akin to attempts to communicate directly with the Supreme Being as that breaks the chains of protocol set out to communicate at that level. African spirituality, in some cases, has adopted the Christian Lord's Prayer not for purposes intended in Christian religion but for the sole intent of showing reverence to the Supreme Being and for its forgiveness essence which resonates with our African spirituality and worldview. For matters relating to our success and general well-being, rituals and spiritual protocols are there to serve that purpose. It is also particularly important to include our *isithakazelo* at the end of reciting the Lord's Prayer, otherwise we attract all sorts of malevolent spirits.

We revere no other gods but the single Supreme Being. We worship or deify no human being who ever traversed this world. Our ancestors are spiritual intermediaries, nothing more than that. Worship and empty prayers are alien concepts in African spirituality and worldview. To be elevated to the status of acting in a godly way, one must commit to serving the greater good and preserving nature.

Understanding Menticide: The Art and Science of Mental Rape and Suicide

To understand how African spirituality was silenced and put outside dominant world belief systems – unsuccessfully, I must admit – one has to dissect persuasion and its subversive techniques ranging from brainwashing, thought control, mental rape (menticide), indoctrination, conditioning, advertising puffery, and education focused on socially empty trainability. Africans continue to practise their belief system despite sustained mental torture from media, church, and education systems. Our African belief system persists and endures as it goes down as the most attacked belief system in the world yet the most resilient and practised across all sectors of African society.

Why such interest in attempting to extirpate African belief system? Who stands to benefit (*cui bono*)?

Many people do not realise that Christianity would have secured its space in African discourses, because its own teachings draw significantly from African spirituality and Kemet belief systems. These belief systems, however, differ significantly in terms of their philosophical outlook (Christianity – transcendence and African spirituality – immanence) as well as the paradigm of practice. There was thus no reasonable basis for Christianity as a belief system to engage in projects designed to undermine others' beliefs except its own capture as a colonial project and part of a Western supremacist agenda. We are yet to be exposed to the **real Christian** belief system free from these shackles of oppression and we are yet to deal with the **teachings of Jesus, whether mythical or real,** that are free from church dogma and doctrine. Jesus' teachings centre on **love, forgiveness and remorse,** the basic tenets of restorative justice, which is the highest virtue in African spirituality. These tenets of restorative justice – love, remorse, forgiveness – are the building blocks of a happy society where happiness derives from *eudemonia*, that is, living well (Parry, 2014).

A society that lives well ensures that all live under material conditions that are mostly evenly distributed. This is what is meant by ubuNtu and Jesus had learnt these values while in Africa during his formative years, even Moses as well, so all Abrahamic religions have a strong African influence, mythical or real. North African spirituality already preached about the one Creator of the universe, the significance of the cross, which they called *ankh* meaning life and life after death, as well as the idea of trinity in the form of Isis, Osiris and Horus all combined into one, long before the existence of Abrahamic religions. This makes Africa the Cradle of Judaism and early Christian belief systems. The ancient ideas that underpinned these Abrahamic religions were not foreign to Africa, as they originated from it.

There is only one plausible explanation for the hostile approach the church, not Jesus, mythical or otherwise, adopted towards African spirituality. White supremacists and colonialists captured the church. In terms of Christianity, we are on the same side, and we should form solidarity to challenge and defeat the monster of white supremacy and coloniality so that we can spread *eudemonia* in the world as captured in the virtue of Justice. Well-being is possible when *suum cuique* (all must get their fair share of wealth), the very tenet of ubuNtu, is practised globally. Justice is about **fairness, truth and equality**, the very credo of African spirituality. Fairness relates to the administration of justice which must be seen by the majority as independent from political and other influences. It must be informed by reliable evidence that can withstand the muster of rigour and effectiveness, that is, ensure that those who transgressed can be seen to have shown remorse and asked for forgiveness as African justice is restorative rather than retributive. Jesus' teachings, mythical or real, demonstrate this restorative African idiom as encapsulated in his first uttering on the gross as he appealed that his tormentors be forgiven thus accentuating his own teachings as deriving from Africa and the accentuation of the African axiom of restorative justice. It is immaterial whether this was an account of what really happened or draws from the mythical Jesus. Either way, there is a good lesson to be learned that strengthens our humaneness. The concept of forgiveness is perhaps a mistranslation of the original Hebrew meaning because atonement appears more appropriate. In this sense, when we use the common word 'forgiveness', we actually refer to atonement that carries a stronger meaning than forgiveness.

While atonement includes forgiveness, it adds the dimension of taking certain courses of action that show the amendment of wrongdoing or the compensation of the harm caused to others or nature. It is a combination of forgiveness and showing remorse. In Hebrew, as in African worldview, forgiveness carries with it efforts to change behaviour, seek pardon, and demonstrate remorse through making real amends to mitigate the effects of harm caused to others or nature. Forgiveness also includes the commitment to abandon the desire to punish or seek revenge. These issues will be elaborated on in later chapters. Justice as equality takes the form of fairness in deciding on signified knowledge or cognitive content as well as social, economic, and political equality. These issues receive extensive elucidation in later chapters. These chapters will lay bare how science, religion, and politics mingled to advance a white supremacist and colonial project at the harm of African spirituality leading to perpetuation of the worst kind of injustice, the epistemic kind that denied the world access to a powerful African cognitive content. It will be demonstrated in these chapters how cognitive domination as a weapon of choice in driving the supremacist and menticide agenda sought to benefit the minority white at the expense of indigenous people of Africa. Menticide was a weapon of choice for Christian missionaries against African spirituality and cognitive domination perpetuated the myth of a Eurocentric model of epistemic development bereft of any African cognitive content.

What Then is Menticide?

It is a technique shrewdly designed to limit free and diverse cultural flow and interplay through subjecting people to enforced mental intrusion that leads to psychological torture and coercion, the consequences of which are loss of identity, extirpation of other cultures in preference of the dominant culture and its values. It is the worst kind of violence on our mental health akin only to a rape or mental suicide. Menticide is a well-planned, carefully calculated and deliberate act of bashing other belief systems to embed its own preferred systems of belief. Menticide is thus organised in ways that lead to betraying one's own indigenous belief system to turn one into a meek, powerless conformist that can be controlled mentally.

It eviscerates the mind of its native cognitive content to not question the 'truthfulness' of religious messages or doubt their veracity so that the view that religious messages are inerrant can be sustained. Meerlo (2006:1) defines menticide as *"the murder of the potentialities of the free creative mind"*. Thought control and intellectual capture waste the creativity of those who are mentally captured and reduce the huge human potential to an orgy of helpless and hapless zombies that dance to the tune of worthless gibberish masquerading as sacred. Its method of mental torture includes the benign art of mental seduction, the purpose of which is to ready the independent, creative mind to become malleable to untested ready-made ideas and routines accepted with woeful docility. The most powerful and egregious aspect of religious menticide was its effectiveness in generating in Africans an antipathy that made their own identity, culture, and beliefs unworthy and entirely irrelevant to their success and good life.

The steps necessary to counter mental rape is to retain a high level of cognitive content deriving from one's indigenous belief system, reasoned arguments about the possible truthfulness of all these beliefs, and a steadfast conviction and commitment to the credo of love, justice and equality. The real locus of love is in finding one's inner kingdom, a special intrinsic place where mental freedom and unconditional affection to act and behave selflessly in ways beneficial to oneself and others including strangers and nature. This meaning of love in African spirituality is closer to the Greek concept of *agape* (Mawere, 2010), the unconditional love bestowed on humans by the Supreme Being, and demonstrable through the human effort to promote and sustain goodness to oneself and otherness in the form of all humans and nature, depicting in form and substance the true trinity of human, physical and spiritual unity with the physical denoting land (fauna, minerals and flora). The breakage of this sacrosanct bond between humans, land and spirituality or ultimate reality (the true trinity in African spirituality) represents the highest form of heretical and treasonous acts of sabotage akin only to a military takeover of a country. Continued lack of access to African land as well as the political and religious structures that enable it violates the virtue of Temperance, which is the building block of African spirituality and the source of spreading goodness in the world.

This should be considered as the ultimate act of treason, sabotage, and constant under-mining of the spiritual order of things in African societies. When a hugely African government fails to reclaim and redistribute land to its rightful owners then such a political formation does not represent the interest of the people, they purport to carry their mandate. It is a hypocrisy of a special kind. It also demonstrates mental capture of the elected representatives of our people who participate actively in their own humiliation and perpetuate the persistent ignominy of a landless majority. This is the highest and sophisticated betrayal of the African masses. These purported representatives of the people lack the inner capacity to love as described in terms of African spirituality because such love promotes general goodness and connects people to their spiritual homes. It also cheapens and takes away the integrity of these public representatives who are willing participants in their own mental capture mainly because of narrow material gains and political expediency. Real public representatives serve public good and work towards a socially just and diverse society where goodness is spread throughout the entire human race and does not become an exclusive preserve of the oligarchy.

The ultimate and most noble role of public representatives is to create conditions where each member of society achieves a state of optimal experience as defined through good health and well-being. This optimal experience is impossible without access to and ownership of land central in the fulfilment of the base virtue of Temperance upon which the other three virtues of Fortitude, Prudence, and Justice depend. Working the land one owns is the most intrinsically rewarding activity which links one's optimal experience with the spiritual energy and ancestral bonds that ordinary humans would find difficult to elucidate. Given the autotelic nature of the experience of working the land, the challenge of working the land has to be matched by requisite skills and capabilities of a collective that combine their expertise for better results and fairer distribution of jointly accumulated resources. This has been the African approach to resource accumulation and distribution since time immemorial. Collective working of the land provides a sense of collective goal setting and a feeling of shared rewards that aggregate to autotelic experience, an experience based on activities performed for their own sake rather than gain in some external goal (Csikszentmihalyi, 1997:117).

It is the experience of performing the activity of working the land that is paramount because it connects one with one's inner being, a lens through which to peep into the other side, the incorporeal reality. It is a psychological level of a spiritual journey into realms inaccessible via mundane activities which are often driven by achieve-ment motives (needs). Autotelic activities are self-regulated and show one who has full command of one's inner kingdom, a mental condition driven intrinsically and powered in ways that reveal a self-assured, confident, indefatigable, and fully in-charge person pursuing selfless acts with others to take all humanity forward. Land ownership and its workings have that effect on the psyche of Africans, hence it is central to our spirituality. **It remains a puzzle why 1 August of each year in Africa** under the political control of Africans is not celebrated as the NEW YEAR and therefore reserved as an African day of celebration and the announcement of the land that it is ready for our autotelic and mundane activities. I have made it my business to celebrate this day as Africa day because even the anthropological cosmologies ready themselves for this crucial moment in the life of an African. It is an annual time for reflection and developing a deeper understanding of **who we are, where we come from, our role in this world and afterlife**. It is achievable when we work the land in an autotelic way as that makes transparent our creative genius which projects of menticide and supremacist dogmatism sought to extirpate.

This strong sense of collectivism in working the land brings forth critical social rituals such as social signalling, solidarity, trust and reliability leading to the African spirituality credo of love, truth, and equality. These concepts will be further elucidated in the next sections of this book as restorative projects that menticide sought to extirpate. Religious menticide is a cruel, egregious, systematic, and systemic strategy deliberately designed to destroy and undermine others' beliefs and values. It is abhorrent and malevolent and for those who continue to practise it under the guise of religion are no better than the lost souls we seek to rescue and restore to a cycle of ubuNtu. There is no greater crime to humanity than to take away people's beliefs and values evolved and developed over time with the sole purpose of imposing one's own version of belief and values.

Destroying a community and a society by taking away their natural endowments, beliefs, and values bequeathed to them by the higher power is a crime and those responsible for menticide must face the full might of the law and religions found to be perpetuating these atrocities against other belief systems must be prosecuted. First, menticide violates the constitutional right to equal treatment of all religions and the protection of every belief system where all of us choose and practise our beliefs and values without hindrance. Second, it violates the right to dignity, because menticide wipes out that right for all of us to be treated with dignity irrespective of our choice of belief and values. Third, no religion has the right to deliberately undermine and destroy other belief systems. Menticide is unconstitutional and illegal even when practised by a dominant religion in any country. **Africa is yet to take Christianity and Islam to a Court of Law to account for their atrocities of menticide and mendaciloquence, which have transmogrified Africans to reconceptualise their identities in terms of foreign beliefs. These were not voluntary exercises but deliberate acts of torture, coercion, and violent persuasion in contravention of Africans' basic dignity and human rights.**

Until Africa has true leadership that serves its interests then African interests in its own land would never be realised. The oligarchy knows how to manipulate the democratic processes to choose those that serve its narrow interests at the expense of the greater good. The true enemies of the people are the oligarchy whose mind is set to serve only narrow, individual interests, with the interests of the majority counting for nothing.

We should isolate the oligarchy and deprive them of the oxygen of societal respect, then society can be on its way to a better life. Focus should be on the oligarchy and their nefarious behaviours and not pliant politicians who often are guided by petty self-preservation issues. There is no greater threat to human stability than the presence and thriving of the oligarchy in any society. This is not a new approach. James Burnham's 1941 book, *The Managerial Revolution*, warned against trying to fix our democracy; focus should rather be on the anachronistic concept of generating the oligarchy as in medieval models of wealth accumulation and distribution. These models were skewed towards the oligarchy, the true enemies of society that distort societal processes to feed their narrow interest, while society itself applauds instead of condemns the acts of these modern leeches.

2

Brief Nature of African Spirituality

In this chapter, central issues of any belief system such as the notion of deity, salvation, embodiment, and reward mechanisms for good behaviour receive attention. The idea that Africans had to renounce their cultures and spirituality and embrace Celtic churches' version of what constitutes proper relationship with a deity is contested and challenged in this section mainly because it is premised on menticide and mendaciloquence. An attempt is made to reconstruct an accurate picture of African spirituality so we can understand what got lost when the church and coloniality as projects of white supremacy unleashed a total onslaught on African spirituality. African spirituality is about **love, truth and equality**, which constitute its credo. The religious deceptions that were imposed on Africans by those who have forsaken love, selflessness, and truth and chose to serve their narrow, selfish interests even against the constitution of our country and in exaltation of crass materialism enter an epic battle with the African spirituality that we restore and reclaim in this book.

The divine essence of African spirituality is ubuNtu, meaning this belief system is glued together inevitably to our relationship with otherness (of all humanity and nature), our unconditional love for them. We have always conceived ourselves beyond the self so that our divinity lies not within ourselves or out there in outer space but in our intimate interactions with ourselves (inner kingdom) and with fellow beings and nature. This is how we chose to prosecute our lives, in celebration of God's creation so that our individual well-being is tied to the well-being of others and nature. Our inner values derive from collective dignity so that individual dignity does not exist outside collective dignity. In the African worldview, dignity denotes a shadow (*isithunzi / serithi*). A shadow appears when light is obscured thus it is the direct effect of a blocked light. This signals integrity, doing right when no one watches or when one is obscured, in our hidden spaces where the light of transparency is inaccessible to the public eye. Integrity is also strongly linked with the second virtue of African spirituality which is Fortitude, meaning deliberately cultivating the courage to meet the demands of fairness (justice, the highest virtue of African spirituality).

Isithunzi is the presence and deep respect for otherness and represents, in form and substance, the hidden yet inherent inner values of worth and respect that must always be extended to others, hence it is community-based rather than rigid individual autonomy as in Western thought. A shadow assumes a positive connotation in the African worldview. It is used in community meetings which have always been conducted under the shadows of the tree. Discussions under tree shadows have always been democratic and freedom of speech was sacrosanct. These rights of engagement meant that all people in the community are worthy and deserving of unconditional respect irrespective of their status. To ensure that dignity spreads across all our communities, basic needs such as food, water, air and homestead were evenly distributed so that not a single person would be considered poor and wanting of these basic needs, including access to land. Access to land was considered fundamental in ensuring the dignity of all people in the community. It represents an essential part of our divinity for without land, humans are denied the basic, divine gift of meeting their own needs which leads to savagery and survivalism. Hence, in African spirituality, our **actions**, not **beliefs**, make us better people and draw us closer to the Supreme Being and our intermediaries in the form of ancestors. Our collective action is always intended to serve the greater good where all people have the dignity of eking out a living through working the land in a sustainable way, hence *letsema/ilima*, functioning in similar fashion as modern-day cooperatives although on a more broader scope.

Where Did it All Start?

It begins with an ancient understanding of three key concepts that define our philosophy and our sense of being:

- The idea that our lives are intertwined with those who came before us, those who live among us, and those that will take over from us (ancestors as intermediaries, the now-living as a collective, and our offspring as heir to our rich heritage).

- The necessity to own our indigenous land so we can meet all the demands of our Temperance virtue (plants, livestock, minerals, sacred places, and so on).

- The need for each one of us to belong to a particular clan (*isibaya*, *lesaka*), whether on the maternal side when a child is born out of wedlock or on the paternal side when all the matrimonial rituals have been performed.

All these concepts form the bedrock of our philosophy of ubuNtu and our African spirituality, which is also based on the trinity of the human world, physical world, and spiritual world. The human world consists of *homo sapiens* who walked this earth more than 3 000 000 years ago right here in Africa, the technologies and cultures that create human conveniences, and cultures that direct our lives in terms of certain precepts built over many years. Africans played a major role in the progress of human societies. We gave the world ancient writings, mathematics, science, and the base upon which chemistry and technology developed. The first higher learning institution akin to a university started right here in Africa, the University of Karaouiyn in Morocco. It was established by a highly learned woman around 859 CE, thus dispelling the myth of women as a lesser, unequal being to men. These issues were sufficiently dealt with in the Preface. **Yes, a woman gave humanity the concept of higher learning and redirected men away from their savagery to civilisation, the struggle that continues to this day.**

All these knowledges were central in shaping and advancing African spirituality and philosophy. The values, attitudes, beliefs, and practices of African spirituality draw from ancient African oral traditions, myths, proverbs, poetry, clan-praises, and parables, as well as the four Kemet virtues of Temperance, Fortitude, Prudence, and Justice as committed to word. These virtues and the six components of African spirituality as identified by Adofo (2016) will receive particular attention in the next chapter of this book and are tersely enumerated below:

◆ Nature of existence

◆ Order and balance

◆ The interconnectedness of all nature – human, physical and spiritual

◆ Cyclical existence

◆ Social signalling as central to health and well-being

◆ Spirit of being understood in terms of immanence and ubuNtu philosophy.

Key constructs under the *nature of existence* in relation to African spirituality are social collectivism, meaningful relatedness, holistic meaningfulness, invitational dialogue, health and maturity (absence of instant gratification and instinctual drives) as well as mythical consciousness. Order and balance refer to the need to sustain the distributive nature of various vitalities from the human, physical, and spiritual worlds also commonly known as vital forces. It explicates how the process of fortifying and revitalising our human bodies using nature's vital forces should be done in ways that do not disturb the order of things or skew the delicate balance between human needs and what nature is capable of providing as any perturbations on this order and balance directly impact our spiritual vitality and render our souls impure. This position builds nicely into our third component of our African spirituality which relates to the interconnectedness of the human, physical, and spiritual worlds so that our own actions, activities, and behaviours in relation to others and nature must always be conducted in a manner consistent with the sacrosanct cyclical existence which constitutes our fourth component. Our strong ubuNtu interconnectedness is the strongest bond we can build with the spiritual world. There is no stronger sacrosanct bond we can build with the spiritual world than our collectivism and reverence to nature.

Social signalling refers to any action or overt activity, mostly non-verbal in nature that is conducted in the presence of other human beings. Examples include gestures, tone of discussion or conversations (prosodic emphasis), conversational turn talking, and so on. It has always been associated with our health and well-being. Social signalling implies a set of self-regulatory behaviours, actions, and customs that get guided through our philosophy of ubuNtu that, in turn, shape our humane essence, collectivism, credo of love, truth and equality as well as our sense of being. It provides us with multiple opportunities to practise our ubuNtu values and principles. It banishes ills associated with lack of human support such as pathological loneliness, depression, panic attacks, and so on. Given that our entire African worldview is based on supporting one another at all levels in pursuance of the Temperance virtue, it serves as a strong deterrence against any sort of ailments. Accepting that most pathologies are psychosomatic, that is, emanate from the mental state prior to being visible at a bodily level then our ubuNtu concept has to be at the centre of all efforts on health and well-being, in particular our cultural non-verbal communication which gives assurance to people that they have full support without saying it in speech.

Social signalling can also be a source of cultural bumping, the phenomenon where social signals are interpreted differently because of different cultures are involved in the interaction or conversations. In cosmopolitan societies with multiple cultural inclinations, social signalling becomes an on-going negotiated construct until some shared non-verbal cues enable communication among people from different cultures. Social signalling can also serve as the predictor of human personalities especially when based on *"thin slices of non-verbal behaviours"* (Ambady & Rosenthal, 1993). When used accurately, social signalling can be an effective capability that can advance our ubuNtu values particularly when social cognition helps us represent all people in our mind in a manner that is accurate and free from cultural prejudice and discrimination. We see the Supreme Being in our daily actions and behaviours as directed by ubuNtu values and principles. There is no greater honour in this world than to treat fellow beings as equals and with love. This is the essence of African spirituality.

3

The African Spirituality

African Soteriology (Salvation)

The concept of *soteria* is foreign in African spirituality because it involves an element of a hero or external force that helps those in need at any level, physical, psychological, and spiritual, by offering safety and protection which is alien in our worldview. Exposure to harm or a dire situation is indicative of broken spiritual protocols and requires restoration, not salvation. Restorative justice is about rerouting people back to the heart of ubuNtu and our Trinity of the human, physical, and spiritual cycles. The interconnectedness of the human and spiritual rests on the physical, that is, fauna and flora (the land). *Soteria* originates from the Torah and is repeated in synoptic gospels, particularly Matthew, which is organised in terms of the Torah's structure. This provides evidence that gospels are more works of creativity and literary devices intended, at the time, to garner support for the Roman Empire. This has led scholars of theology to suggest that the authorship of the gospels can be traced from the Roman Empire propaganda machinery (123helpme, 2022; Hatch, 1895; Le Roux, 2007). In terms of these religious beliefs, salvation involves accepting three things:

1. The doctrine of ontological sin framed in terms of the relationship between humans, their reality, and the divine. In the human reality, there are two important considerations: free will and fate. Free will is considered the gift of deciding and making choices about one's life without the influence of the environment, propaganda, persuasion, or any other means of influence. Free will is that inner mental agent that makes decisions and effect courses of action without undue environmental influence and tends to be inimical to external pressures. Free will links the soul to voluntary human action. In this sense, free will gives greater freedom and responsibility to humans, allowing them space to make choices and decisions freely thus increasing the prospects of accountability and accepting responsibility for one's actions. Free will rejects the idea that our lives are preordained, predetermined, and predestined. African spirituality rejects the idea that somehow our reality from day one is grounded on four types of sin:

◆ Transgressions of **commission** such as murder, adultery, violence, envy;

◆ Transgressions of **omission** including lying, withholding truth, ignoring call for help;

◆ **Venial** transgressions such as bad habits, negative attitudes, avarice, selfishness; and

◆ **Mortal** transgressions that include evil intentions against humans, environmental degradation stemming from avarice, revenge, anger.

While these transgressions are recognised in African spirituality, they are considered as deliberate acts committed by those who have abandoned the values of ubuNtu. Our collective efforts as Africans are to help these people regain their ubuNtu values and restore them into the cycle of love, truth, and equality. In this sense, the notion of salvation becomes meaningless and just gibberish in African spirituality given its origins from fatalism and hard determinism. Fatalism is this idea that people have no free will, are born in sin, and their lives are predestined and determined by actions of others that preceded us, such as Adam and Eve, and that some kind of superhero will save us and ensure a safe passage to a place called heaven. This must pass as the greatest achievement of an imaginative mind, however harmful to our soul and mind. Hard determinism is the idea that human actions and choices are casually determined by external forces which a person has no meaningful control over or freedom to change the course of action or choices. Fatalism and hard determinism serve as mental prisons that ready people for manipulation, persuasion, and propaganda to sway their choices and actions to those preferred by external forces often serving nefarious agendas. Both these constructs create conducive environments for spurious concepts such as salvation which is based on learned helplessness and that fatalism and hard determinism breed.

2. The denigration that ancient Africa had no notion of God and relied on idolatry as spiritual guides. One of the most shocking things about Western thought and its belief systems is their insatiable reliance on destroying others' thoughts and beliefs to insert their own version of 'truth' as universal and unproblematic. These other cultures' extirpation project smacks of a supremacist agenda, which is highly racialised, condescending, and outright disrespectful.

A powerful thought and belief system must be able to stand on its own merit without needing to extirpate equally deserving thoughts and belief systems. More importantly, it is the West that practised idolatry and paganism until we saved them from these dangers. Christianity itself is based on stories with strong Greek mythology influences such as the god Zeus and draws other information from ancient beliefs such as Zoroastrianism and African Kemetic system. For instance, Jesus has no present-day Hebrew analogy because such a name never existed in Hebrew. The closest is *Yeshua* meaning Joshua. Despite efforts to dissociate Jesus from Zeus by Christian apologists posing as scholars, the strong association between Jesus and Zeus remains and is more plausible. In any case, all gospels were written in the Greek language making the connection between Jesus and Zeus even stronger, more so given the Greek political undertone of the time which sought to promote Christianity for its own political interests and marginalise other belief systems. Such an approach vitiates the strength of Christian thought and its belief system. We need to be invited into conversations of thoughts and beliefs outside the dictates of extirpation, persuasion, and menticide. We are here not to reject alternative thoughts and beliefs, but to take the view that they could enhance our own African spirituality on the strength of their reasoned logic, evidence, and irrefutable facts – not suppression. For instance, we find no difficulty adopting the Lord's Prayer because it captures key aspects of our African ubuNtu, particularly the forgiveness motif. However, in reciting the Lord's Prayer, we omit "our father", because in African spirituality the original source of all the energy that moves the universe has no form and cannot be reduced to a human attribute or even to our fallible understanding. It is considered blasphemous and arrogant to even consider that we can attempt to describe this ultimate reality. Our Lord's Prayer begins with "*Tlatlamatjholo, senesa pula, uNkulunkulu wethu, omazuluni, Muumba wetu mkuu* **(our Supreme creator of the sun and lighting stars)**", then follows through with the rest of the Prayer.

In African culture, we also do not promote dependence so we do not ask God for a daily bread. Rather, we request health, means, and good weather so we can irk out our own living (daily bread). We complete the prayer with a terse clan-praise because we seek to beacon only our benevolent ancestors to acknowledge our efforts. Other departed lost souls are trapped in rancorous malevolence and require our spiritual intervention to resume their journeys to ancestral homes for their lives nourished avarice, envy, hatred, malice and darkness.

We further ask for an opportunity to do it ourselves (*vukuzensele*) so God can be proud of us. At the end of the prayer, we make a solemn oath that we shall live our lives in a way that leads us to be one with the Supreme Being. Our lives, in African spirituality, are deeply intertwined with our journey towards oneness with the Supreme Being (*Hae – mohloding, Ikhaya – umthombo, chanzo*, where it starts and ends, the source of all sources).

In our darkest hours, in our deepest despairs, through our sorrows, in our trials and tribulations, our turbulences, in our deepest pain, through unbearable storms and our greatest weaknesses (*phalo e eme le lesemelo*), the African elders counsel: *Hae, hae, hata mabala, kmumbul' ekhaya, nenda nyumbani* (go home and reconnect with your spirit and source of power). This is why the parental home (the source of true love, *agape*) is a sacred space, a spiritual shrine, our Mecca, our Jerusalem, our temple, if you catch the metaphor. It derives from immanence; that is why our sacred space is grounded on the smallest unit that forms the African nation, our parental home, *hae, ikhaya, nyumbani*. The mediumship space is the intermediary space (consulting with spirit mediums, psychic, clairvoyances, *inyanga, dingaka*) that assumes the role of the elders in modern times and advises people to reconnect with their source, their roots, *ikhaya / hae / nyumbani*. A rooted tree weathers all sorts of storms. It never changes, never fades in the face of formidable forces:

> [It] *looks on tempests* [huge storms],
> *and is never shaken.*
> *It is a star to every wondering bark* [a beacon to lost ships,
> lost souls]
> [...] [it] *bears it out even to*
> *the edge of doom.*
>
> (Shakespeare, n.d. Sonnet 116)

Our homes are a pathway to our spiritual portal that leads to the ultimate reality. My former primary school principal, Makhale Makhale, who was also a Christian pastor, wakes up on a Wednesday, this particularly eerie 2022 Wednesday that proved to be his last on this earth, and says to his family:

> *Ke ya ho mme le ntate* (I am going to my late mum and dad).

He also gave another instruction:

> When you enlarge a photo for my funeral, use the one where I am wearing my traditional clothes, not my doctoral or church garments. The food to be served must be simple not lavish.

When his family asked him why, Makhale Makhale answers:

> *Ke ya hae* (I am going home), *ikhaya* (a place of humility and simplicity).

When his son inquires as to why, because he has been preaching Christianity all along and has a doctoral qualification in theology, Makhale Makhale answers:

> *Ke tsa fatshe lena* (those are of this world).

LET US PRAY TO VENERATE THE SUPREME CREATOR, OUR **ONENESS**:

> Bitsong la / Sikhonza / We call upon
> Tlatlamatjholo senesa pula, uNkulunkulu wethu, wezimanga,
> Mungu-Murungu, the Supreme Creator
> Hallowed be thy name;
> Thy Kingdom come,
> Thine will be done, on earth as it is in the sun,
> the source of all energies.
> Allow us this day, to irk out our daily bread,
> And forgive us our trespasses,
> As we forgive those who trespass against us.
> Make us aware of things
> That lead us into temptation;
> And to all malevolent forces,
> so we can defeat them and become one with You
> (Own isithakazelo / sereto / thella / clain-praise)
> uMthimkhulu, Bhungane,
> uMangelengele, Shwabade!
> aMahlubi amahle!

We also find the Gospel of Thomas resonates well with African spirituality. Islamic notions of solidarity are also consistent with our ubuNtu philosophy. In our increasingly complex society, thoughts and beliefs, which seek supremacy over others instead of equality and diversity, risk irrelevance. There is no honour in denigrating other thoughts and beliefs, and in building a world of domination.

3. The existence of demiurge, the creator of the material world, often opposed to anything spiritual.

Why It Matters to Reconstruct and Reclaim African Spirituality

All religions are based on:

1. A theory of **salvation**: being saved from something. African spirituality does not embrace the concept of salvation rather incorporates something similar under the Temperance virtue – being saved from mortal needs (physiological needs of food, water, air) to ascend to higher levels of African spirituality virtues. Life revolving around meeting these basic needs leads to self-centred behaviour and lots of problems such as corruption and avarice. Greeks call it being an idiot from idiocy, meaning own, private, serving only self. In psychology, it is called native egocentrism, serving self often at the expense of the other. Salvation includes **purpose**. The purpose of African spirituality is the liberation of the soul from mortal needs so it can develop an inner vision of attaining spiritual consciousness.

2. Rituals: feasts, ceremonies, assisting departed souls to cross over to assume new lives (accessing one's inner space and inner kingdom). Spiritual consciousness is about making it your mission to serve the greater good at different levels: working towards the interests of fellow beings and preserving nature as a path to spirituality or attaining ultimate reality, protecting nature for posterity, roles and responsibilities as junior spirits, belonging to a particular *isibaya* (ancestral home), protecting your home spiritually by inviting ancestral power, strengthening children's fontanel, and so on. All these rituals will be elucidated in later chapters.

3. All religions have **teachings**. African spirituality teachings revolve around four virtues or striving for these higher ideals:

i.   *Temperance:* being in charge of your emotions and passions (emotional maturity / emotional intelligence), the ability to control your feelings even in the face of provocation, and the ability to resist immediate gratification and greed. Understanding the basic right that all people are entitled to nourishment and offering such even to strangers because, in African spirituality, the concept of 'stranger' does not exist.

ii. *Fortitude:* steadfastness of purpose, having the courage to stand your ground in defence of the African spirituality ideals – Temperance, Fortitude, Prudence, and Justice.

iii. *Prudence:* deep insights and intelligence to figure out deceptions and illogicality, and to solve complex problems by learning critical thinking and studying science and philosophy.

iv. *Justice:* controlling one's thought and action, unswerving righteousness of thought and control, striving for fairness in everything you do. Preserving one's integrity – the courage to meet the demands of fairness and doing right when no one is watching.

Each religion has its training process and African spirituality follows this pattern:

1. **Probationary stage:** mortal state, dealing with **Temperance.**

2. **Perspicacious stage:** insights and intelligence capacity, compulsory study of science and philosophy, gain **Fortitude** perspective.

3. **Illumination stage:** attaining the state of spiritual consciousness that enables one to gain inner kingdom, liberation of independence and one's soul, understanding one's life purpose, moment of clarity (epiphany) – knowing why you are on earth, practical wisdom, gaining **Prudence.**

4. **Acme stage:** becoming creative and innovative, enabling one to serve the greater good, advocacy for restorative **Justice** and all types of justice – social, emotional, economic, epistemic. This is the highest stage of African spirituality that qualifies one as a mentor, a guide that can discern when dark forces mislead and attempt to use us as their portals for their nefarious intentions.

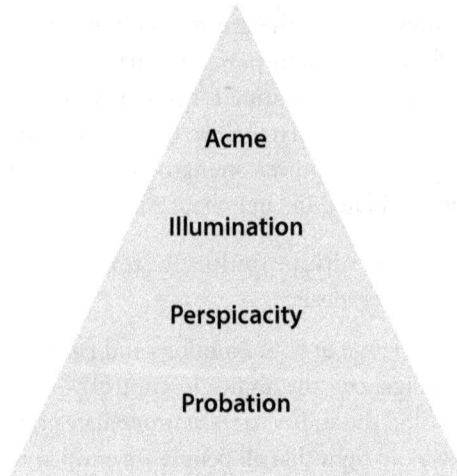

Acme

Illumination

Perspicacity

Probation

Diagram 3.1   Stages of Training

To attain the highest virtue in African spirituality (Acme stage), one has to effectively meet the basic needs expressed under the Temperance virtue. It is in this sense that poverty is such an abhorrent notion in African spirituality because it stunts the growth and development of humans to their creative genius stage to become epitomes of justice. Hence, any political formation that fails to eliminate poverty and distribute land in a fairer way works against the interests of Africans in general and is unworthy of their support. Understood from an African spirituality point of view, these politicians are nothing more than imperialist voices and rancorous, malevolent, dark forces. People who have defeated poverty and own land develop the capacity to be courageous and tackle life's challenges with confidence. This way, people become fortitudinous and effective in resolving their challenges and making the world a slightly better place, a legacy worth celebrating. Following the ability to tackle challenges is practical wisdom which allows for powerful decision-making, which often leads to creative genius and a strong sense of justice. These are the main teachings of African spirituality.

4

Temperance Virtue

Introduction

It is important to note that Temperance constitutes the base element of African spirituality upon which the other three elements of African spirituality, Fortitude, Prudence, and Justice, are built. It has a strong resonance with the physiological needs-based structure of Abraham Maslow. Temperance is also central in organising human societies economically and deals with that side of the human condition that gets motivated through sustaining their physical structure.

Unlike Maslow's theory of needs, Temperance excludes sex which is given a separate consideration in African spirituality because it could not be lumped together with base, primitive urges of hunger and thirst. Sex and sexuality form an integral part of creating and sustaining human existence, thus forming a big part in carrying family and communal values as well as continual perpetuation of ancestral home through newly born children. Given that Temperance includes controlling human urges for satisfaction or gratification, it is tempting as Maslow did to locate sex under primitive urges. However, in African spirituality it falls under the Prudence element because it requires deep spiritual insights to understand and engage in it in the most responsible way as will be expounded in Chapter 6. There are also laws and protocols that govern sexual activities in African spirituality, both intellectually and morally, thus locating sex under Prudence. The sacredness of sexual activity warrants its inclusion in higher levels of cognitive development necessary to achieve the ultimate goal of African spirituality.

Sexual activity is thus a ritualistic sacred shrine that deserves the utmost reverence, because it brings mortal life into this world. It is closer to the highest element of African spirituality, Justice, because fairness is the hallmark of the laws and protocols that need to be observed before any sexual encounter takes place. It thus cannot be lumped with basic human needs that require immediate gratification such as food, air, and water. Choices can be made about sex and deep reverence for what it stands for as a life-giving exercise. It is sacred and not a toy for our mundane games.

It deserves the highest human order, hence ritualistic efforts have been accorded sex to show human veneration of this spiritual privilege.

What then is Temperance in African spirituality?

The next sections of this chapter attempt to delineate this important virtue from the perspective of African spirituality.

Temperance

To develop the spiritual meaning of Temperance as understood in African discourses, it is important to understand that African spirituality finds real expression in the **ownership and control of land** in ways that makes land its embodiment. In terms of African spirituality, there are three worlds – the human, physical, and spiritual – whose integration is crucial in the success of human societies. The human world consists of biological organisms that contain superior vital forces that give these organisms a distinctive characteristic of being spiritual and linked to the ultimate reality in the form of the spiritual world. These organisms lay claim to past events through reconstructing histories in ways that define property relations including land, shape the present, and imagine futures beyond the mortal coil. It is their exercise of imagination and creativity that compel these organisms to hold strong views about the nature of ultimate reality, that is, reality beyond our *ante mortem*. Presently, these organisms (humans) derive sustenance from fauna and flora as lesser vital forces via a cumulative process of nourishment. This is why land is so central and highly contested, because the being of these organisms depends on it for food, air and water.

In terms of African spirituality, control over these lesser vital forces and their proper utilisation leads to the next higher level of our spiritual ladder, Fortitude. It is impossible to ascend to the higher state of Fortitude if the Temperance state was not fully resolved. Self-control or voluntary self-restraint derives from the ability to adequately meet all one's basic needs of food, water and air. Hence, Temperance is considered as the virtue responsible for restraining and constraining passions as it moderates pleasures and pain so the greater good becomes the principal concern of all humans. Avarice, the acme of selfishness, is the outcome of a lack of this Temperance virtue.

There is some kind of overlap between Temperance and Fortitude as Fortitude helps one to have the courage to moderate fear, lust, and avarice necessary in Temperance. In the face of formidable challenges, perseverance, indefatigability, and resilience, sources of Fortitude, are key in upholding the Temperance virtue. Perseverance as a virtue of bonding is not, as Aquinas suggests, just a response to the demands of value (success). It is persisting with one's project and the objectives that bond an individual with the mission to succeed even at the risk of the greatest of dangers or possible failures. The belief that one will succeed and triumph amidst the greatest of the storms followed by specific intentions (objectives) and specific courses of action commits one to the enterprise that is anticipated to generate greater goods and benefits. The need to achieve well-being for an individual or a collective becomes the supreme driver to persist with actions designed to achieve that particular goal. It reduces hardships, pain, and challenges to secondary considerations.

When an internal strength sustains specified activities designed to achieve well-being then perseverance is at play. It is possible when a clear **well-designed plan** is available. There is no point in persisting and persevering when there is no plan. Perseverance becomes meaningless. Indefatigability is some kind of advance perseverance where a person at the point of despair, fatigue, and sustained but vitiating persistence continues tirelessly even against the forces that attempt to wear them down. It is about beating fatigue and succeeding whatever the odds. Resilience, on the other hand, involves emerging from the vortex of defeat and trying again. It is a recovery from a loss, a defeat, and a sense of being vanquished. It is learning how one was defeated and developing the mental agility and a mindset to try again and win. It is about reorganising resources in the social space and reconnecting with others to build a collective social system that will lead to better results. It is about acknowledging the fear and threats to success but acting and persisting in spite of them. All these attributes of Fortitude are necessary in Temperance and explains the overlap. While hunger can compel one to seek its satisfactions, one does so in a weakened state and thus lacks Fortitude, hence its centrality in Temperance.

One does not ask a hungry person to be brave and courageous. It is an impossibility. A hungry person cannot voluntarily self-control. Such self-control is often extirpated from the poor via threats, legislated dependence (social grants), and force of harm exercised via various forms of politics, media, religious puffery, and dirty tricks. A hungry, desperate person is easy to manipulate. A hungry person is unable to deal effectively with meeting the demands of immediate gratification for we all need lesser vital forces to gain strength to pursue higher virtues. Temperance is strongly associated with the powerful force of immediate gratification as we are biologically wired to respond to basic needs without delay or deferment. You cannot delay hunger, thirst and breathing, but you can delay sexual encounters, hence they cannot form part of Temperance. However, breathing, thirst and hunger in that order are all essential aspects of our being.

Temperance, the basic virtue of African spirituality, is based on the following tenets. Total elimination of avarice so there is greater equality in the production and distribution of basic necessities of life such as food, water, and air. This includes the responsible use of land and less contamination of the land, air, and water. The concept of poverty does not really exist in African spirituality because the hunger of one person, family, or clan represents an abominable affront to our sense of being as humans. It is also the ultimate ignominious act that can be visited upon fellow human beings. There is no honour in a situation where some are super rich and others languish in the cesspool of absolute penury. It is so inhumane and dehumanising that its very existence in our lives reduces all of us to an animalistic, barbaric and primitive status, sensible only to those who are demented and narcissistic.

Avarice defined as individualised insatiable desire and lust for riches is the greatest enemy of humankind. Temperance which demands absolute moderation and restraint in wealth accumulation, thus rejects outright any system, ideology, or religion that advances unfettered use of the land for selfish self-aggrandisement. Avarice is at its most dangerous when it functions as a pretext for virtue especially in modern societies where it is shrewdly conceptualised as securing the future prosperity of an individual, family, or clan. It is a morbid capital vice fit only to sub-humans. It is the main source of injustice and has caused immeasurable harm to fellow humans, destroyed dreams, and ensured that many do not achieve their full potential. Avarice is an immodest and unreasonable urge to accumulate riches often at the expense of other humans and is the main driver of unfettered use of raw materials and skewed private property relations that often deny others the inalienable right to land, a big factor in the satisfaction of basic human needs.

The concept of Temperance is embodied in access to land and without land, the entire African spirituality collapses because it is the plinth of this belief system and its philosophy of ubuNtu. Land is the basic, fundamental tenet of African spirituality. It is the very essence of our sense of being. Ameh (2021:1) defines it as something that "*should be seen as an ancestral trust, committed to the living, the dead and the ancestors*". Land is the source of African ontology which "*views and represents traditional African beliefs of their land, their ways of life* [**Fortitude and Prudence**], *food supply* [**Temperance**], *spirituality and moral views* [**Justice**]" (Ameh, 2021:10), aggregating to an embodiment of African spirituality. It is considered a gift from the Supreme Being to the universe, hence all indigenous Africans have a birth right to access and possess land. The denial of land to its indigenous, rightful owners is not only an abominable affront to the Supreme Being but also a blasphemy of massive proportions which should shame those who claim to know the Supreme Being irrespective of their belief systems.

Temperance also deals with emotional maturity and intelligence. Emotional maturity is about reaching a position where the emotional and mental capabilities of an individual human being are fully developed, including the ability to delay immediate gratification, a key source of avaricious behaviour. Emotional maturity thus compels us to act and behave in a particular way, mostly in a constructive manner leading to harmony in human affairs, an essential element of African spirituality. Emotional intelligence, on the other hand, refers to the ability to harness one's emotions and feelings in ways that are productive, emphatic and accommodative of others. There are, at least, five dimensions of emotional intelligence, including self-awareness, self-regulation, motivation, empathy and social skills (Goldman, 2006, 2013; Goleman, 1995). The most powerful aspect of emotional intelligence is that once a person is in charge of the five faculties of emotional intelligence then that person becomes capable of entering the ubuNtu cycle and function optimally in human affairs leading to a strong connection with the spiritual world.

In our African spirituality, **emotional awareness** involves choosing guiding ubuNtu values and setting goals that serve the greater good. It is also about engaging in discussions that lead to gaining new perspectives and learning. Another benefit of these discussions on emotional intelligence is gaining sound decision-making skills and the capability to function under conditions of uncertainty and unpredictability. **Self-regulation**, in our case, entails the capability to control and manage one's emotions and feelings as one acts ethically all the time in ways that builds trust, integrity, and a sense of humility. In African spirituality, only **intrinsically motivated action** is the apex of our behaviour as it draws from our sacred inner space. Self-initiated, innovative, proactive behaviour is paramount in advancing our spirituality and help people set challenging goals and take calculated risks, the outcome of which must benefit the greater good. The ability to share the pain and hardships of another human being as one takes steps to assuage the pain and hardship of another human being to the best of one's ability represents the highest point of emotional intelligence within an African perspective.

Unlike in some cases where **empathy** is processed at an intellectual level and therefore maintains some distance between one and the person suffering, African empathy involves not only feeling the pain and hardships of another but taking decisive action to assist the person to overcome the pain and hardships. *Cognitive* or *intellectual* empathy gets processed via thought, understanding, and intellect and comes handy in communication by inviting people into meaningful conversations, negotiations, and discussions where all are treated as equals and the intent to influence is kept at bay. *Emotional empathy* involves the ability to feel the pain and hardships of others in ways that lead not only to understanding these pains and hardships but taking decisive action to assuage the pain so it is related strongly with emotional maturity essential especially in spiritual mentoring and coaching of others. *Compassionate empathy* is the one strongly associated with African spirituality because it combines a deep understanding of others' pain and hardships plus the shared feeling which compels a collective effort to jointly overcome the pain and hardship in the spirit of ubuNtu.

Temperance is closely linked with safety and well-being. In African spirituality, a sense of security and well-being is dependent largely on a sense of community and a community is built on ownership of land from whence people eke out a living. People derive sustenance and an aura of reverence (*serithi, isithunzi*) when they work the land they collectively own as a community to which there is equal share of the land and its resources. Reverence is achieved when one gains collective *dignity*, only possible through ownership of land which leads to communal *integrity*, the courage to meet the demands of justice, and deep *respect* for the right of all to live a dignified life where there is no poverty and all own land. Security, in this case, refers to two main issues: advancing the ideals of social justice in particular when it relates to property rights and the dominant resource accumulation project of a particular society. The extent to which social justice determines the accumulation and distribution of resources provide the basis upon which a community or society gains collective dignity and respect.

The greatest threat to our security is lack of ownership to land, which limits our ability to banish poverty. No freedom can be achieved without land ownership and the best tribute a community or society can pay to our collective ignominy is to deny a community or society access to and ownership of land. Temperance is about land, which elicit all sorts of emotions and curtail human rights. Our relationship with land is not only an unalienable right, but it defines our fundamental essence as a human species. There is no greater, ignominious violation of a community or society than to deny it its birth right on ownership of land.

Well-being, on the other hand, deals first with the degree to which one is integrated into a community and the positive emotions that social integration elicits. Second, it involves the contribution that one makes in a community as part of a collective so that one remains actively engaged in community affairs to the betterment and benefit of that community. Third, as all these things on well-being are part of Temperance, relationships with fellow human beings and nature become paramount, the exercise of which should be guided by the ubuNtu philosophy. A strong sense of beneficence, Prudence, and Justice draw from meeting all the conditions of Temperance. Without it, the other virtues are difficult to attain. One's well-being is greatly enhanced when one employs one's cognitive abilities to discern and understand the needs of others then applies one's emotional intelligence to fashion behaviours that assist others in the process to build social cohesion. This is the true meaning of beneficence or kindness.

Kindness is closely linked with authenticity. Caldwell (2017) argues that one cannot be self-serving and manipulative while also being kind. For instance, a person cannot amass riches via exploitation of other humans, then demonstrate munificence to the very people one exploited. That is a guilt trip. Our interconnectedness obliges us to live with others in a humane, kind way where respect for all is sacrosanct and poverty is defeated. Once we show kindness and respect to others, then our sense of justice improves and we become ready to exercise the highest virtue in African spirituality and our lives proceed on the basis of trustworthiness. Kindness increases our integrity as we commit to the courage to be fair, meaning Temperance is at the heart of our need to be courageous (Fortitude).

There is no greater injustice than denying the indigenous people their inalienable right to land ownership particularly if such land ownership leads not only to physical well-being but also to spiritual fulfilment given its embodiment status in African spirituality. This crime of massive theft needs to be tackled with vigour for without land, the physical and spiritual needs of Africans will never be fulfilled. Failure to redistribute and restore land to its original, indigenous owners remains the key factor in collapsing any political mandate of any democratic formations, because it is tightly linked to African spirituality. Any democratic formations that betray this inalienable right of indigenous people to access land and its minerals to meet their Temperance suffer from the possession of *spiritus immundus*, a *daemon* of the worst kind. A daemon, in this African spirituality context, refers to a super malevolent force that weakens humans to a point of reaching a critical point of hopelessness. Their own African politicians who are essentially possessed and captured as *spiritus immundus* weaken Africans. The purification of these kinds of politicians involves resolving the sticky issue of land.

Land is not a commodity, not an individual possession (Ameh, 2021), but God's gift for all humanity, not some exclusive preserve of the oligarchy, the demented, abominable *spiritus mundus*. It is a critical factor of production and productivity, hence its centrality in Temperance, the foundational virtue. Its appurtenance, an inalienable right owner of land, is the Supreme Being who is the worthy owner of it.

5

Fortitude Virtue

Fortitude, firmness of mind in the face of formidable odds, as an African spirituality virtue has a strong meaning of mental toughness and is always preceded by well-being, emotional maturity, emotional Intelligence, and stability (attributes of the Temperance virtue). It plays a major role in the development of mediumship because mentally weak spirit mediums are incapable of connecting strongly with the spiritual world and it makes a spirit medium susceptible and vulnerable to the manipulation of lost souls or those humans with malevolent intent. Various theories have been developed over time in the scientific world on mental toughness, but our concern is understanding mental toughness (Fortitude virtue) as it relates to spiritual medium-ship development. From this perspective, the key constructs relevant to our notion of mental toughness are mindscape (cultural knowing, spiritual ethics, spiritual power, attitudes, self-efficacy, confidence, coping with adversity), courage, self-control, commitment to the African spirituality credo, and the philosophy of ubuNtu and con-centration. The African spirituality credo entails truth, love, and equality.

Spirit mediums that are open to untruths risk becoming portals for malevolent forces so they must be truthful and strive for it all the time. There can be no spirit mediumship without complete commitment to truth, however difficult it is to articulate and share with others. It is an indispensable part of spirit mediumship, a non-negotiable. Those who lack the courage to persist with truth against all formidable odds are not worthy of being spirit mediums. They are caricatures of a grotesque kind, shameful actors of phantasmagoria, dreams of horror, and *fata morgana* (a mirage to lure people to their death). True love, the essence of our being, is a beacon to lost souls to reclaim their stakes in the grand parlance of ubuNtu. Those residing in these great spaces of love, a resolve of steadfastness to appreciate and show deep affection and intense emotions to fellow humans and nature are an indispensable requirement. It is impossible to be a spirit medium without the steadfastness to love unconditionally. All humanity are of equal status and standing, and should have equal opportunities to realise their goals, missions and talents. The right to land and its opportunities is inalienable and non-negotiable.

There is no greater malevolence than to deny Africans and all other people the right to land so they can stand as equals in the wonders that the Supreme Being created for all of us to enjoy and celebrate. Access to land represents the primary sense of equality followed by equal social, civil, political, economic and legal *locus standi*. Any spirit medium worthy of such a title must abide by this credo of truth, love and equality at all times, or risk irrelevance.

Mental toughness (Fortitude virtue), in African spirituality, is the developed capacity of a spirit medium to be persistent, indefatigable, and resilient in the face of extreme spiritual adversity, attack, and provocation because the tests of spiritual adversity are integral to our work as all sorts of spirits exist in the spiritual realm, the realm we work in. It is in this sense that mindscape is the first critical construct in our understanding of the Fortitude virtue. Impurities of the mind become our first focus when training spirit mediums so that they possess the mindscape that is suited to our work as spirit mediums. This mindscape is already pre-prepared by the Temperance virtue described in Chapter 4. Without strict adherence to the Temperance virtue then Fortitude is impossible.

Mindscape

Mindscape is the region of the mind where cultural knowing, spiritual ethics, and the power to connect with the spiritual realm and serve as the interventionist agent between humans in antemortem reality as well as the spiritual beings at a postmortem state reside. It includes positive attitudes towards one's work as a spirit medium and appreciating the privilege and humility of being chosen to perform spiritual tasks. It further involves self-efficacy, the strong belief that a spirit medium can successfully complete spiritual tasks and help people to restore their state of good health, good life, and strong connection with their spiritual *isibaya* (ancestral home, *hae*, *ikhaya*). There is no greater honour than to be chosen by a higher power to serve as its servant. It is not easy but it is rewarding. It is also crucial that one has faith that one can deliver the assigned spiritual tasks (confidence). Times will come when a spirit medium experiences extreme adversity and spiritual attacks. These are times of steadfastness, firmness, and total resolve to persist and overcome great adversity.

The coping strategies of a spirit medium will be tested and need to withstand that test of time. These are opportune times to strive, persist, and push with sheer grit until the actual goal of helping others to overcome challenges is reached. Many of the consulting persons go through a process from consulting, being exposed to information about their lives, becoming confused as the entrenched reality or way of life meets the reality that the ancestors seek, through to either accepting the new reality or reverting to entrenched ways of knowing. It is when a consulting person reaches a moment of clarity (epiphany), the acme of spirit mediumship, that the real purpose of consulting or initiation becomes clear, leading to working on impurities until a state of purity is achieved. This state of purity is marked by the credo of African spirituality, truth, love, equality, humanness, and ubuNtu.

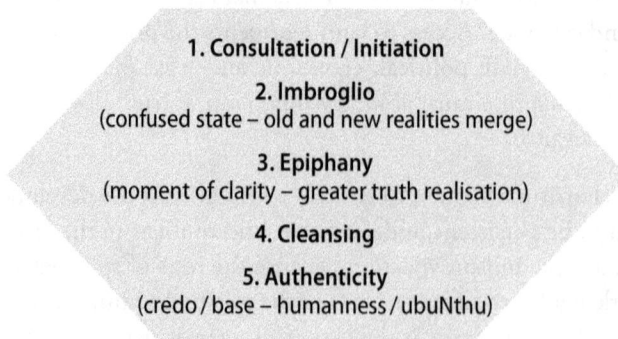

1. Consultation / Initiation

2. Imbroglio
(confused state – old and new realities merge)

3. Epiphany
(moment of clarity – greater truth realisation)

4. Cleansing

5. Authenticity
(credo / base – humanness / ubuNthu)

Diagram 5.1 The Stages of Spiritual Growth

The responsibility and role of the spirit medium during these difficult times is support and deep understanding as we encourage initiates and consulting persons to persist until the goal of authenticity is achieved. In each stage, the initiate or consulting person must be exposed to evidence and all must be revealed to them so that primary data, not secondary information, from the spirit medium should be the driver of this spiritual growth. No evidence, no spiritual growth. The spirit mediumship process is evidence-led, it is science and must meet all criteria for a scientific endeavour along the lines of the quest for truth. Séance serves as the peer-review mechanism where various spirit mediums share a consistent spiritual message otherwise some are then used as portals for *spiritus umundus*, daemon.

Cultural Knowing

One of the key components of mindscape is cultural knowing. Cultural knowing refers to the state of accessing and gaining knowledge and knowing of the identity, history, values, beliefs, and heritage of a particular human grouping to know the rituals and customs that need to be performed to spiritually link a consulting person with their spiritual *isibaya*. Without this link, the chances of resolving the problems of a consulting person are almost zero. Cultural knowing means to be in touch with the being and understanding of the consulting person including embedded, tacit knowledge the person possesses. In the case where a person is not in touch with their identity then the spirit medium has the sacred responsibility to help the consulting person get in touch with their identity, history, totem, heritage, and clan origins (*hae, ikhaya*, home).

Knowing one's culture is about knowing the knower within and things as they really are because assistance comes from knowing oneself, aboding in inner space, that sacred, hallowed part of oneself that many struggle to access. It requires persistence and tireless effort to reach those hidden, remote crevices of one's heart. It also seeks selflessness and abandonment of avarice. Additionally, once one has found inner kingdom then one banishes the fear of death because in African spirituality, people do not die but proceed from one time-space zone to another to assume new roles and responsibilities, hence the concept "*ho hlokahala*" meaning to be needed on the other side. This way, we do not talk about *rest in peace* when a person crosses over. Rather, we say "*tsamaya hantle, morena wa kgotso a be le wena/ hamba kahle*", meaning go well, let the true spirits accompany your soul.

When we say *go well*, we recognise that one is still alive but in transition to a different time-space zone. In one instance, an initiate was accessing the spiritual world through a normal ritual (*ho phahla*) of a white candlelight and *imphepho* (incense). The initiate describes the scene where he was in some kind of deep conversation with the spiritual elders (*imbizo/ lekgotla/* meeting/ council). In the conversation, he was asked what his greatest fear was. He responded by saying: "*It is death.*" The elder responded: "*You do not know your father. If you know your father then fear of death is meaningless.*"

It is quite clear that if one does not know one's own culture, identity and the source of all as embodied by one's own father, then one will forever remain in the grip of fear. Fear disturbs reason. It weakens one's resolve to succeed in life, making one lack persistence (Fortitude), the courage to face formidable odds on one's way to success. It so proved to be correct as the initiate has been struggling with knowing his father for the rest of his life and his mother has refused to share that kind of information with him despite his persistent insistence. This case study reveals the absolute necessity to develop cultural knowing, the basis of which is one's own father (the father to one's father, also called paternal grandfather in the European sense). When all that fails, the child has to belong to the maternal grandfather through a ritual.

Another crucial aspect of cultural knowing is the implicit, tacit understanding that all things, the human, physical and spiritual, are all connected to a single cyclic whole and disturbances in that delicate balance have dire consequences for humanity. When consulting with a person, it is crucial to reach a **moment of clarity**, that stage when greater truth is achieved (epiphany). This is the heightened stage of cultural knowing and the optimal level any spiritual consultation must, out of necessity, reach. It is achievable when the consulting person reaches a stage of cultural knowing as expressed in *isithakazelo* and a thorough understanding of one's spiritual home (*isibaya*).

Spiritual Ethics

This sub-section of mindscape deals with the centrality of African spirituality in ethical decision-making. In this African spirituality sense, ethical decision-making includes recognition and appreciation of the dignity and sacredness of otherness (other human beings and nature) and the dire need to preserve and protect the sanctity of the relationship between humans and nature as a means of accessing ultimate reality. The relevant consultation methodology for African spirituality ethical decision-making follows this pattern:

1. Identify and critically examine the underlying beliefs and values of the consulting person.

2. In a case of incongruence between the beliefs and values of a consulting person and ubuNtu beliefs and values, the need for the consulting person to appreciate that their help will come from embracing the basic principles of ubuNtu and connecting with their spiritual home (*isibaya*) must be created and articulated. In other words, achieving cultural knowing and spiritual growth.

3. When the consultation fails to achieve its intended purpose, terminate it and do a referral to the belief system that may be consistent with the beliefs and values of the consulting person. We do not abandon those who consult us but refer them to relevant institutions even when we know that help is comes from understanding one's own culture. **Spiritual consulting is a voluntary exercise and under no circumstances should a consulting person feel coerced or manipulated into an undesirable belief system even African spirituality.**

It is particularly important to note that all consultations:

◆ Cannot harm or have an adverse effect on the physical and psychological aspects of a consulting person.

◆ Cannot take the free will of a person away. The person remains in the consultation voluntarily and can leave as and when they so desire. No form of persuasion must be attempted during or after consultation. There are no follow-ups on consulting persons and under no circumstances should such follow-up be entertained. Persuasion, whether by conquest, conversion, or advice, is not allowed in our African spirituality framework. We invite people into a cordial conversation where no form of mental violence is permitted including benign violence such as persuasion or puffery. Consultations are about invitational dialogues where the intent to persuade is rejected and a person can self-persuade based on available evidence. Our responsibility as spirit mediums is to create conditions where the consulting person can meet up with their departed elders (spiritual home) and hold meaningful conversations. We inform, they choose.

◆ Must include an explicit explanation that the consultative process is voluntary and can be terminated at any time without explanation. It is an inalienable right a consulting person possesses and is protected by the constitution and our highest African spirituality virtue of Justice.

◆ Must ensure informed consent. Informed consent means that the consulting person has the full understanding and information to decide on whether to continue with the spiritual consultation or séance. Without this provision, the consulting person is within their right to reserve all their rights.

◆ Ought to ensure confidentiality and privacy so that the information shared in the consultation session or séance remains protected at all costs and where someone's story or experience is vital to the consultation then *nom de plume* must be used to protect the true identity of a person.

◆ Must be concerned and ensure consulting person's beneficence, that is, ensure well-being and safety of the consulting person at all times.

◆ Ensure that all the principles of our African spirituality credo are adhered to in each consultation or séance.

Spiritual Power

The most profound aspect of spiritual power is finding one's inner kingdom and being fully in charge of it as a personal fiefdom to which one has full command. The inner kingdom of a spirit medium has to be free from any impurities be they past transgressions of infidelity, fornication, pledges in *selva oscura* (dark) spheres (faiths, cults, religions that engage esoteric and dark practices), criminality, or deviations from ubuNtu principles. Inner kingdom can only be achieved when a person has undergone a soul-searing journey of extreme pain, sorrow, melancholy, and troubles.

We experience and process deeper pain, because we have greater purpose. These extreme pains and setbacks compel one to find one's true self and experience one's full humanity as well as real purpose in life. Often it is our false sense of love that can lead us astray but it is also true love that will restore our inner kingdom. Inner kingdom involves:

- The deep understanding of one's intrinsic worth and how to preserve it in the service of humanity and nature. This is the surest way of gaining one's spiritual power. For instance, the idea that one can only share one's body through sexual and emotional contact once all the rites of *lobola* (gifts to the ancestral home of the bride often using cows) have been properly performed or there is a solemn commitment that such rituals will be performed. Another way is the deep understanding that preservation of our natural resources is our primary purpose and the surest way to gain spiritual power. Once one has transgressed some of these solemn commitments to a fellow human such as one's life partner through infidelity then one needs to confess or as a spirit medium ensure that the confession is made, especially if it involves an initiate. One also needs to join pressure groups that seek to reclaim our land and redistribute to its rightful, indigenous owners and those seeking to preserve nature. This is one path of gaining spiritual power.

- The inner spiritual realm where one has full control over the decisions one makes, also called free will, and its exercise within ubuNtu principles of selflessness and recognition of otherness is our source of inner space.

  Free will is the strong connection between one's soul and behaviour framed within ubuNtu principles. Free will, in its conceptual essence, is about the freedom to behave and act without constraint or coercion from anyone or any formation whether religious or otherwise, hence menticide is so malevolent, because it impugns our basic right to dignity and freedom. Spiritual power comes with intelligently guided behaviours that occur in an ambience of free will, freedom, and dignity. As active agents in society possessing free will, we need to actively participate in societal structures, practices, and situations that affect us. To exercise our spiritual power, there is an absolute need to "*embrace a holistic and autopoietic self*" (Franz & Gillet, 2011) in ways that use appropriate language to guide our actions and behaviours as framed within the ubuNtu philosophy. In line with the four cardinal virtues of African spirituality, all the needs of a person must be met for a person to possess spiritual power. The highest form of attainment in African worldview is not self-actualisation but a strong sense of restorative Justice and the courage to meet the demands of fairness as well as the ability to be responsive to the needs of others and nature without outside influences. This is a holistic and autopoietic approach to spiritual power.

- Recognition of one's identity and culture including beliefs and values that shape one's vision and life's mission dedicated to the cause of humanness and preservation of nature. Cultural identity, in African spirituality, is a socially-constructed concept that embodies the ancestral home (*isibaya*), clan totem, history, heritage, and clan-praise (*isithakazelo/ho thella/sereto*). The responsibility of a spirit medium is to connect the consulting person with their cultural identity and where it is not clear then a ritual to connect with this identity is a prerequisite as already stated. It is a critical source of spiritual power because without cultural identity, it is near impossible to know who belongs to which clan and how to connect with the ancestral home, which is a source of accurate diagnostics and solutions to the problems that beset a consulting person.

Courage

The second most important aspect of Fortitude is courage, the willingness to take decisive action to achieve set goals including working towards achieving one's life purpose which often refers to working towards a just society ruled by ubuNtu principles. Courage is defined originally in terms of the four-factor scale (Woodard, 2004) to which I have added a few others:

◆ Willingness and readiness to know the truth, defend it at all costs, and strive to serve general good. Willingness and readiness to work to meet all conditionalities of Temperance and assist others to do same. *Letsema/ilima* is an African concept developed to ensure that all members of a community or society work together and forge collective efforts to meet the basic needs of all members of society as described in Temperance. The type of courage that applies here refers to the courage to eliminate poverty, unemployment, and inequality through collective communal efforts or joining activist groups that seek such ideals or challenge political and economic ideologies that seek to entrench poverty, unemployment, and inequality.

◆ Willingness and readiness to live life in terms of the principles of ubuNtu, service to others, and preservation of nature. In this sense and in addition to combating poverty, unemployment, and inequality, one has to join the pressure groups on the green economy.

◆ Willingness and readiness to exercise ethical and spiritual power.

◆ Willingness and readiness to start a family and adhere to all protocols of matrimonial rituals.

◆ Willingness and readiness to belong, defend, and revere one's cultural identity, history, and heritage against dark forces of menticide masquerading as legitimate religions that compels one to pray to foreign gods.

Self-control

One of the fundamental aspects of African spirituality is finding one's inner kingdom which signifies the profound importance of self-control, foregrounding the significance of self-governance and self-determination within the parameters of ubuNtu philosophy and African worldview. Self-control, in African spirituality, is a deliberate, well-calculated effort to bring consistency to one's actions decided upon to serve the greater good and the intentions to serve the greater good with the necessary patience and reasonable **persistence** and **assertiveness**. It involves intentional, patient, and persistent directing of one's behaviour towards general good. It contains strong elements of emotional maturity and emotional intelligence plus the cognitive ability to restrain oneself in the face of the desire for instant gratification and setting up achievable goals that benefit the greater good.

A thorough understanding of African spirituality and its associative rituals have positive effects on self-control. A ritual is a predefined course of action arranged sequentially in a strict protocol, because its performance leads to some positive results in terms of solving the problems of a consulting person. Pro-social behaviours tend to contribute to self-control which, in African spirituality, means acting in the best interest of a collective and demonstrating selfless commitment to the interest of a collective. Studies show that enacting rituals lead to a strong sense of self-discipline which, in turn, enable self-control. Self-control means the agency to act and achieve goals in society in a voluntary, free way and without any form of external persuasion or coercion. The best way of ensuring self-control is to instil and strengthen one's **willpower** and **self-discipline** all the time. Self-control is about providing a superior response in situations of great temptation where the need to succumb to immediate gratification is strong. We develop a strong sense of self-control when we do not bow or pray to an assigned god particularly from those that oppress and steal of our land. An assigned god is one from foreign beliefs because such acts lead to **othered self**.

Commitment

Commitment is understood as consisting of three very powerful constructs: **belief**, **intention** and **action**. Each construct is explicated below.

Belief

The concept of belief is closely analysed with doubt and differs in the sense that belief leads to intentional action and doubt delays it. Belief brings some sense of stability to our minds and is a key aspect of practical rationality generally lacking in actual factual knowledge but sufficiently motivates humans to take intentional action often on the basis of faith and hope rather than well-reasoned, factual information. Humans act on a firm belief whether its veracity or mendacity can be proved or not. This makes a belief quite a powerful but dangerous force in our lives that requires doubt for moderation.

In African spirituality, belief in ubuNtu, the role of ancestors as intermediary, and the existence of the Supreme Being, frame our lives and how we relate to otherness (other humans and nature). We do not proceed because of doubt or faith, rather based on accurate evidence. No evidence, no African belief. This African belief premised on evidence leads to intentional action designed to benefit the entire community of people and nature as it serves as a key determinant of our relationship with ultimate reality. It is a belief formed over many years whose practical rationality has built solid communities of people and banished avarice and poverty. It is based on the superior logic that the interests of a collective humanity are more important than individual riches that lead to the suffering of other humans and nature. Belief understood this way, brings forth elements of tenacity and steadfastness required as the fundamental basis of commitment, that is, required as a mental condition that intrinsically motivates intentional action. Belief, in African spirituality, is about collective empowerment and universal freedom accorded each and every human being. Beliefs that enslave and degrade other people's identities and cultures are in violation of the basic right to dignity and represent an ignominy in our collective consciousness.

Our collective African belief transcends an anthropocentric conception of the universe as the universe in our view subsumes a pantheon of ancestral spirits and those of deities that account to the Supreme Being and that also serve as intermediary between the human world and ultimate reality. Our universe also includes spirits marked by caprice and deviation from the cycle of ubuNtu, who require an intervening space between the transition from earth to ultimate reality where the cleansing of the departed soul is conducted. This way, our belief is premised on the understanding that souls never get extirpated, but are lost and restored. Lost souls still require our collective effort for restoration as junior spirits with a positive role to play.

Kin of the same ancestral home have to perform rituals that enable lost souls to resume their journeys back home. One such ritual is the **crossover ritual** where an outer bark of a particular tree is used to crossover souls that left the body before its time, such as in cases of abortion, stillborn, miscarriage, or those bewitched to die before their time. Such lost souls tend to wander around the human world. The outer bark of this specific tree wards off malevolent forces when the soul is ordered by kin to proceed with the journey back home. It is expected that within 72 hours of performing the ritual, the soul will indicate its safe passage to the ancestral home, otherwise the ritual protocols were flouted. This sign from the departed soul comes in the form of a dream or vision. I have facilitated more than 50 such rituals to date and all were successful based on the personal accounts of kin that conducted such rituals and have attested in recorded videos and notes of such dreams or visions of confirmation. For those who have had the humbling experience of a departing soul, such moments are special, especially when encountered for the first time.

Belief, in African spirituality, is meaningless without the support of experiential evidence. Indeed, the crossover ritual is performed *a priori*, prior to actual experience of being contacted by the departing soul, but must be confirmed by experiential evidence leading to an *a posteriori* sense of knowing. Blind faith is not acceptable in African spirituality as it reduces humans either to a child-like status or sub-human level. There is no honour in such a belief as it affects how one prosecutes one's life (intentions, plans and action). It also compromises the intent to be perspicacious all the time, which guides prudent judgement and actions based on norms produced from a prudent judgement.

Intention

Intent is at the heart of our behaviour, conduct, and action. It is the basis of internal psychology that we, in African spirituality, examine and attempt to understand from the behaviour, conduct, and action of another human. Based on inductive inference, we are able to determine whether a person has the courage to function within a cycle of ubuNtu. In real situations, the clarity on actual intent can be blurry as intent can take multiple forms thus making discerning the most accurate intent quite a challenge.

Intent thus can be understood in various ways. Intent as purpose is considered a narrower definition because it involves a deliberate desire to act or behave in a particular way to achieve a set goal such as a need to function within the cycle of ubuNtu. The purpose is clear and unambiguous. Intent as knowledge, on the other hand, is the view that a behaviour or act will appear but coupled with indifference towards the outcome (Crump, 2010). Central is the need to accurately prove the actual intent and deal with multiple possible rebuttals of intent that occur in various circumstances (Crump, 2010). It is therefore important to consider which intent applies under what kind of situation, meaning one has to have the courage or fortitude to make prudent judgements of character, behaviour, or conduct. As Crump (2010:1064) explains:

> A person acts with the intent to produce a consequence if: (a) the person acts with the purpose of producing that consequence [intent as purpose]; or (b) the person acts knowing that the consequence is substantially certain to result [intent as knowledge].

This dual meaning of intent provides a powerful basis to measure the behaviour and conduct of a person and makes a determination of whether the act or behaviour under consideration was warranted.

Was the purpose to behave in a particular way warranted and deliberate?

Was the person fully aware of the consequences of their behaviour or conduct and would they willingly, with full awareness of the consequences of such behaviour or conduct, continued and sustained the behaviour?

These are the main analytical tools that are helpful in assisting one to determine the internal psychology that informed external and observable behaviour or conduct. Without these tools, prudent judgement is difficult and the courage to persist to act on certain behaviours and conduct could prove to be difficult. It is also about the courage to be fair to a person under consideration to meet the criterion of the Justice virtue.

Based on our African worldview, our collective intention is to practise all four virtues of African spirituality (Temperance, Fortitude, Prudence and Justice), hence ensuring that all humans live within the cycle of ubuNtu and our evaluation of a person under certain situations or circumstances is fair and accurate. All these considerations apply under all types of intentions. For instance, collective intention is when individuals plan to work together and execute joint action to, in terms of an African worldview, generate outcomes that benefit the greater good. The we-intention involves at least three aspects: collective agency, conventions, and the power of collective agency.

Collective agency (typically *letsema* / *ilima*)

It is essentially collaborative and entails the active participation of all the people involved in an enterprise designed to benefit the greater good. All participants contribute towards the planning and designing of intentional action and have the common understanding that individuals alone cannot perform actions that only the collective can execute with precision and efficiency. Individuals within the collective do not necessarily lose their ingenuity as that would vitiate the power of the collective and dissent is considered vital to ensure the collective does not descent into norming, thus compromising the collective ingenuity necessary to execute a we-plan. Ideas that shape we-intention are socially constructed and driven through the ubuNtu philosophy. Collective agency is thus a deliberate intent undertaken by a collective to perform certain courses of action acceptable to all as well as based on evidence and reason whose consequences benefit the greater good.

This is fundamentally the difference between capitalism and African *letsema* / *ilima* in that the factor of production is, in both cases, conducted collectively yet the proceeds of such effort, in the case of capitalism, ends in private hands, while under *letsema* / *ilima* it becomes a public property that ought to be distributed in a fairer way among all of us. The same applies in the distribution of indigenous African land which, by dint of common sense and natural justice, should not exclude any indigenous African from its possession. African spirit mediums have the spiritual necessity and *chutzpah* to ensure that all Africans have land.

Conventions

Without attempting norming which the collective ought to fight against to ensure collective ingenuity remains at the heart of the collective intent, some basic guidelines and rules are necessary to bring a certain level of collaborative effort and ephemeral stability within the collective. Such conversions include the affirmation of the right to participate actively in a collective, the right to dignity, non-discrimination, free expression of one's views, and suggestion within the collective. A common language usage has to develop where there is a high degree of shared meanings and all members of the collective feel invited to a conversation without condescension. The collective intent is always to arrive at a moment of clarity, that is, the level at which the plan, its execution, and joint action are so clear and understood by all in the collective that it leaves no space for ambiguity or vagueness. All these matters must be ventilated within a highly democratic environment where the intent to persuade others is banished and only ideas-sharing triumphs.

The power of collective agency

It refers to the ability of a collective to co-initiate and maintain a programme or plan of action that leads to joint action and yields results that benefit the greater good. Collective agency derives from willed, voluntary participation in activities designed and planned to pursue intentional action, the outcome of which leads to the greater good. This way collective agency accentuates the volitional, purposive, and intentional aspects of human activity, the power of which derives from serving the greater good. The intent to serve the greater good and create opportunities for such action to occur as well as generating resources to actuate the plan aggregate into joint action that leads to outcomes that benefit all people. This is the power of collective agency.

Joint action

It is coordinated activities of a collective directed at achieving end results intended by the collective. A typical joint action in African spirituality is *letsema/ilima* as expounded elsewhere in this book. It manifests itself also in processes of achieving restorative justice as in truth and reconciliation as elaborated on elsewhere in this book. Joint action, in its broadest sense, refers to joint enterprises such as running big brand companies, marriages, *letsema/ilima*, truth, and reconciliation forums. Miller (1992:275) refers to joint enterprises as "*long term projects involving planning [...] are the collective analogue of an individual making plans for the future*". Joint action leads to entrenched joint practices as guided through undergirding values of ubuNtu and principles of humaneness. In the post-truth era, real joint action is often replaced with quasi-joint action so a pretence can be sustained that modern societies driven by avarice can genuinely serve the greater good. A typical example is when political parties rooting for a capitalist state use African nomenclatures such as *imbizo, letsema/ilima*, and restorative justice as a pretext, the intent of which is to deceive and serve post-truth.

Further examples include using *letsema/ilima*, truth and reconciliation, and ubuNtu in marketing puffery. These sacred concepts have so been soiled that their saliences drawing from African spirituality are vitiated. These are the examples of how post-truth theories twist facts to achieve narrow gains that seek to protect and justify avarice and the abhorrent capitalist ideology and, in the process, thwart real joint action. It is such a terrible public relations exercise whose primary purpose is to fool and deceive people that it is surprising how the masses can so gullibly be hoodwinked. When a multi-billionaire talks of *letsema/ilima* or ubuNtu, then the contradictions are too transparent to express in any other way. It is pretension of the highest order, because such feats of riches can only occur at the expense of exploitation of joint action that leads to private ownership.

Society needs to develop collective courage to challenge avarice and capitalist ideology to frame a new formation in society guided by a universal cultural heuristics. A society that justifies injustices of any sort is abhorrent, an ignominy of the highest order, and those that preside over it are not worthy of our respect and honour. They are the worst kind that needs spiritual cleansing and indeed some ostracisation – scoundrels in suits and designer pants, and I am saying this in moderation and with some level of measure. They deserve the worst descriptions.

6

Prudence Virtue

In this virtue, Temperance and Fortitude coalesce into a complete whole that enables humans to tackle issues that vitiate the achievement of a just, noble, and equal society. It includes matters of sex as the most noble act and gift of life, worthy of deep reverence because it is a source of bringing life to earth. It has to have a strong sense of justice where engagement in sexual matters has to be preceded by protocols that observe the Justice virtue. Prudence is vital for living a good, meaningful life. It is encapsulated in the concept of *praeceptum*, referring to teachings, lessons, precepts, and spiritual orders and commands. Once one reaches the stage of Prudence, then one has achieved the highest level of **perspicacity** and **spiritual authority** to guide and help others attain this significant level of African spirituality. This is the level of virtue that a spirit medium must reach to practise and access the ultimate reality. The Prudence virtue follows these guidelines:

1. Gather reliable knowledge, solicit sufficient evidence, follow logic, and heed advice, then evaluate all this information accurately before curating it to aid judgement.

2. Make a prudent judgement based on curated information above (perspicacity).

3. Direct one's actions, activities and practices in terms of the norms established from a prudent judgement.

African Teachings

Some of the fundamental teachings of African spirituality are:

◆ Ongoing communication between living beings and those who have crossed over to the realm beyond the azure dome is the source of our spirituality.

◆ Knowing that the spiritual world consists of junior spirits (ancestors), senior spirits (deities), and the Supreme Being. Communication between the living and the spiritual worlds involves a strict protocol where the living communicate with ancestors that share a common genealogy with them. The living do not attempt to communicate with ancestors in general, but specifically with those that share their genealogy. Furthermore, it is forbidden in African spirituality to attempt to communicate with the Supreme Being directly, especially when such attempts relate to well-being, because humans have the capacity to resolve such mundane activities. It is blasphemous for a capable human to seek spiritual intervention in matters that can be resolved by joint action, hence the greedy and avaricious will do everything to divide and lie to society, because the might of such societal solidarity can easily defeat their narrow interests.

It is not the fault of the Supreme Being that there is misery, poverty or inequality, but rather the impact of human systems guided by avarice. Judging such injustices correctly is a centralising aspect of Prudence and there is no point praying to the Supreme Being to intervene in human affairs. Humans cause suffering and misery driven by selfish interests, and that has nothing to do with the Supreme Being.

People are poor and miserable because of avaricious humans. We need to judge this accurately and understand this basic logic. There is no greater blasphemy than humans pleading for rescue on matters caused by humans themselves, or creating the expectation that the Supreme Being will alter inexorable laws of nature to suit individual interests. These laws apply equally to all of us.

♦ Senior spirits or deities are those ancestors who have earned the right to communicate directly with the Supreme Being and influence the affairs of the living. The living are prohibited from communicating directly with deities and the Supreme Being, except through the adopted Lord's Prayer. Even then, the purpose for prayer is for reverence and veneration only, not for resolving mundane problems that humans can sort out themselves.

The origin of the Lord's Prayer is highly contestable with a significant number of Biblical scholars suggesting that Jesus, real or mythical, knew nothing about it and those Abrahamic religions adopted it from North Africa. However, in African spirituality, it is unusual to attempt to communicate with the Supreme Being directly because that will be in breach of accepted spiritual protocols of communication. In trying to understand whether the Lord's Prayer has an African origin, there is a need to analyse it more accurately.

Given that African spirituality emanates from immanence makes it highly unlikely that the Lord's Prayer is an African concept, because it addresses the Supreme Being directly, which is forbidden in African spirituality. Our spiritual protocols suggest we communicate with the spiritual world via our genealogical ancestors, who then convey our messages to the Supreme Being. It further refers to a place like heaven, which reflects a belief in transcendence which is not part of our African spirituality nomenclature. The gendering of the Supreme Being as "our Father" is considered blasphemous in African spirituality, as the Supreme Being has no form and cannot be reduced to human attributes.

There is a more plausible explanation of how the Lord's Prayer became part of our African spirituality nomenclature. Cyprian and Tertullian, early Christian church scholars, are considered responsible for normalising the Lord's Prayer in African spirituality, although it was intended for the African Christians. There has always been an understanding that African spirituality, like all other belief systems, is an evolving belief system, which could adopt or adapt other belief systems' teachings. The question is whether we need the Lord's Prayer in African spirituality and if it adds anything to our worldview and spirituality.

First, it can be used for purposes of reverence for the Supreme Being only, but it also adapts the original Jewish concept of *Abba*, referring to a level of personal intimacy with the Supreme Being rather than to gender. We reject outright any notion that gives the Supreme Being a human attribute. It is distasteful and ignominious. *Abba* is strictly used in African spirituality as meaning "personal intimacy", nothing more and nothing less. This way, we do not violate the normal spiritual communication protocols, because the purpose is to acknowledge our intimacy with the Supreme Being in this first petition of the Lord's Prayer.

◆ When recited purely for reverence or veneration, the first petition of the Lord's Prayer is harmless and of no negative consequence to our African spirituality, because it does not violate the African spiritual communication protocols. However, the gendered aspect is extirpated as shall be shown below.

The location of the Supreme Being in terms of the Lord's Prayer is heaven, which is immaterial in African spirituality, because we do have a concept that our time-space zones are different to those of our ancestors, deities and the Supreme Being. However, our African spirituality essence is that the Supreme Being resides in us and can be discerned from our conduct towards otherness. Reverence to the Supreme Being is consistent with our protocols that the Supreme Being is too high up in the spiritual hierarchy to be addressed directly ("hallowed" meaning greatly revered to a point that no human can address the Supreme Being directly).

In African spirituality, therefore, the kingdom of the Supreme Being is depicted in our own search for inner kingdom. This way, the kingdom of the Supreme Being is already within us and is accessible via how we relate to otherness. The command of the Supreme Being resides in our ubuNtu philosophy. In banishing poverty and ensuring that all the Temperance virtue tenets are met, we ensure that the we-petition in the Lord's Prayer finds expression in our *letsema/ilima* projects, which serve as an intercession on behalf of all humanity and to ensure that all humanity's needs are adequately met (*give us this day our daily bread*). We do not ask the Supreme Being to give us bread like spoiled brats, rather we ask for opportunities and good health to enable us to irk out our own bread and find something that makes the Supreme Being proud.

The second we-petition is also significant and refers to a very important aspect of humans as fallible beings who are prone to hurt others and cause harm to humans and nature, hence the need for forgiveness (*forgive us our trespasses…*). One of the central tenets of African spirituality is restorative justice, that is, the power to forgive and the expectation that we too can be forgiven, in particular when our request for forgiveness is followed by corrective action. Again, we ask for opportunities to forgive and when such is granted in terms of deep pain, we tend to back off, making us great pretenders and hypocrites.

Temptation, in African spirituality, comes in the form of avarice and hedonistic narcissism, because it creates self-serving despots, tyrants, and social parasites with their selfish, egocentric personal interests. The search and work towards hedonistic utilitarianism is closely associated with ubuNtu philosophy because of its attempt at collective happiness. Again, we cannot ask the Supreme Being not to lead us to temptation, because then we suggest such intent exists on the part of the Supreme Being which is blasphemous. We ask the Supreme Being to help us become aware of these temptations, including malevolent spirits, so we can tackle them. The Supreme Being cannot be the source of temptation. We do not recognise the concept of evil, but rather associate it with deviation from the cycle of ubuNtu, therefore evil is used in this book only in this context. Instead, malevolent force is the preferred concept, as the possibility to repent and rejoin the cycle of ubuNtu remains probable.

The last part of the prayer reveres the Supreme Being and is consistent with our African spirituality. When the Lord's Prayer is used in African spirituality, it is in the sense described above, that is, within the immanence framework. In African spirituality, it is recognised that those souls who depart prior to their restoration to the cycle of ubuNtu, which is a prerequisite for accessing a higher level of existence, or those who depart earlier than the original time of departure because of witchcraft, enter an intermediary time-space zone called *celestial hades* (similar to but different from purgatory), which is located somewhere between the sun and the moon. *Celestial hades* is thus an intermediary space between earth and the ancestral home where lost souls can spend an undetermined period after death before proceeding to an ancestral home to resume new roles and responsibilities.

The period of stay in this place is dependent on two things. First, one could stay there for an indeterminate period until a living relative can perform a ritual of atonement or crossover ritual. Often messages of this kind come in the form of a vision or a dream. The difference is that a vision depicts a real situation and can be interpreted literally, while a dream requires an allegorical interpretation and may require a spirit medium to explicate. In the case of a vision, one might think it is hallucination, but the condition for hallucination is that one needs to be unaware that one is hallucinating.

The crossover process is conducted by any of the qualifying family members. It is an extremely delicate ritual whose protocols must be followed at all costs and without exception. Within 72 hours of performing the crossover ritual, the departed soul must indicate via a vision or a dream that they have ascended to a higher existence and has arrived safely in the ancestral home as stated elsewhere in this book. Second, some kind of spiritual amnesty can be offered, but this remains an unexplored area of African spirituality. A separate book might be needed once clarity is achieved on spiritual amnesty, the forgiving of transgressions and failure to live within the cycle of ubuNtu.

Precepts

The following represents our overarching African spirituality guiding principles that regulate our behaviours, conduct and actions:

- Everything that we do must be godly, that is, intended to create a collective benefit for humans and steadfast determination to preserve our nature.

♦ Each human being must be within the ubuNtu cycle to ensure continual presence of the spiritual to human life.

♦ All human beings must thrive for the highest virtue of Justice through first, meeting all the requirements of Temperance, Fortitude, and Prudence plus participating in all efforts to restore ownership of indigenous land to its rightful people. There is no greater injustice than denial of a basic right such as land ownership.

♦ Each human being must thrive for a just society where all humans are treated equally and poverty is banished, including its most ignominious version in the form of government safety nets which perpetuate rather than eliminate poverty. Safety nets serve as a justificatory warrant for the perpetuation of an economic system based on individualism and avarice. African spirituality is not opposed to private ownership as long as the production and distribution are fair and just so that poverty is banished.

♦ Sex is a sacrosanct activity designed to bring human life on earth and all protocols of accessing it must be observed such as *lobola*, the exchange of gifts and all matrimonial rituals. These matrimonial rituals serve the purpose of exchanging a woman and the children that will be born to the husband's ancestral home. Lobola is not a bribe but a spiritual status issue thus it is sacred. It determines where the offspring of the marriage will be accepted, in which *isibaya*.

♦ Free will (right to choose freely) is sacrosanct in African spirituality and anyone or institutional system including beliefs that seek to deny people this birthright must be challenged and considered as anti-human.

♦ Each spirit medium must adhere strictly to the African spirituality **credo** of **truth, equality and love**. Any exceptions to the credo render the spirit medium spiritually impotent.

♦ The concept of death (end of life) does not exist in African spirituality as only a change in time-space zones occur where new roles and responsibilities are assigned, hence "*ho hlokahala*" (to be needed in a different time-space zone). This explains why the epitaph on African graves should be "*tsamaya hantle/ hamba kahle*" then the first stanza of *Isithakazelo*. In my case, it is "*hamba kahle Mthimkhulu, Bhungane, Ngelengele, Shwabade*". When we say "go well", we mean you are still alive but in transition to a different time-space zone.

♦ The first three months of an infant's life are crucial and every effort must be made to minimise contact with more people who could bring malevolent spirits that could be detrimental to the child's health. Within this period, an experienced elder performs a ritual that strengthens the child fontanelle, the soft spots on the child's head. An enema is also conducted to cleanse a child for impurities and ensuring that the child remains healthy during the childhood years.

Spiritual Orders and Command (not prescriptive; rather serve as spiritual guidelines)

The following orders and commands are non-negotiable:

1. All Africans have a sense of community and must participate actively in activities designed to promote collective happiness and preserve nature.

2. The concepts of heaven, salvation, hero, evil, or any other concept that seeks to reduce us to learned helplessness or passive agency are forbidden. Any use of fear, crude persuasion, or manipulation in the so-called service of God is blasphemous.

3. We do not recognise the concept of worship. Rather, we believe that our deep commitment to selflessness, identification of our inner kingdom, nature preservation, and collective happiness are the surest ways to join ultimate reality as a legitimate member. Further, our profound appreciation of the Supreme Being is via the privilege of living as a human being rather than as other animals as defined through developing one's creative genius and intellectual capacity. Ancestors serve the role of communication intermediaries between the living and the deities as well as the Supreme Being only. They are accorded no other status than that of being intermediaries. The distortions that suggest that Africans perform gory rituals of appeasement or worship of ancestors were intended to undermine and extirpate African spirituality. African spirituality must be critiqued on its own logic not hatched caricatures, outright lies, and clutching illogical straws. Fair critique is encouraged and welcomed in African spirituality because its essence are values and these can always be refined, particularly in light of universal cultural heuristics.

4. Taking away a life and all unethical acts are forbidden, including intentional pregnancy termination, tubal sterilisation, vasectomy and any kind of treatments intended to affect fertility, disrespect of elders, abuse or distortion of sexual activity, unequal treatment of others, and diversion from the cycle of ubuNtu. Rituals are performed to fix all these malevolent acts.

5. Poverty and avarice are the greatest enemies of all humanity and every effort must be made to eliminate them from society.

6. Dishonouring other belief systems, religions, and faiths is forbidden including using menticide, persuasion, or manipulation. Every human has the inalienable right to the dignity, culture, and identity bequeathed to each of us by our previous generation.

7. Each of us belong to an ancestral home (*isibaya*) which links us with the ultimate reality and is the basic source of our success. This is the most important part that a consulting person must fix prior to any further help.

8. When we finally transit to the other time-space zone, only our blood ancestors will come and accompany us to our final destination. Such accompaniment is pleasant when one has achieved all their missions on earth.

———————————————

7

Justice Virtue

The highest and most revered virtue in African spirituality is Justice. There is sufficient scientific evidence that indicates that the Justice virtue comes from a caring community. A community involves people engaged in some collective activities designed to benefit all its members while functioning as equals free from any form of oppression, disadvantage, or poverty. This way, community life functions within a sacrosanct African spiritual decorum and adheres to strict protocols of fairness.

In this light, African spirituality does not believe on imposing and dominating one belief over other legitimate beliefs as this position violates the right to fairness and a sense of justice. Contemporary Western conceptions of a science-oriented culture and its isomorphic tendency towards a single, universal culture dominated by science represents a sophisticated form of injustice. First, it occurs within a global societal framework that marginalises all other alternatives and imposes a single scientifically-driven perspective which is still a form of belief in the idea called science-oriented culture, some kind of cultic dogma that breeds scholasticism. Scholasticism is about narrow-minded dogma or tradition. It is a habit of mind that compels one to stick obdurately to one line of thinking, leading to philosopher Alain to suggest:

> Nothing is more dangerous than an idea, if it is the only one you have. (Alain, n.d.)

Justice is multi-perspectival and multi-dimensional but adheres to strict protocols of logic, prudent judgements, and the courage to meet the demands of fairness and evidence. It is essentially restorative rather than punitive. Indeed, there are those who commit unspeakable acts of atrocity and are unworthy of forgiveness but retributive justice has not proved to be efficacious rather quite recidivistic, with repeat offenders on the increase. An offender repeats criminal behaviour after being convicted leading to many believing that these criminals are incorrigible and weak sanctions are set to promote recidivism. Others attribute recidivistic behaviour to poor access to economic benefit. Societal failure to ensure proper values and that all people function within the cycle of ubuNtu is, in African spirituality, a measure contributor to the behaviour of these lost souls.

Second, in the societal era that recognises a multi-perspectival approach to life, science-oriented culture becomes a dogma. Third, this science-oriented culture emanates from the traditions of scholasticism which combines religious and philosophical understandings of reality as the basis of education in Medieval European universities. In this sense, the Christian belief system was given the decorum and aura of being a scholarly endeavour worthy of higher learning considerations, thus originating the idea of a science-oriented societal culture. Science-oriented culture is nothing more than a myopic insistence on traditional doctrines of Christianity as the main driver of global society and creates, both in substance and form, an egregious injustice. A sense of justice is restored when Christianity is considered as one of many belief systems that enrich our global society, and a strong sense of equality is established among all worldly belief systems. Fourth, a science-oriented culture represents some kind of Western and Christian ethnocentric puffery with its implied claims of superiority and forced subjugation of other cultures to its own standards of measure. Our African spirituality does not seek to be superior to all other cultures or impose its own standards because that would be contrary to its highest virtue of Justice.

Fifth, given its propensity towards superiority, science-oriented culture and its ethnocentric tendencies has tended to impose its own nomenclature. For example, demonic possession, evil, Satan, and so on have gained universal usage mainly out of processes of subjugation that marginalised the terminology and nomenclature of other cultures and beliefs. In African spirituality, these concepts do not exist as those who might be working in dark spaces or succumbing to the dictates of dark forces (witchcraft) are considered as deviating from the cycle of ubuNtu so that our collective responsibility is to restore them to this cycle of ubuNtu. The idea of Satan or hell is not applicable in African spirituality mainly because of its immanent nature and firm belief in restorative justice. We do not believe there is a negative powerful force (Satan) that works against the will of the Supreme Being residing somewhere in a place called hell.

These are foreign concepts that destroy our cultural structure and belief system which only sees those who work within the cycle of ubuNtu and those that deviate from it who require some restoration into that cycle. This way even the dignity and humanity of ubuNtu deviants are recognised as is their potential to be restored into the cycle of ubuNtu. There is always a sense that all they need is love because their home of origin was broken and correct values of ubuNtu were not instilled. It is also noteworthy that even *thokolosi* (a short malevolent spirit of infirmity) was originally only meant to co-shepherd livestock until others used it with malevolent intent. These people with malevolent intent (*baloi*) have the potential to cause considerable harm to others and must be treated with the necessary care but our primary purpose is to help restore them into the cycle of ubuNtu and not judge them, an activity which is the exclusive reserve of the Supreme Being. Even our ancestors can only send recommendations to the Supreme Being who is the ultimate administrator of Justice. We do not underestimate the serious harm or fatality that *boloi* (witchcraft) can cause and how other ubuNtu deviants might be lost causes or lost souls that are beyond redemption in our mundane world. We know that witchcraft is not the sole preserve of Africans but a general practice in other nations otherwise why do they have names for it.

However, our strong sense of fairness suggests that the thriving of witchcraft should not be because of a lack of trying on our side. We need to defeat such wicked behaviours because they go against ubuNtu. African spirituality is not opposed to science. It created it. It is however opposed to its use to generate injustice.

Our sense of justice is based on the idea that we need to create and sustain a society that is premised on a system of cooperation, consisting of equal and free citizens that pursue lofty ideals of selflessness, love, truth, integrity, and equality. A system of cooperation must meet the following criteria:

◆ It must have a publicly recognised set of **values, principles** and **credo** that all citizens can identify with and help regulate their behaviour, conduct, and activities including social signalling. In our sense, the source of all these social constructs is ubuNtu and there is a reasonable expectation that all people involved in a cooperative enterprise ought to belong to a cycle of ubuNtu. In this sense, the concept of citizenry is meaningless, in our worldview, when not defined within the framework of ubuNtu with its emphasis on selflessness, fairness, love, equality, and truth.

◆ The cooperation must have strong **work ethics** and a strong sense of **reciprocity**. Reciprocity goes beyond mutual exchange of benefits accrued from joint action and pays attention to voluntary participation in efforts that serve public good to which mutual benefit is the primary driver of behaviour. Honesty, a strong sense of justice, and collective dignity define the parameters upon which reciprocal cooperation is practised. There is a reasonable aversion of inequitable distribution of resources that are collectively generated in African spirituality because inherent in that concept is an injustice which is frowned on in the African worldview.

◆ A clear **intention** to serve the greater good through productive joint action and equitable distribution of resources collectively generated. Intentions have three crucial aspects. First, intentions are accessible through a clear consciousness meaning there is a high degree of awareness of what the collective seeks to achieve. Without this awareness, it may be difficult for people to understand the terms of engagement in cooperative enterprises or even plan appropriately. Second, intentions derive from a particular belief or worldview that defines parameters of cooperation. In our case, those parameters include functioning within the cycle of ubuNtu. Third, intentions also lead to subsequent action which, in African spirituality, relates to joint action that leads to outcomes that benefit greater good. Intentions, drawn from literature, consist of two distinct types. The **immediate** intention, in the case of cooperative enterprises, may involve actions designed to set up the cooperative enterprise within the context of the African worldview and the enterprises are essentially communal and non-individualistic. There is also **prospective** intention which refers to actions planned and hoped to be performed in the medium to long-term basis and include visions that ought to be realised to spread the spirit of ubuNtu. There is also a higher degree of intention recognition in cooperative enterprises which is closely linked with commitment to the ideals the cooperative enterprise seeks to pursue and achieve. Intention recognition in cooperative enterprises refers to a heightened awareness of the collective goals being pursued, the rationale behind the goals, and the responsibilities of a group of other agents within the cooperative enterprise. In our African spirituality, it adds the dimension of constantly examining the actions and behaviours of others in terms of whether they remain selfless and beneficial to the greater good plus whether the actions of the cooperative enterprises remain committed to preserving nature and reducing environmental harm. Cooperative enterprises are one of the surest ways of building strong cultures. In this sense, intentional recognition is central to human optimal social functioning, hence its relevance to cooperative enterprises (*letsema / ilima*), the equitable agency in the production and distribution of collectively generated resources and benefits.

The strong link between cooperation and justice implies the centrality of ubuNtu values in the administration of justice but what kind of justice would benefit from values of ubuNtu?

Distributive justice involved in the fair distribution of benefits and resources to all members of society reflects a critical element of ubuNtu, which is equality. However, distributive justice, in African spirituality, builds from the three other virtues of Temperance, Fortitude, and Prudence. In this sense, distributive justice has to ensure that the societal distribution of resources and benefits lead to all members of society meeting their basic needs of food, clean water, clean air, and living in a healthy environment. Another aspect of Temperance is emotional maturity and emotional intelligence and often conditions of fair distribution play a major role in making people matured and emotionally intelligent. Once the fundamental virtue of Temperance is achieved, then such a society is premised on fair distribution of resources and benefits.

In this sense, such a society ascends to the second virtue of Fortitude, which deals with the courage to meet the demands of fairness, equality, and truth. In this society of equals, distributive justice ensures that all members of society get involved in cooperative enterprises that produce resources and benefits that can be distributed equally. In the African worldview, communal life is more important than individual aggrandisement so that distributive justice becomes the most crucial type of justice.

Restorative justice applies under conditions where some members of society have deviated or moved out of the cycle of ubuNtu to pursue self-interested activities that accrue benefits and resources to individuals instead of the collective in society. This includes committing acts that harm others and the environment. Unlike in Western thought where the tendency is to administer retributive justice against those who wronged society based on the understanding that justice is essentially retroactive, in the African worldview, it assumes a proactive and restorative stance. In retroactive approaches to justice, there is a high degree of justification of punishment meted out to the wrongdoer to correct past injustices or unfair advantages the wrongdoer positioned themselves against all other members of society so that this type of justice is assumed to reset the balance of fairness in society. Retributive justice is based on corrective action premised on punishment, deprivation, and collective revenge against the wrongdoer. The African worldview seeks not punishment in the sense of meting out pain or taking away a privilege such as depriving the wrongdoer the right to be a member of society for a certain period, hence the concept of prison or, in some cases even taking away their life.

Our first problem with punitive measures as part of justice administration is that these measures perpetuate harm and contradict our moral values of ubuNtu. A harmed individual through punitive measures even when done in the name of justice cannot easily be restored to the cycle of ubuNtu or live a normal life in a society that harmed them, so this particular society assumes the same status as the wrongdoer because both cause harm to one another, leading to a vicious cycle of harm. Punishment has a weak deterrent effect in societies premised on retributive justice. The rate of recidivism is very high because wrongdoers, upon being reunited with the society they harmed, tend to seek revenge and revert to harmful acts. Rehabilitating wrongdoers outside of society is almost impossible, because it is based on an artificial environment where there are limited rights such as a lack of free association with members of society and free movement.

There are three main schools of thought that drive retributive justice, which are anti-human and ineffective. The consequentialists argue that punishment is justified for the wrongdoers, because it prevents future repetitions of an offence, thus having a deterrent effect (general prevention of wrongdoing) and leading to greater good in society. Consequentialists understand punishment as a form of dissuasion, that is, discouragement of further harm to society and restoration of general happiness. Thus, it assumes a hedonistic stance. As already argued, the rate of rehabilitation success is very low. Instead, a culture of harm becomes entrenched in society wherever punitive measures are used against wrongdoers.

The retributive exponents view punitive measures as essential in responding adequately to the transgression, but represents in form and substance a sophisticated form of collective vengeance against wrongdoers. Even the application of the proportionality principle in retributive justice where lesser wrongdoing calls for lesser harm to the wrongdoer or greater harm leads to greater harm to the wrongdoer does not lessen the severity of a culture of harm in society. Using the forfeiture of rights to be a member of society for a period, reprobation (moral censure), and just desserts in retributive justice shows how far a retribution-driven society is prepared to sink into a cesspool of moral decrepitude. Just desserts deal with the principle of proportionality, determinate sentences, and disparity in sentencing, meaning sanctioned societal harm to wrongdoers has to fit wrongdoing.

The abolitionists take a different view that rejects punishment in the administration of justice. However, abolitionists seek a non-punitive approach to justice, preferring societal non-intervention or minimum restrictions for wrongdoers. This is an extreme end of the administration of justice that could lead to *laissez-faire* society in which clear societal values are not inculcated ito serve as guidelines for appropriate behaviour. In our African worldview, these values and guidelines are undergirded by ubuNtu philosophy. In this sense, restorative justice one premised on reconciliation and reintegration into a cycle of ubuNtu makes for the highest moral virtue that the administration of justice should aspire to achieve and one that is second nature in

African worldview. Restorative justice invites both the wronged and the wrong-
into a powerful conversation of reconciliation, atonement (forgiveness plus
itive corrective action), and restoration into a cycle of ubuNtu. ubuNtu values
love, support, and care form the bedrock of restorative justice. Despite the seve-
y of wrongdoing, what the wronged need is not further wrongdoing, even when
nctioned by society. Rather, a sense of closure is needed that comes with the
oluntary acknowledgement of wrongdoing, its severity, and the considerable harm
has caused to the wronged as well as a commitment to unconditionally rejoin the
ycle of ubuNtu. Vengeance, even when sanctioned societally, would never bring
real closure. In restorative justice, a mediation process plays a major role in bringing
the wrongdoer and the wronged together in a fruitful conversation that leads to
reconciliation and reintegration into the cycle of ubuNtu.

For those who misunderstand restorative justice within the framework of African
worldview and its philosophy of ubuNtu, it can be seen as illusory and too idealistic.
This is typical of those whose hearts are filled with vengeance and a sadomasochistic
mindset that derives pleasure from self-harm and harming others. It is self-harm when
one's heart is filled with vengeance and rage (masochism) and peace is only possible
when forgiveness and corrective action from the wrongdoer is genuinely attempted.
This is the meaning of reintegration into a cycle of ubuNtu through sustained
cycles of healing, mediation, community service as well as truth and reconciliation
processes. While variations in restorative justice are acknowledged and have wider
scope of use, we restrict our understanding of it within ubuNtu values because that
is our Africanist ways.

It has always been part of our culture and our lives since ancient times and its distortions and use in modern times assume meanings that are generally inimical to our
African conception of it. I now describe the restorative justice procedure from the
perspective of the African worldview. All efforts of restorative justice, in terms of
the African worldview, are intended to restore the wrongdoer back to the cycle of
ubuNtu and allow the wronged an opportunity for forgiving, recovering, and healing
respectively.

Mediation

Mediation, in the African worldview, involves arranging an inquiry into wrongdoing,
understanding its nature, severity and scale of psychological, emotional, and physical
harm inflicted on the wronged. The inquiry is often led by respected elders of the
society or spirit mediums and entails a dialogic engagement with people affected
by wrongdoing. There is a greater understanding that dialogic engagement must
give recognition to the sensitivity of the matter at hand and provide a conducive
environment for diverse views to thrive, including understanding wrongdoing from
the perspective of the wrongdoer, the wronged, and ubuNtu values.

An inquiry is followed by conciliation efforts, which pays attention to activities designed to achieve healing and a sense of closure for the wronged as well as create rehabilitation conditions for the wrongdoer so that both parties can rejoin the cycle of ubuNtu. The inquiry process involves setting up a meeting between the wrongdoer and the wronged with elders or spirit mediums playing a mediatory role by facilitating amicable but powerful conversations between the parties affected by a harm. The facilitation itself involves understanding the wrongdoing and the nature of its severity such as those with the most severity, including murder, rape, molestation aggravated assault, and others, including robbery, theft, arson, and so on. The most difficult and complex wrongdoing is murder, because it involves permanently removing a person from this time-space zone and causing them to enter the ultimate reality early. This leads to egregious and permanent damage and deprives those murdered of the right to live.

The facilitation needs to be conducted by highly experienced mediators, preferably respected members of society or spirit mediums. The wronged needs to be made aware that even state-sanctioned vengeance such as lengthy imprisonment or the death penalty for the wrongdoer will not bring lasting peace in their lives as only a culture of harm is the real beneficiary of such self-defeating actions. Those who have wronged us in the most egregious way deserve our unconditional forgiveness that goes with the wrongdoer's compensatory action of reparation. The terms of reparation must be clearly outlined during the inquiry and must be endorsed by those who are wronged so that the conciliation process should deal mostly with the implementation of the outcomes of an inquiry. An inquiry must thus meet the following criteria:

♦ It must involve those most affected by harm, that is, the immediate family members of the wronged and the wrongdoer(s).

♦ It must be mediated by highly respected elders in the community or spirit mediums. Those affected by the wrongdoing must agree on the mediators as well as terms of mediation.

♦ **Full disclosure** of what actually occurred is a precondition of engagement and makes other subsequent processes possible.

♦ The framing values of engagement should be that of ubuNtu, atonement (forgiveness plus corrective action), and rehabilitation. Rehabilitation, in the African worldview, deals with efforts designed to restore the improved functionality of those who were wronged of which proper functionality means full participation within the cycle of ubuNtu. The wrongdoing itself, depending on its severity, adversely affects the proper functionality of those harmed by wrongdoing so that rehabilitation serves a restorative purpose. Unlike in Western thought, rehabilitation serves a therapeutic purpose to the wronged rather than the wrongdoer whose responsibility in the mediation process is full disclosure of wrongdoing, understanding the full scale of harm and its impact on the quality of life of those wronged by such acts, committing to a clear corrective action that is driven by values of ubuNtu.

◆ It must be driven by a strong sense of we-intentionality and deontic relations, that is, relationships driven by a strong moral obligation undertaken by all parties focusing on ubuNtu values and a collective commitment to resolve the matter amicably and in the best interest of the entire community and broader society.

The conciliation process, in the African worldview, entails voluntary participation in activities designed to correct wrongdoing. It follows the first phase of restorative justice which is inquiry and all conditions of such an inquiry as stipulated above should be met unconditionally. It is about implementing the mutual agreement reached during the inquiry which seeks to correct wrongdoing and start the therapy sessions (rehabilitation) for the wronged. The mediator(s) continues to monitor progress in both instances and keeps the parties involved updated on progress.

The mediator(s) may give advice on areas that are likely to be effective in fast-tracking corrective action and rehabilitation as well as provide evidence of progress and constraints. Given the general marginalisation of African thought in our complex, global society, it is important that mediators are properly trained in the ways of African philosophy that guide mediation within the framework of restorative justice. Each of the two processes of mediation must be properly understood and the ubuNtu values that guide them must be paramount in both processes.

Truth and Reconciliation

Closely linked with the mediation process as part of restorative justice, truth and reconciliation ensure that the incidents or activities that led to causing harm to others are well understood and practical mechanisms are set in motion to prevent the recurrence of the incident or activities that caused harm. The issues raised and documented during the mediation regarding causes of harm are further analysed and critically engaged on a broader scope to determine how they affect the culture of human rights and ubuNtu in society. The fundamental principle is that the rule of law that protects human rights across the board is restored even in incidents that involve an individual or family. In other words, specific cases drawn from the mediation process are analysed and understood within the broader scope that affects the entire society. The democratic constitution across the globe protects the dignity of every individual in society even those who wronged society although, in some cases, their rights may be temporarily revoked to protect the greater good in society. In the African worldview, this temporary withdrawal of rights is conditional to kick-starting the restorative justice processes.

The truth and reconciliation process examines whether the purpose of the mediation processes was clearly outlined to all parties concerned in the mediation and their basic human rights were upheld during the mediation process, otherwise the mediation process may have to be redone because restorative justice processes cannot cause new harm to all the parties. The truth and reconciliation process may even determine whether the circumstances of the case in some mediation process warrant that some parties in mediation require legal representation. There is also another determination that is important during mediation, which is that the process is entirely voluntary and withdrawal without explanation is perfectly acceptable. In cases involving minors, the parents / guardian must participate actively and fully in the mediation process, and this must be established upfront and emphatically.

This process must also determine whether there was proportionality between harm committed and the agreement reached in the mediation process, that is, corrective action to be undertaken by the wrongdoer and the scale of therapy offered to the wronged is sufficient to restore both to the cycle of ubuNtu. There is also a need to find out whether the wrongdoer shows remorse and a willingness to embark on corrective action. In this sense, conciliation deals with the process of bringing peace and harmony, ending harm, while reconciliation involves re-establishing healthy relationships and ensuring that the cycle of ubuNtu is restored within a community and the broader society. Reconciliation considers all aspects of the Temperance virtue to ensure that poverty and its accompanying violence and harm on human dignity are eliminated in communities and broader society.

Reconciliation is quite a complex concept because it is a goal and a process. The goal is to ensure that all the mediation processes were done in terms of a democratic constitution and values of ubuNtu so that peace and harmony are restored in a community and broader society. As a process, reconciliation deals with specific steps that are undertaken to evaluate the truthfulness of the mediation processes and ensure that procedural fairness as well as the basic human rights of all concerned in the mediation process were strictly adhered to without exception so that conditions for a shared future and society driven by ubuNtu values are met and sustained. The definition of truth and reconciliation that fits our African worldview is best captured by Asmal, Asmal and Roberts (1997:46):

> [It] is about facing unwelcome truth in order to harmonise incommensurable worldviews so that inevitable and continuing conflict and differences stand at least within a single universe of comprehensibility.

In restorative justice understood within our African worldview, this *"single universe of comprehensibility"* is possible when values of ubuNtu undergird the processes of mediation and reconciliation where truth is the ultimate arbiter of the success of these processes. Truth deals with the exact nature of the harm, its scale of damage, collating expectations of those affected by harm, negotiating terms of engagement and agreed-upon processes of mediation, including compromises and sacrifices to be made to restore harmony in communities and broader society. As a shared, arduous journey guided by ubuNtu values and ethics, the end of which is harmony and peace, restorative justice is about restored societal values and harmony accompanied by peace because peace is possible when justice has been achieved and understood as the full disclosure of the truthfulness of circumstances of harm and appropriate corrective action and therapy. In our case, restorative justice is the very essence of our being Africans.

Letsema / Ilima

Claiming its origins in the farming practices of African communities and permeating every aspect of African community life, *letsema/ilima* can best be described as a collective effort designed to build communities and broader society through voluntary contributions to the productivity, development, and growth of a community and broader society. It is an epitome of the ubuNtu cycle where collective sharing, caring, loving, and supporting are second nature. It is one of the most effective programmes used in African society that builds solidarity and makes use of the voluntary power of community members for socio-economic activities and building solidarity. It includes activities such as farming (crops and livestock), house construction, youth training, care for the frail and weak, environmental preservation initiatives, and so on.

Letsema/ilima eliminates wrongdoings such as theft, stealing and murder, because there was always enough for everyone and sharing is a normal part of communal life. There is no concept of scarce resources in African communal life as the food production, animal rearing, and all related economic activities were done not for profit but to ensure all members of a community have enough to sustain themselves as they meet all requirements of the Temperance virtue. Community members brought their various skills and competencies into community projects designed to optimise productivity and ensure fairer distribution of resources collectively generated.

Its use as a restorative justice programme is intended to achieve the following:

◆ Restoring wrongdoers into communal life and the cycle of ubuNtu.

◆ Serving as a deterrent for future wrongdoing within the framework of restoration in lieu of punishment and retribution.

◆ Rehabilitating the wrongdoer and inculcating principles and values of working together for the development and benefit of the community thus upholding the basic virtue of African spirituality which is Temperance.

◆ Allowing those harmed by wrongdoing to heal and undergo therapy, safe and secure in the knowledge that justice, the highest African spirituality virtue, has been served and achieved.

◆ Building in the moral arsenal of the wrongdoers the courage to meet the demands of fairness (Fortitude virtue) and the caring attitude (Prudence virtue) that qualifies the wrongdoer to be a productive and effective member of the community, resulting in a more caring society.

♦ Creating conditions for wrongdoers to benefit in ways that meet all the requirements of the Temperance virtue. In the African worldview, this process of allocating resources to those who lack them is referred to as *ho tshwahela*, meaning a piece of land, livestock, and other relevant resources will be identified and allocated to those who lack such resources. This explains the centrality of land ownership in African societies as an embodiment of African spirituality.

♦ Using wrongdoers to raise awareness and educate others on the consequences of wrongdoing and its impact on communal solidarity, ubuNtu values, and the sustainability of harmony and peace within the community. This would also reduce an entrenched traditional gerontocratic approach to education, mediation, and leadership in African communities, assuming that most wrongdoers would normally be younger adults or the youth. However, in no way should this be construed as a way of turning African communities into a paedocracy where young adults and the youth occupy positions often reserved for elders who boast vast wisdom. The role of the youth and young adults should be limited to awareness and education programmes where they learn from one another as part of *letsema*/ *ilima* rehabilitation programmes.

8

Mediumship: Becoming a Spirit Medium

Introduction

Mediumship, in our sense, is about creating conditions for people to connect with their spiritual beings. To understand the concept of a spiritual being, it is important to note that no distinction is made between living and incorporeal beings as both represent variation only in time-space zones and their profound connectedness derive from their status as essentially spirits that occupy different time-space zones. These differing time-space zones assign different roles and responsibilities to these spiritual beings. The living is tasked with creating a peaceful and sustainable world that our children should inherit and progenitors (ancestors) serve as divine mediators and act as benevolent guardians who ensure that this divine mandate is executed properly in the land of the living. A spirit medium is a person assigned spiritually to create conditions where this divine connectedness between the living and their progenitors can be facilitated and sustained eternally as well as guide people through the process of establishing and sustaining this divine connectedness. Understood this way, life is about subscribing to something bigger and richer than material possession.

The binary between the living and their progenitors in some scholarly analyses is flawed because a spiritual being is the **oneness** of the living and their progenitors. It is a divine connectedness that is fundamental to our very being and a source of creating a humane, peaceful society based on restorative justice. The divine role of the spirit medium is to ensure that this divine connectedness is restored, repaired, and corrected all the time. Spirit mediums can receive spiritual messages or connect eidetically, clairvoyantly, clairsentiently, or clairaudiently to identify **vitiated divine connectedness** between a consulting, living person and their ancestral home / *isibaya*. This is the primary purpose of a spirit medium. The fundamental intent in every effort of a spirit medium is to create conditions that reconnect people with their spiritual beings. In this chapter, the initiatory learning process and mediumistic development of the spiritually gifted are described in detail.

The initiatory learning process involves the initial stages of the mediumship in which the cleansing and purification of the spiritual initiate take place. It also represents a transition in which four behavioural patterns manifest themselves and particular care must be taken to observe and advise the initiates on this paradigmatic shift and how its effects on their mindset can have a negative impact on their routinised behaviour (entrenched ways of thinking and doing). The key traits of this transition are therefore:

◆ The reality that an initiate ought to jettison and abandon old certainties and predictability of their life (entrenched efficiencies) and embrace new efficiencies. This has the potential to weaken and even eliminate existing relationships and comfort zones, leading to a breakdown of shared meaning that defined a sense of self for the initiate over a certain period. This part of the transition is important to ensure that old habits which might have given oxygen to the initiate's impurities are destroyed so new ways of doing things can be inculcated. Josephides (1999:144) calls it "**disengagement**", doing away with **sentiment**. **NO SENTIMENT on matters of spirituality.** In most cases, those closest to us who we entirely trusted for most of our lives prove to be hyenas in sheep apparel. Most of my initiates struggle with this new reality and some even abandon the mediumship process. Given that it is a voluntary exercise, no action is taken to convince them of the error of their ways. Free will reigns. Many who left this corporeal world did so before their time and without completing their missions mainly because of **SENTIMENT** which leads to false trust and similarly to fake news. These hyenas around us are nothing more than fakes and hypocrites. Hypocrites have the intent to exaggerate their role in one's life in ways that beholds one to them. They often are biased, inaccurate, deceptive, and dangerous to our lives while pretending to love us for manipulation purposes. In the service of justice, the spirit medium needs to be exposed to the reality of the cycle of ubuNtu so both can be made available to the spirit medium. Second, both realities will then create some level of confusion which is necessary for choices to be made between the two realities.

Without exposing the initiate to the cycle of ubuNtu, it would be wrong to judge them. An opportunity for exposure to the cycle of ubuNtu must be granted unconditionally. The reaction of the initiate or consulting person can either be disengagement from the cycle of ubuNtu reality and regression to old reality or entry into this new reality. Initiates or consulting person must be given the opportunity to decide without persuasion from the mentors. This exercise is voluntary and no form of coercion must be used at all. The demands of justice call for nothing less than the freedom and right to decide without persuasion or coercion.

♦ I know that disengagement leads to some kind of **identity imbroglio** marked by extreme confusion. This is the next phase of spiritual transition where the initiate seeks to keep faith in old habits and behaviours that defined their identity and hold on to the significant others who they trusted with absolute conviction. This is the most crucial phase of the transition as it prepares the initiate to assume a new identity as a spirit medium. It is important that this phase is handled with the sensitivity it deserves as it can lead to some panic or anxiety attacks including all sorts of psychological pathologies. It can break or build the character of the initiate and can easily make the initiate abandon the spiritual journey at this point as already stated. However, handling this stage of confusion with care should not degenerate into sentimental blackmail, a stage where malevolent significant others try to manipulate the initiate through emotions to abandon the mediumship process.

♦ It is important to assure the initiate that this is a normal phase of their mediumship development and that things are changing for the better where they will be elevated from ordinariness to becoming a crucial link between living human beings and their ancestral homes / *isibaya*. The fact that they were chosen to fulfil such a life purpose should be a source of humility and appreciation. It is a spiritual privilege for the chosen few and indeed as is the case in all other areas of our lives, there will always be charlatans who claim speciality in spirituality without meeting the requisite criteria. The three most important criteria are to adhere strictly to the credo of truth, equality, and love as well as the ability to communicate directly with one's ancestors and those of the consulting person plus creation of conditions for an initiate to be trained and inaugurated by their ancestral home. In addition, the initiate must be able to identify the exact spot where they will collect their spiritual gift as instructed by their ancestral home. If an initiate is unable to receive the spiritual message of where they will be collecting the spiritual gift, then an initiate does not graduate and conditions for achieving this feat continues. Spiritual mentors cannot inform the initiate about these things. The initiate must receive them from the ancestral home as clear evidence of communication at that level. Anything less is unacceptable and the initiation process is dropped because its basic plinth as evidence-led was not achieved. It is rare that initiates can collect their spiritual gifts at the exact spot simultaneously although it can be at a similar place. This is because these are highly sacred spaces and must be hallowed at all times. While it is a prerequisite that the spiritual mentor(s) accompany the initiate to the sacred space, once there, it is between the initiate and their ancestors. No interference at all from the spirit medium.

The spiritual mentor(s) become observers and have no control over the inauguration moment and process. It is a special, sacred moment for the initiate. For purposes of research and memento, pictures and videos are taken and all ethical issues apply. For instance, this pictorial and video information cannot be used for research or any other intent without the informed consent of those involved in it. The research is essential to provide evidence and reasoned logic that spirit mediumship is as much science as any other scientific enterprise.

◆ The next phase of the transition that follows an identity imbroglio is **psychological disorientation**, which involves a loss of meaning and direction, anger, extreme frustration, and a sense of loss, grief and deep-seated of doubt. At this stage, the initiate struggles with a new reality and can either make a breakthrough or have a breakdown. It is marked by extreme doubt and some initiates fall on their swords, especially if the spiritual mentor is not sufficiently trained to deal with this stage. Fear of failure is strong and past indiscretions bear heavily on the initiate. Care must be taken to assure the initiates that the outcome of the mediumship process is way more important than current uncertainties and doubt. Those who have worked outside the cycle of ubuNtu and might have acted malevolently might carry the quilt of past indiscretions and might seek to correct them. This action often exacerbates the quilt and must be discouraged. Spiritual consultations are voluntary exercises and cannot be forced onto people. Assist only those who volunteer to participate in the spiritual consultation and assure them that they can leave the spiritual consultation anytime without explanation. The voluntary exercise in spiritual consultation is sacrosanct.

♦ The initiate has to, out of necessity, steam and regurgitate regularly so as to open the vertical spiritual communication lines where they receive messages directly from the spiritual realm. Evidence of such spiritual presence is crucial so as to reorient the initiate into a new spiritual path.

♦ The last phase of the transition is when the initiate with the guidance of the spiritual mentor achieves a **moment of clarity** which is also called **epiphany** (Diagram 5.1 and Diagram 8.1), the point at which the realisation of a greater truth is achieved. This is the phase where the real mediumship journey of the initiate begins.

Mediumistic development entails the spiritual growth and attainment of the spirit medium status which includes collecting one's spiritual gift at a designated sacred place as shall be revealed to the initiate during the process of mediumship and is commonly achieved at the epiphany phase, a **moment of spiritual clarity**. The process of becoming a spirit medium takes approximately **21 days** but could last up to six months or more in some cases, especially if disengagement, identity imbroglio, and psychological disorientation were not dealt with prudently. The initiatory learning process begins with the knowledge of self (inner kingdom), origin, identity, and *isibaya*. *Isibaya* is a traditional African village that mostly consists of people of the same clan who share a common totem, bloodline, and *isithakazelo* (clan-praise). It emanates from a kraal, a place where animals such as cows are kept. A cow is a key economic currency in the African worldview. When an initiate does not belong to any *isibaya* then a ritual is conducted to inaugurate an initiate into their proper *isibaya*. Without this precondition, the initiate cannot start their mediumistic journey, as their spiritual connectedness with the ancestral vitality cannot be guaranteed.

Another precondition is that the mediumship development involves creating conditions for the initiate to connect with their ancestral spirits who guide the initiate throughout the mediumistic development process. The role of the spiritual mentor is to create these conditions for those spiritual conversations of connectedness between the initiate and ancestral spirits to take place unhindered by impurities of the initiate, hence the first 10 days of mediumship development are focused on cleansing the initiate so such connectedness can occur. In case there are unresolved issues in the life of the initiate such as unresolved trauma, psychological pathologies, or acts such as abortion, fornication, murder, rape or past molestations and so on, then these issues must be made transparent as the process of purification or cleansing intensifies.

These processes are evidence-led, and without evidence that the initiate is reconnecting spiritually then the mediumship is terminated. It is also expected that the initiate learns the four virtues of African spirituality and practise them in day-to-day activities. Furthermore, the initiate gets to know how to conduct diagnostics through connecting and inviting the ancestral spirits of the consulting person into the diagnostics process and charting a way forward. In some cases, a séance is conducted.

The Integrated Model of Spirit Mediumship Development

This model is based on a two-year study of initiates that underwent the spirit mediumship development. It went through various iterative stages until its refinement into its current form. It is a purely scientific endeavour true to the essence of African spirituality. African spirituality is based on the study of observable behaviour to understand the internal psychology of individuals whether it is based on othering (reconceptualised identity) or selflessness/ubuNtu (authenticity). In one instance during the refinement and final iteration of this model, a consulting person went through séance overseen by me which sought to establish why the family was beset by troubles and struggling to achieve well-being and a good life. In fact, her son was incarcerated for drug dealing. During the online consultation, I indicated that her son will be released without a charge but must come over with the entire family so we can conduct a séance. Indeed, the son was not charged and the séance happened. During the séance, the following interaction occurred between family and spirit mediums:

◆ *Spirit medium*: Your late father-in-law implores you to abandon the church (she has been a staunch member of A.M.E. Christian church for more than two decades) and focus on your spirit medium journey.

◆ *Consulting person*: I was taken to A.M.E church by the same father-in-law when I got married, how could he be the one suggesting we leave the church.

◆ *Spirit medium*: He wishes you abandon the church pledges including its attire, the Bible and everything associated with the church. Throw all that in the river.

◆ *Consulting person*: I am sorry. This is too big, I need time to think.

◆ *Husband of consulting person*: We have known this reality for the rest of our lives, so it will be difficult to just abandon it. Give us time.

◆ *Consulting person*: I am now seeing the vision of Bobo (father-in-law) and he repeats the instructions and demand that I do this urgently.

The next morning, the consulting person (her version of events of that morning) begins to collect all church things and place them in the plastic bag to dispose of them. In the meantime, the husband had prepared tea and saw the teacup fall on him in such speed that it was impossible to do so without some push from somebody. There was nobody around and the push defied all laws of nature. The husband disposed of his church attire and both began their spirit mediumship development. This very day, the consulting person was able to spiritually diagnose people accurately.

This family has agreed to be interviewed on condition that the interview is not based on testing or experimenting, but rather a normal consultation process is followed then questions can be asked around the experience itself.

Abrogation of Pledges

1. Identify all pledges one has made in cults, churches, other religious formations, and secret churches and commit to abandoning them unconditionally. These are nothing more than *manufactoriums* of iniquities with emphasis on manufacture.

2. Get rid of all things associated with these formations, books, attire, symbols, and so on.

3. Receive some cleansing from these impurities.

4. It is expected that some form of light will appear to the initiate once all these impurities have been removed.

5. Once the spiritual light appears, never make any pledges including on African spirituality. African spirituality is evidence-led and does not proceed on faith and extreme conjecture.

The Initiatory Learning Process

This spiritual learning process is based on the four spiritual virtues that are hierarchically structured in some kind of pyramid similar to Maslow's Hierarchy of Needs. At the base level of the pyramid resides the Temperance virtue. As described in detail in Chapter 4, the Temperance virtue occupies the middle space between *the vice of excess* such as avarice, pursuit of crass materialism, dipsomania, nymphomania, greed, emotional immaturity, and cantankerousness and the *vice of deficiency* such as celibacy, soberness, extreme poverty that leads to hunger, lack of clean water, contaminated air, denial of ownership of land, good health, and so on. Temperance reflects the spirit of ubuNtu and excludes sex, which is considered as part of the highest virtues of African spirituality, Prudence and Justice because its exercise brings life to earth. The initiates are taught to ensure that this base virtue of Temperance is adhered to unconditionally and without fail. When the initiates do consultations and séance, they are implored to do the following in line with **Temperance**:

◆ Ensure that each person that enters their homes or consultation room partake of some beverages and food within the limits of what they can afford. This is crucial to ensure consulting persons feel welcomed and a sense of belonging, thereby experiencing first hand the true spirit of ubuNtu. This serves to build a strong rapport between the consulting person and the spirit medium, who invites a consulting person into a powerful conversation among equals. Because a person is consulting one does not place one on a higher pedestal than them. One of the tenets of our credo is equality among human beings so that it must be adhered to at all costs.

The spirit medium must have a sense of being privileged that the consulting person chose them over multiple available possibilities, including modern medicine, and must proceed ethically and in terms of ubuNtu.

◆ Identify and deal with the mental and emotional dynamics of each consulting person and develop the patience and perspicacity of judgement that will not trigger negative emotions or lead to some mental instability that could unsettle the consulting person and collapse the consultation.

◆ Develop a strong sense of caring and identify the need that compelled a consultation. Decide if you are the right person to resolve the matter or whether a referral might be necessary.

◆ Promote the principles of ubuNtu, collective solidarity, and the need to advocate for African land ownership because it is the embodiment of our African spirituality. There must be a high level of awareness on land ownership.

◆ Adhere to the African spirituality **credo** of **love**, **truth** and **equality**. In executing our spiritual tasks, our love for otherness (all humans and nature) must trump any other considerations and our profound commitment to truth must be unconditional and without any distortions or sugar-coating. We tell the spiritual message as it is. **NO SENTIMENT**. The major source of distorted spiritual messages is emotional sentiment and puffery. It diverts the spiritual message to human attributes of sympathy and empathy which are entirely irrelevant in the conveyance of the spiritual message. There is also an absolute need to detach oneself from the spiritual message however painful it is, because doing so is offensive to the spiritual world for it is not one's message. As a spirit medium, one is a link between the ancestors of the consulting person and that person so the spiritual message one receives is not meant for one. This abstinence from sentiment applies only to the spiritual messages and their conveyance to the consulting person.

◆ There are two additional powers that initiates should possess and use prudently: concupiscible and irascible powers. Concupiscible power refers to the ability of initiates to do what is in the best interest of the consulting person and bracketing off personal biases and emotions so the spiritual message can be conveyed in its purest form. Irascible power deals with the solemn oath to adhere strictly to the African spirituality credo of love, truth, and equality including the resistance to anything that may cause any form of harm to the consulting person whether emotional, physical, or psychological.

Once all the conditions of the Temperance virtue are met, then the initiate can ascend to the second virtue, Fortitude. Fortitude refers to the courage to adhere to all principles of Temperance and ubuNtu. Initiates must demonstrate the virtue of **Fortitude** through:

◆ Rescuing the concept of the Fortitude virtue from conceptions of Western philosophy, Christian dogma, and other formations that claim exclusive right to the meaning and understanding of the Fortitude virtue so a level of equality, one of the African spirituality credos, is achieved. Spirit mediums must have the courage to challenge the epistemic inequality that exists in society and marginalisation of not only others' equally legitimate epistemic conceptions of Fortitude but also all other epistemes that create imbalances in society. This is crucial because spirit mediums must be seen to challenge patterns of oppression, marginalisation, and the flourishing of injustice in society. The thin, nominal meanings of Fortitude, a Western and Christian epistemic preference, has to be replaced by multiple and broader understandings of Fortitude so that a medley of different conceptions flourish in the global society marked by a multi-perspectival approach to everything. Understood as a society driven by productive complexity, our society requires thick meanings and descriptions of key concepts that undergird it. Jaladoni (2015:12) argues:

> A virtue like fortitude is 'thickened' through the details and particularities of fortitude in specific local, cultural instances.

◆ It is in this sense that its meaning and understanding is context-specific so that a universal understanding of it is unattainable unless forced upon through an oppressive political project. This is where the activism of spirit mediums become crucial in combating these epistemic injustices. Spirit mediums need not be overly fearful or overly confident in pursuing epistemic justice. Rather, they should be at the centre of the fear and confidence dichotomy to demonstrate the kind of courage vital for challenging epistemic injustice. A certain level of fear is necessary for a person to be courageous otherwise what would be the point of having courage.

In this case, the fear that inequality and epistemic injustice lead a complex society such as ours towards isomorphism is legitimate and become a strong motivator for activist to challenge such undesirables. Isomorphism (equal in shape), in this sense, refers to universal meanings allocated to key societal concepts but derived from Western thought and excludes all other alternative meanings. This is a sophisticated form of epistemic injustice which is undesirable in our society marked by a multi-perspectival approach to everything. True courage entails serving the greater good in society and appreciating multiplicity of meanings derived from multiple contexts.

True courage also involves ridding oneself of superiority over others in ways that place equality and justice at the heart of every endeavour. For instance, Christianity should stand on its own rationale and not on the grounds of bashing other cultural formations. As Aristotle's conception, true or mythical, of fortitude virtue goes, courage is the mean between fear and confidence so that a cultural formation such as Christianity that uses fear as a persuasive instrument takes away true courage among its converts who must build confidence to tackle inconsistencies, inaccuracies, and contradictions in their own religion. Instead, its ignorant congregation or converts build a false sense of courage / confidence that it uses to spread and defend its message. Philosophy scholars call this kind of false courage "*sanguineness*", overconfidence based on ignorance. True courage is based on **magnanimity** (generously forgiving where justice has been attained), **magnificence** (the courage to pursue excellence in all things), **indefatigability** (the courage to go on even in the face of extreme hardship), **perseverance** (the courage to be persistent and patient in pursuance of an ideal), plus **resilience** (the courage to recover from setbacks on the way to achieving an ideal).

◆ Accepting and acknowledging their own vulnerabilities, because there is no courage without vulnerability. The very essence of courage is vulnerability, doubt, and fear. A spirit medium requires strength of mind and emotions to face adversities that may be visited upon them by various lost human souls alive or in an apparition form.

◆ They must always be ready to be tested and vitiate attempts to block their duties as spirit mediums and have the courage to overcome the unsavoury acts of these lost human souls who need to be restored to our cycle of ubuNtu posthumously.

◆ Understanding the deceptive nature of discarnate spirits that operate outside the cycle of ubuNtu. These incorporeal spirits are masters of masquerade and would use the human form of those one admires and holds in high esteem to come closer to one and destroy one's spiritual mission. Spirit mediums must have the courage and wisdom to discern these unsavoury forces and overcome them. Another form of deception is when forces of darkness (*baloyi*) use other humans as a shield so that when one does diagnostics, these innocent souls are purported as witches (*baloyi*), whereas they are nothing more than victims of these dark forces who require rescue.

The spirit medium must reach a level of courageous discernment that would allow them to distinguish between a witch impostor and the real witch. It comes with spiritual growth and increased diagnostic capabilities of the spirit medium. Where the spirit medium is unable to make such a distinction then a referral to the spirit medium mentor may be necessary.

The next virtue that initiates should embrace and practise is the **Prudence** virtue and this should happen through:

◆ Deep understanding that practical wisdom involves two main constructs: "*intellectual humility and recognition that our society is informed by productive complexity*" (Pitso, 2021). Intellectual humility is about openness and willingness to accept that there are diverse ideas, beliefs, and values that are equally valid and can influence our actions and behaviours. Intellectually humble spirit mediums are not close-minded, dogmatic, authoritarian, or hang steadfastly to the inerrancy of their beliefs or sets of ideas. Furthermore, intellectually humble spirit mediums proceed on the basis of concrete evidence that leads to truth and accept nothing but the truth. Those consulting that are not ready to face the truth or reveal everything through the full disclosure of relevant information that can assist to unravel the truth render themselves unsuitable to receive further attention from the spirit medium. Without obtaining and evaluating the correctness of the information from the consulting person (*ho hlapholla*, clarify) in relation to the received spiritual message, establishing truth becomes difficult yet the solution rests with establishing the truth. Intellectual humility is understanding the limitations imposed upon the spirit medium when the process of clarification (*ho hlapholla*) is not thorough and the spirit medium must be humble enough to admit that they cannot resolve the matter without the direct input of the consulting person. It also involves the idea that the spirit medium does not hold exclusive rights to matters relating to the consulting person or is superior to the consulting person. There has to be a recognition that the spirit medium is also not perfect and goes through their own life battles. Intellectual humility also involves learning from the experiences of consulting persons and gaining practical wisdom from them, including tacit knowing, the kind of heightened awareness and deep understanding of very esoteric information relating to life in general and issues relating to consulting persons more specifically. Spirit mediums must also have a thorough understanding of the society we live in and its main drivers. As things stand now, our society functions on a global scale and in real time because of the capabilities of advanced technologies, which makes it a highly diverse and complex society full of multiple perspectives, beliefs and values, which coalesce when handled properly and not in a dogmatic way for some beneficial productivity. Practical wisdom derives from recognising that our society is too complex and diverse to rely on a single perspective plus it functions within uncertain, unpredictable, and multi-perspectival conditions that require higher levels of flexibility and open-mindedness.

◆ Gaining practical wisdom that derives from the Temperance and Fortitude virtues as outlined above and a strong sense of justice. Spirit mediums must document their experiences and derive patterns that inform their practices and guide their mediumship. Given that the Prudence virtue combines the mental and moral virtues, it stands to reason that its purpose is to build capabilities of practical wisdom necessary for spirit mediums to function optimally in the interstices between living humans and their ancestral home and to promote good life (*eudemonia*). A good life is possible when spirit mediums pursue only things that are just, noble, and filled with moral integrity.

◆ Practising intellectual humility as described earlier to include the ability to inter-twine reason and action to cope with uncertainty, unpredictability, and change as well as function in a multi-perspectival environment where equality of meanings and epistemic justice are sacrosanct. These attributes are essential in a spirit medium who must at all times be open-minded enough to accommodate various consulting persons with their vast and varied personalities, which must be treated equally irrespective of their conduct and actions.

◆ Practical wisdom, deriving from intellectual humility and recognition of diversity, uncertainty plus complexity in society, and in relation to spirit mediumship can be considered as ethereal, delicate, light, and spiritual in the sense of its exercise and understanding so that its acquisition takes time and exposure to hardship that bring humility and perspicacity into our work as spirit mediums.

◆ Practical wisdom clarifies our life purpose and mission in ways that make spirit mediums understand that they came **through** their parents but not **from** their parents, meaning their conception in a human form was decided from an ancestral home acting on the permission of the Supreme Being so that each one of us have a mission that transcends the wishes of our parents. It also brings a sense that we are not beholden to our parents or siblings purely on grounds of birth. Rather, our mission is bigger and more profound. We also have no basis to allow manipulative tendencies or emotional blackmail from our own children. Practical wisdom helps us navigate these unsavoury spaces of human interactions.

The highest African spirituality virtue is **Justice**, particularly restorative justice, which the spirit medium should attain by focusing on:

◆ All aspects of justice such as *economic* justice at the level of all people being able to meet all conditions of Temperance, highlighting particularly fairer redistribution of land including its productivity. *Social* justice in pursuance of equality among people irrespective of their colour, gender, orientation, or belief. *Epistemic* justice with attention paid to equality among all forms of epistemes and ontological orientations. *Axiological* justice where values deriving from all forms of beliefs and cultures are recognised so that people from our complex society can choose those values that better serve their purpose without being coerced to follow values decided upon by dominant societal forces whether political, economic, or religious. Spirit mediums must always be careful not to impose their values on consulting persons except to inform them thoroughly about ubuNtu values so they can choose for themselves whether these are the values that should guide their actions and behaviours. This is also part of intellectual humility that derives from practical wisdom. Spirit mediums must be actively involved in matters dealing with the achievement of a just and fairer society and should therefore not limit their activities to spiritual consultations. It would be a great spiritual travesty to our spirit mediumship if our active agency in matters relating to justice and land is compromised. Land is the embodiment of our African spirituality.

◆ Spirit mediums must also be actively involved in mediation, conciliation and reconciliation efforts intended to establish the nature of hurt to those wronged, appropriate courses of action to restore the wrongdoer back to our cycle of ubu-Ntu, and provision of some therapy as well as counselling for the wronged. There is nothing more powerful than for people to realise that revenge, vengeance, and anger towards the wrongdoer makes the wronged person a character in the story of the wrongdoer and letting go of these undesirable feelings makes one a protagonist in their own story. This is the purpose of restorative justice, reclaiming one's own story and letting go of victimhood and psychological incarceration.

◆ Closure is about reclaiming one's status as a protagonist in one's story rather than a harmed antagonist seeking revenge and the visiting of some sadomasochistic pain to those who hurt us. There are no winners there, only two ignominious graves, that of the wrongdoer and the wronged.

◆ Spirit mediums must be involved in activities and programmes that ensure the rate of recidivism (return to behaviour that hurts others) is substantially reduced as a result of using restorative justice programmes as designed in ways that serve as a deterrence for future hurt.

◆ Restorative justice must be directly linked to the Temperance virtue so that all society have sufficient resources to live, including wrongdoers. There is no greater honour than to strive for an equal and just society. Spirit mediums must be at the heart of such endeavours. When conditions of Temperance are not fully met, it leads to all kinds of psychological pathologies, which tend to contribute to wrongdoing. There is no evidence to suggest that in a society full of resource fecundity as conceptualised within the Temperance virtue, wrongdoing can be eliminated but it is possible to surmise that it can substantially be reduced and possibly eliminated in the long term. It is, in this sense, that spirit mediums must play an active role in the productivity of their communities. Not only should they join already existing empowerment programmes but must innovatively initiate programmes and projects with strong ubuNtu values. The role of a spirit medium is to build communities and the broader society and this must happen at a practical level whether fixing the spiritual side of things or dealing with the physical, emotional, and psychological aspects of humans.

◆ Spirit mediums must also empower themselves in terms of formal education so they can acquire the technical ability to do research that challenges epistemic injustice and restores ubuNtu values in society (exhortation). The spirit medium must have a strong sense of epistemic equality and ethical conduct based on fairness and diverse value systems minus dominance and imperialist tendencies. Exhortation in African spirituality deals with (1) teachings about ubuNtu and how to function optimally within the cycle of ubuNtu. For the spirit medium to teach effectively on Africanness, extensive research on the history, culture, and heritage of Africans is crucial to correct errors in history and distortions about our culture and heritage. (2) Past and present trials, tests, and tribulations that visit a spirit medium or those that consult them are intended to build courage and testimonies that can be used in exhortation teachings. (3) Adherence to the African spirituality credo of equality, love, and truth ensure that the teachings of the spirit medium are within the confines of the ubuNtu principles and values. (4) Spirit mediums serve as therapists in the commission of restorative justice precepts and provide counselling and advice, hence they need to receive basic training on these important psychological tools.

Mediumship Development

The mediumship process refers to creating spiritual conditions so that the discarnate spiritual elders of the initiate dictate the terms of spiritual initiation where the spiritual mentor serves as a purifier and guide. Mediumship development is thus about learning to do a proper diagnosis of the actual spiritual affliction that beset a consulting person or family, the primary one of which is a lack of ancestral home (*isibaya*). This is the most basic and fundamental affliction that results in misfortune, shattered dreams or visions, spiritual attacks, and so on. Once the diagnosis is done then some well defined intervention is advised which might include the performance of some ritual. The last responsibility of the spirit medium is to monitor the progress and outcomes that must be supported by credible evidence. In this sense, mediumship development is a three-stage process – diagnostics, intervention, and outcome.

There is, however, a pre-mediumship stage which comes before the initiatory learning process. In this pre-mediumship stage, the type of spirit mediumship is discovered through steaming and spewing. The initial activities of purification involve these steaming and spewing exercises. Spirit mediums can either be auditory, ventriloquist, eidetic, tactile, or intuitive spirit mediums, concepts that receive further attention in the next sub-section.

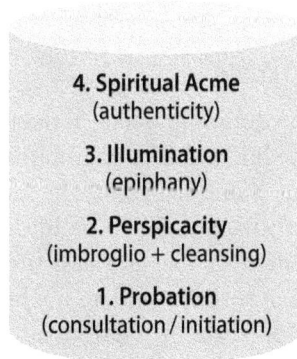

4. Spiritual Acme
(authenticity)

3. Illumination
(epiphany)

2. Perspicacity
(imbroglio + cleansing)

1. Probation
(consultation / initiation)

Diagram 8.1   Mediumship Development Process

Pre-mediumship – Purification stage – Diagnostics training and practicals (spiritual interventionist techniques) – Collecting a spiritual gift at a designated sacred place

Pre-mediumship

In this stage of development, initiates can experience various bodily challenges which emanates from an increased supply of ectoplasm, the type of energy that allows initiates to access a world beyond matter and allows for the manifestation of spirits (Pierini, 2014), also called discarnation or incorporeity. The purpose of this excess production of this particular energy is to allow the initiate to use it to heal others. In some cases, the initiates can viscerally feel the pain and symptoms of the consulting person or they can experience excruciating headaches or stomach aches. Disturbances in the solar plexus (digestive system) of the initiate are one of the strongest indicators that the initiate is ready for mediumship development. In other instances, initiates can experience the presence of an incorporeal body giving instructions that the initiate must take up a spiritual gift. This can come in the form of a vision or dream.

There are therefore **auditory** spirit mediums that listen to spiritual messages from the ancestral home of the consulting person and convey the message or instructions to them. The **ventriloquist (power mimicry)** spirit medium assumes the voices of the ancestors and conveys the spiritual message directly from the ancestral home of the consulting person. **Eidetic** spirit mediums are capable of visualising the exact spot where certain spiritual activities takes place and communicate it to the consulting person, mostly seeking confirmation from the consulting person as the actual spot of spiritual activity is lucidly described. The **tactile** spirit medium uses bodily touch as the basis of diagnosis, receiving spiritual messages, detecting malaise, and recommending treatment or resolution of a specific problem. The **intuitive** spirit mediums just look at a consulting person and are capable of diagnosing them even without touch or listening to the ancestral home. The **auditory-tactile** spirit medium uses both listening to the spiritual messages conveyed and touching consulting persons in spots linked to spirituality to diagnose malaise. The spiritual message comes automatically. These different approaches to diagnostics often get determined during the purification stage.

Purification (cleansing) of the initiate

When initiates commence their mediumship, focus in the first 10 days of the 21 days of mediumship is on cleansing the initiates of their impurities so the chosen spiritual guides from their specific ancestral home can access the initiate and provide instructions and guidance on how the initiate ought to be initiated. There is an absolute need for the initiates to be cleansed of the filthiness of the flesh and spirit. This could include hurts or wrongdoing that the initiate might have committed or were committed to them such as the infliction of physical pain that leaves psychological scars and creates emotional instability or psychological pathologies such as depression, rape, miscarriage, cheating, and many other acts of hurt.

The primary cleansing relates to *isibaya*. It is impossible for an initiate who has no ancestral home to undergo mediumship training because the training is conducted by an ancestral home where the initiate belongs. For instance, a married initiate has to call upon the ancestral home of the husband to conduct the mediumship. If the marriage rites were not done correctly then that ought to be fixed prior to the initiate starting her mediumship.

The second primary consideration is cleansing the spirit medium of the impurities emanating from death such as abortion, miscarriage, death of child or family member. The purification rites are performed at the relevant family home prior to starting mediumship. Where cheating is involved then mediation takes place and the necessary mechanisms of atonement including marriage counselling take place and can be conducted by a competent spirit medium or they can make a referral to a competent professional. The list of purification rites is not exhaustive.

Once these impurities have been attended to then initiates can start the actual cleansing, beginning with disturbances in the solar plexus through the rites of liquid mixture spewing, steaming, and enemas which includes rectal douching as the first stage of enema. The most complex purification rite, in African spirituality, is akin to an act of exorcism which is conducted by all initiates to determine whether acts of ensorcellment (state of being possessed by lost spirits that place one under their spell so one functions outside the cycle of ubuNtu) have been visited upon the initiate. The purification process can be divided into rites that are performed during mediumship. **Familial rites** (*isibaya*, cleansing, crossover ritual), **catechumen rites** (rites of acceptance into mediumship), **intra-cleansing rites** (liquid mixture spewing, general and sacred steaming – must have communicated directly with ancestral home, enema and rectal douching, de-ensorcellment), and **ancestral Spiritual Gift Impartation rites** (a stage where the ancestral home of the initiate assigns a physical place where the initiate will receive their spiritual gift).

General steaming is a purification ritual that entails getting rid of man-made impurities such as negative forces imposed on a person through bewitching to make a person unattractive in society either when seeking employment or love. In the case of spirit mediumship, general steaming involves removing all these man-made impurities and enabling the spirit medium to communicate directly with their ancestral home. Furthermore, initiates must also undertake séance steaming. Séance steaming for initiates takes place when the initiate has unresolved issues such as a lack of closure on one whose death was not resolved, divorce, abortion, miscarriage, doubt on any matter, and many other things that have some psychological impact on the health and well-being of an initiate. It is important that an initiate is purified before proper communication can take place between the initiate and ancestral home.

As earlier stated, mediumistic development in African spirituality is about creating conditions for the initiate to be spiritually developed by their ancestral home including providing a place where an initiate must collect their spiritual gift. Spiritual charlatans would claim that they conduct a mediumistic development as a spiel for money-making rather than be humble enough to understand that no human being can conduct a mediumistic development of any initiates as that is the exclusive reserve of their ancestral home. We, spiritual mentors, merely create an enabling and conducive ambience for initiates to be developed by their ancestral home.

Tactile diagnostics

Vitalism 1: Metacarpus reading (palm-to-palm analysis)

The first stage of tactile diagnosis is palm-to-palm analysis. In this stage, the spirit medium touches the palm of the consulting person using his or her own palms. This is called metacarpus reading. The most important aspect of the metacarpus is the transverse arch which creates the capability that allows fingertips and thumb to work together for purposes of diagnostics, meaning this reading is about the productivity of the consulting person, whether they own a business, are employed or unemployed, or due for promotion conditional to expectations from the ancestral home that the initiate becomes pure.

Vitalism 2: Carpus reading

This form of diagnosis is strongly linked to pulse rate, which determines the health of one's heart and blood flow. In African spirituality, it signals the general health of the consulting person at a physiological level. It identifies things like blood pressure, sugar levels, blood circulation, and any other physiological ailments. The reading from the wrist is thus intended to achieve similar goals as conventional medical diagnosis and be enhanced by using normal reliable tools of diagnosing blood pressure and sugar diabetes available in any pharmacy at a reasonable price. There is a need for greater integration between Western and African health tools.

This serves to indicate that African spirituality is not opposed to advances in science and conventional medicine. Rather, the incorporation of these modern capabilities strengthens our practice. Integration of both traditional and modern capabilities enhances the quality of health provision and spirit mediums have a responsibility to refer consulting persons to modern health services when such is warranted and here is a reasonable expectation that conventional medical practitioners would extent such courtesy to spirit mediums. This cooperation between traditional and modern medicine would prove beneficial to a society marked by a multi-perspectival approach to education, medicine, health, leadership, and so on. Western health field must cease the arrogance that it has all the answers.

Vitalism 3: Scalene reading

The scalene reading deals with enervated people, that is, those with reduced mental and moral vitality thus lacking the vigour to live optimally within the cycle of ubuNtu. They are often weak and tired, losing the zeal for life. People often feel depressed and enervated, because they have ignored a spiritual message or have been functioning outside the cycle of ubuNtu. This reading drawn from three groups of muscles at the lateral neck – anterior, middle, posterior muscles – provides the basis for understanding why the consulting person is weakened by the ancestral home. This reading is strongly linked with the third to the eighth cervical spinal nerves which innervate the scalene muscles, meaning the entire mental condition of the consulting person can be detected and a determination made as to the reason for its weakened state.

The spirit medium has the responsibility to connect with the ancestral home to find out what needs to be done to invigorate and revitalise the consulting person. In other words, the spirit medium needs to be guided as to the purification rites that need to be performed to restore the consulting person into the cycle of ubuNtu and thus to *eudemonia. Eudemonia* is a state of living one's life in terms of ubuNtu principles and values in ways that create collective happiness because individual happiness, in the African worldview, is meaningless without collective happiness.

Vitalism 4: Cranial reading

The cranial part of our body relates to our skull that is linked to our spinal cord and begins at our medulla oblongata, the part of the brain that controls the autonomic aspects of our lives such as respiration and heartbeat. Respiration and heartbeat determine whether our stay in this corporeal life continues or not. In African spirituality, these two brain activities are the exclusive preserve of our ancestral homes so that by making a cranial reading, we are in essence determining the strength of the relationship between the consulting person and ancestral home. A weakened relationship between a consulting person and ancestral home suggests that the life of a consulting person in this world is threatened or is coming to an end. The responsibility of the spirit medium is to find out the reasons for such a drastic decision and what can be done to save the life of a consulting person.

Often, it is a matter of *isibaya* or some rites or rituals that were not performed correctly and need fixing. Given the strong reliance of African spirituality on restorative justice, the highest virtue, threatened lives of consulting persons can be salvaged once necessary corrective action is done.

Setting up a séance

A séance, in African spirituality, refers to a specialised ritual that involves a session where, as per the request of the consulting person(s) or as the need arises, spirit mediums as a collective enable a communion to take place between the consulting person(s) and their ancestral home. Other spirit mediums join the séance as per request. It is often necessitated, particularly when the cranial reading shows a strained relationship between the consulting person(s) and their ancestral home.

A séance is a more advanced, participatory process of connecting at a spiritual level with those who have gone before us and serve as conduit between living beings and the world of the Supreme Being. Séance is a form of advanced and specialised diagnostics. As clarified many a time in this book, African spirituality knows no worship or the notion of some individualised hero who rescues people spiritually. The ancestral home is part of a communication channel with the spiritual world in which the spiritual protocols dictate that living human beings cannot communicate directly with the Supreme Being. There are protocols to be observed when setting up a solid séance encounter with a high degree of a successful communion. Spirit mediums serve as spiritual intermediaries, not some superman swooping to save souls. Such superman spiel is the stuff of legends that depends on learned helplessness, a mental state achieved through the exercise of conditioned learning that one is incapable of resolving one's challenges and needs some superhero for assistance or salvation.

There is the preliminary setup that must be arranged to communicate effectively with the departed. First, there is an absolute need to differentiate between mediumship séance and séance conducted for consulting person(s) under the guidance of a spirit medium. The purpose for mediumship séance was outlined earlier and focus here goes to séance for consulting person(s). A word of warning on conducting a consultancy-based séance is that it comes with experience and insights developed over time so that a novice spirit medium must undertake consultancy-based séance in the presence of an experienced spirit medium. This is because there is a strong likelihood that on conducting this sacred rite, one can unknowingly summon lost souls with malignant intent who can inhabit and possess humans attending séance insidiously. These malevolent forces once in possession of humans act out their wicked intentions that seek to avert people from the cycle of ubuNtu with dire consequences for humans' *eudemonia* (good spirit) and well-being. This is possible mainly because séance of any type works on multiple spiritual portals and there are always unfiltered spiritual portals where malevolent lost souls and malignant forces can invoke themselves for a free ride on these séance portals to commit acts of wickedness. It is, in this sense, particularly crucial that each séance is preceded by *isithakazelo* of the consulting person(s) so the appropriate spiritual portal could open up and communication with the right ancestral home is possible.

Secondly, it is very important that the reasons for séance are clear and discussed in advance between the consulting person(s) and the presiding spirit medium so the séance communication is focused with clear direction. Thirdly, the number of people in a single séance should not exceed five people, excluding the presiding spirit mediums. Fourthly, it does not matter whether there is a table or some furniture item when a séance is conducted. Fifthly, no candle should be used during séance as this is reserved for "*ho phahla*" (ancestral summon ritual) often intended as a communication line between humans and their ancestral home.

A white candle depicts one's spiritual path or journey. When the candle burns until completed with no sign of protruding waxes depicts *diritta via* (the righteous path or journey). When the white candle produces protruding waxes normally called a "crying candle" then we are in *selva oscura* (dark path) spaces which necessitates a spiritual intervention. A yellow candle without protruding waxes indicates a smooth spiritual contact and a crying yellow candle means a disconnect between the consulting person(s) and their ancestral home then purification rituals must be conducted to reconnect the consulting person(s) with their ancestral home, a source of *eudemonia* and well-being. A red candle with no protruding waxes represents the weak presence of malignant forces and lost souls and the crying red candle is indicative of the strong presence of malignant forces and lost souls leading to spiritual intervention such as spiritually securing a home against these forces and lost souls.

All sources of artificial light including television and mobile phones must be switched off and this must include extraneous sources of noise or other distractions. There is no need for holding of hands during séance although it may not affect the quality of sessions if it happened. The séance process entails the next steps:

◆ Let the consulting person(s) recite their *isithakazelo* and the spirit medium should, at the end of the recital, make it clear that only the spiritual portal of this specific ancestral home is invited to the séance. In some cases, and when the consulting person(s) request or feel comfortable doing that, the adopted Lord's prayer can be recited but at the end of the recital then *isithakazelo* should be recited before saying *amen* (invitation of appropriate spirits from relevant ancestral home to join the séance session and assist with diagnosis of the consulting person(s) and describing the intervention rituals and rites).

◆ At this point, the spirit medium should be able to access the appropriate ancestral home and spiritual messages would then be communicated. In most cases, the spirit of individual ancestors would identify themselves and when the matter is rather complex often the third to fourth generation ancestral spirit will appear and elucidate grounds for misfortunes and how they can be fixed. In the case where the ancestral spirits refuse to identify themselves then one or more of the consulting person(s) has some impurities and the spirit medium must be able to identify the particular impure participant and request them to recuse themselves from the séance session so progress can be made. The recused person should then receive further attention after the completion of the séance in the form of diagnosis and rites as well as rituals. This is to ensure that all consulting persons receive the necessary attention and resolution of their problems. No person is left behind.

◆ Once in contact with the other side, questions should relate to **relationships** (family, workplace, friendship, marriage, social events, including death and matrimony) and their state of health. Furthermore, questions should relate to **values** that are inherent in African communities as undergirded by the ubuNtu principles of love, equality and truth.

Of particular importance during the séance is for consulting persons to find their **life purpose** (inner kingdom), which will be expounded, in the next bullets. Given the importance of searching for one's inner kingdom, a strong sense and understanding of African spirituality as immanence is crucial. This way, séance serves the purpose of assisting humans to find their inner kingdom. An inner kingdom draws from immanence (finding the power of the Supreme Being within ourselves) as such deals with:

◆ The principles and power of priorities. In African spirituality, these principles emanate from ubuNtu such that the total well-being of all members of a community and broader society including the preservation of natural endowments are non-negotiable. Power (who decides and who stands to benefit) talks to our own abilities to focus on important things first (priorities) and the choices we make in serving the greater good or private interests. In other words, inner kingdom is about control over our own lives and doing things that enhance the collective well-being of a community and acting in the best interest of nature so the next generation of humans can find it in pristine condition. The source of our inner kingdom is the priorities we make everyday and serving selflessly towards achieving goals that benefit all humanity and nature. Séance must allow the ancestral home of those consulting the spirit medium to listen to the priorities they make relating to relationships and the ubuNtu values of selflessness, love and equality. It is this truth that must preoccupy those seeking inner kingdom and their relationship with their ancestral home. It is in this sense that all forms of religion are themselves the **search for an inner kingdom**. Those religions based on transcendence tend to locate this kingdom somewhere outside the human world such as the kingdom of God is in heaven and that Jesus, Moses, or Muhammad (PBUH) are the surest way to salvation, redemption, and occupancy of the kingdom beyond the azure dome. Our immanence-based philosophy and spirituality posit that finding inner kingdom on this earth and within one's soul is the surest way of transitioning smoothly to ultimate reality. The concepts of heaven, hell, and superhero as the passage to God's kingdom are foreign to our understanding. We surmise that living a healthy and effective life involves a deep understanding of the power of priorities because in priorities we learn how humans select certain tasks and goals they seek to achieve, and whether these tasks and goals are intended to serve the greater good. Prioritisation of certain tasks also reveals choices humans make in pursuit of a good life defined in terms of ubuNtu values. These choices and decisions that compel humans to act and behave in a particular way illuminate the search for inner kingdom whether the human being is aware or unaware. Priorities are strongly linked with inner kingdom, that is, the actions and behaviours we display in public reveal the mental signification process that preceded these actions and behaviours. The signification process is about what one has considered important and actualised it in practical action and external behaviour. In essence, the search for inner kingdom is about knowing one's life purpose and once that is achieved then fear of death or any kind of fear gets eliminated as the agent of fear, ignorance, and lack of empowering information is removed. The most basic of fears is "*fear of the unknown*" (Carleton, 2016:5).

Most of the belief systems, including Abrahamic religions, thrive on this fundamental fear of the unknown. Our human propensity towards self-preservation and an intolerance of uncertainty and unpredictability predispose us to this basic, primitive fear which leads to anxiety and neuroticism, a sustained experiencing of negative energy. Fear brings a state of mental paralysis that grips and compels one into submissiveness as the logic faculty is shut down so a person becomes an easy target of manipulation and intellectual capture. One of the key goals of séance is assisting people to connect spiritually and discover their true mission on earth. Solemnly summoning the ancestral spirits during séance involves helping consulting person(s) to reconnect with their spirituality and achieve a moment of clarity about their life purpose which leads to a better understanding of one's inner kingdom and the principal values that structure this inner kingdom. Once this is achieved fear is banished and a person ascends to a higher and greater level of understanding. During séance, it is important that the ancestral home of consulting person(s) help make transparent the person's inner kingdom. Often, humans lead their lives without a clear inner kingdom which in, African spirituality, means living a worthless life bereft of any life purpose. Without a deeper understanding of how inner kingdom shapes and guides actions and behaviours of people then the life of such people without an inner kingdom is worthless. We connect with our spirituality once we have discovered our inner kingdom which, in turn, eases us into communicating directly with our ancestral homes. Every effort to connect with the other side during séance is intended to help people find their inner kingdom (life purpose, meaning of life, universal values of ubuNtu). There are only two priorities that define the inner kingdom of people. First, it must ensure that our actions and behaviours contribute selflessly to the greater good.

The second priority is about conserving our natural resources. These are the priorities that help us connect with our ancestral homes. Those who prioritise private interests and unbridled exploitation of nature function outside the cycle of ubuNtu and are aptly described as idiots not in the sense of lacking intellectual capacity but in terms of its etymological meaning of serving one's interests even when those interests breach the dignity and rights of others.

◆ Inner kingdom subsists on Temperance, Fortitude, Prudence and Justice. The basic needs of the consulting person(s) must be met fully; if not, this matter must be dealt with during séance. African spirituality rejects poverty and inequality, and it has to be tackled where it exists during séance sessions.

Avant garde séance

This advanced, radical form of séance denotes a vanguard of spirit mediums that wage a war against malevolent forces, or negative spirits that seek to destroy the general well-being and happiness of a family. It is thus an advanced form of de-ensorcellment that is led by highly experienced, seasoned spirit mediums intending to drive away the malevolent force or negative energy. These forces or energies were originally summoned to bring wealth and fecundity to a family but have now turned dark. The process itself is quite laborious and requires thorough preparation and readiness to challenge the most formidable force of immense power and strength. Those who have doubts or are in the grip of fear need not participate in this type of séance.

Phase 1: Spiritual reconnaissance

◆ Conduct a preliminary survey of the haunted family home through a pre-séance session where all spirit mediums involved in the process connect to identify places of interest, that is, spaces where the negative spirit tends to spend most of its time. They too have favourite places to hang out and these places must be identified and a kind of map is drawn to determine its routine and movement patterns.

◆ Once identified, the most common place where the negative spirit is strongest needs to be cleansed via painting and using Jeyes Fluid or similar cleaning liquids that can tackle a hidden negative spirit.

  This cleansing exercise will not chase away the negative spirit but will help identify it and dislocate it.

◆ The cleansing occurs a day before the actual séance. It is important to conduct it while the negative spirit is unsettled and disoriented.

Phase 2: Making contact

◆ All the doors of the haunted home must be opened, including trap doors or garages.

◆ Mphepo and other African incense drawn mainly from trees should be burnt prior to the séance process.

◆ All the spirit mediums should be in possession of their sacred spears or knobkieries (rods) and ensure that they are cleansed and ready for the struggle of removing these energies.

◆ All spirit mediums connect to identify the presence of the malevolent force or negative energy, including deciphering its apparition.

◆ Once all spirit mediums have made contact, then each shares how this negative spirit(s) manifests itself and the tricks it uses to escape detection or weaken spirit mediums.

Phase 3: Adjuration

Adjuration is intended to protect the spirit mediums against these formidable, negative forces by:

◆ Reciting one's *isithakazelo/sereto/ho thella* so that the ancestors of each spirit medium can offer such protection and safety.

◆ Ensuring that the spiritual authority to conduct such a specialised séance is offered by an ancestral home and a spirit medium without such spiritual authority has to recuse themselves from the séance.

Phase 4: Theurgy

◆ This phase involves persuading the malevolent force or negative spirit to leave the home and never return. This is done via hitting one's spear or knobkierie three times on the ground and it is expected that the negative spirit would voluntarily leave or desist from attacking or bringing unsavoury things to the family.

◆ Once this persuasion fails then the spirit mediums hit the ground harder and faster until a particular rhythm is established and sustained over a longer time until there are signs that the force is vacating the home. The rhythms continue until the *henosis* or mystical oneness that existed between the negative spirit and the family members is broken and entirely extirpated. This can take several hours and should not be ceased until the negative spirit is defeated. It is important to note that the negative spirit can mimic the demiurge (divine mind) as an attempt to deceive or end the extirpation process. The semblance of 'union' that existed between the negative spirit and family members could have been installed in childhood so it is important that to those traumatic and painful childhood memories as that is a strong antidote against this negative force.

Phase 5: Pathway to oneness (our way back home, *hae, ikhaya*)

The family must now begin a journey towards reconnecting with their benevolent ancestors and becoming **ONE** with the ancestral home, nature, and fellow beings, often called "*journey towards oneness*". Oneness is a living reality, a presence that attracts all positive energies and leads to real well-being and fecundity. It is often experienced inwardly in what is called "***the beloved***" situated in the deepest repositories of the heart. It refers at a higher level to the fact that everything in the universe is connected with all other things, hence science seeks "*the theory of everything*" in recognition of this "*oneness theory*". Oneness is in essence "*a manifestation of the divine*" to which everything aggregates. The greatest destroyer of oneness in oneself, in family, in a clan, country, and the source of narrow individualism, religious bigotry, racism, narrow culture, patriotism, patriarchy, and supremacy of any sort including white supremacy is egocentrism, a deep-seated solipsism (me, me, me...).

This means that the first step towards journeying to oneness is to step out of oneself and onto the path towards oneness. Scholars in the Theory of One call it "*a sigh in the soul*", a *primal longing* for the ultimate reality referred to in as many names, God, Allah, Modimo, Tlatlamatjholo, uNkulunkulu. It is a return to the most powerful source to which the selfish, avaricious, and demented have no access and only those who truly attempt access to this source stand a chance of successfully completing the journey. It is important to note that there are many oppositions, malevolent forces of ego and avarice that misdirect and create detours along the way so one is denied the smooth path to oneness. There are those who call these detours "*the veils*" that misdirect us to ensure that the union with oneness is not achieved, the inter-connectedness with Divine Oneness is frustrated. In the African worldview, it is about returning to the cycle of ubuNtu. "*The veils*" live among us and some are very close, very close – habits, rituals, religious bigotry, brainwashing, menticide, routines, sentiment, malevolent people. Basotho have an expression to signal the first step towards oneness:

"*Ya kgaola, ya ya*" (breaking the bonds and journeying towards oneness).

Practical Training (intervention)

There are several rites and rituals that must be observed when attempting to resolve issues that came out of diagnostics and séance. Each of these cultural tools must privilege the needs and interests of the consulting person(s). The first step in the spiritual intervention process relates to *isibaya,* which is a prerequisite in resolving problems besetting the consulting person(s). The ancestral home must provide guidance as to which rites or rituals need to be performed to resolve the issues raised during diagnostics and séance.

There has to be evidence that the performed rites and rituals adequately addressed the challenges the consulting person(s) had because African spirituality is evidence-led. Without proof or evidence then the rites or rituals performed must be repeated because the protocols of each rite or ritual must have been violated one way or the other. As indicated earlier, African spirituality meets all criteria of being an evidence-based practice defined as the integration of traditional and clinical interventions in resolving problems besetting consulting person(s) driven by a combination of traditional and modern medicine. In all these interventions, evidence of efficacy must be sought and referrals to clinical intervention must be done when the matter relates to physiological challenges.

When using traditional medicine, care must be taken with the existing condition of the consulting person(s). For instance, before administering traditional medicine, the health history of the consulting person(s) must be explicitly known such as high blood pressure, sugar diabetes, cancer, and so on. Each spirit medium must have basic testing equipment for high blood pressure and sugar diabetes and must work closely with a qualified medical doctor. In cases where clinical intervention is necessary then a referral to a medical doctor must be made. Spiritual mediums have to understand that spirituality is one aspect of a very complex human being.

It is in this sense that the definition of an evidence-based practice adopted by Hodge (2011) fits into African spirituality intervention efforts with some significant modifications:

◆ Meeting the needs of a consulting person. The ethical principle that a consulting person voluntarily consulted a spirit medium and puts trust in them means that the best interests of a consulting person must trump all other considerations. If the best course of action is for a consulting person to be referred to a medical doctor, that is exactly what should happen. Spirit mediums should develop a deeper understanding that they are part of a broad therapeutic enterprise and that meeting the needs of a consulting person should firstly be premised on an accurate assessment of their condition. Secondly, decide whether spiritual intervention would suffice to resolve and meet the needs of a consulting person. Thirdly, the nature of intervention must be clearly articulated so as to make a determination of whether a relief care is necessary often involving assuaging pain, corrective care entailing restoration of good health whether physiological, psychological, moralistic, or whether wellness care would be the best course of action to meet the needs of a consulting person. Wellness care is particularly important because it entails taking steps to restore a person's optimum well-being at a spiritual, emotional, physical, psychological, and social level. All this progress towards optimum wellness must be recorded and evaluated constantly for efficacy.

Spiritual wellness, in the African worldview, refers to a state of health that compels people to make sacrifices and act to achieve the greater good.

◆ Evaluating evidence from diagnostics and séance to determine the suitability of an intervention. Diagnostics would include clinical tests such as high blood pressure and sugar diabetes readings, meaning a more holistic approach to optimum well-being makes for a better therapeutic approach.

◆ Making referrals where necessary to relevant clinical experts and expecting them to also develop an understanding that the spiritual well-being of people is as legitimate as all other wellness aspects, so that a referral to credible spirit mediums should not be difficult. A database of accredited spirit mediums should be developed and shared with clinical experts.

◆ Ensuring that the spiritual competence of each spirit medium is fit for purpose so that charlatans are eliminated from the therapeutic regime and database. Spiritual competence involves high levels of awareness about the value-laden worldview of the consulting person and the need to bracket off one's own worldview to develop a deeper understanding of the consulting person's worldview. It is the worldview of the consulting person that is relevant in the intervention process and no persuasive efforts should be made to convert a consulting person's worldview, unless evidence suggests that a change in mindset would be beneficial to the consulting person. In such a situation, the specialisation assumptions, limitations, and biases of the consulting person's worldview must be made transparent and their inefficacy in resolving the pressing problem of a consulting person must be made clear. There has to be some discussion between the spirit medium and a consulting person as to why an alternative spiritual paradigm would be the best course of intervention action. The approach should be that of sharing information on spiritual paradigms and of letting a consulting person choose the best intervention option. There has to be greater emphatic understanding of a consulting person's worldview (Hodge, 2011:153) so that intervention can be within its framework, unless otherwise suggested, in which case a thorough discussion as to why it cannot resolve a consulting person's predicament must ensue until consensus is reached.

Where possible, the design and implementation of spiritual intervention should be in line with that of a consulting person's worldview, unless there is a compelling case that this spiritual paradigm would not yield the desired outcomes.

◆ When making referrals, the full scale of intervention whether spiritual, physiological, or psychological must be succinctly elucidated and informed consent of a patient or consulting person must be secured in writing. Spiritual intervention is a value-guided approach which, in our case, would involve ubuNtu values and principles as the spiritual framework of choice.

A spiritual framework reflects a set of implicit specialisation assumptions about the nature of ultimate, supreme reality which, in our African worldview, entails the recognition of an informed inter-subjective reality that draws from the experiences, perceptions and meanings people attach to their lives. Our ontological stance is that there are multiple social realities out there which are not fixed, measurable or observable. It is this position that compels us to focus on people's inner kingdom in lieu of searching for it out there outside our own experiences and understandings. The path to ultimate reality is through embracing values of ubuNtu and working within its cycle, which we can illuminate through making transparent the embedded tacit knowing in each person.

Such knowing enables us to differentiate between idiots (those serving private interests, modern primitives in gilded cages) and cultured humans that serve the greater good.

◆ Tacit knowing is more important than objective knowledge since focus is on the experiences, perceptions, and meanings people attach to their lives. These lived experiences of people are fundamental in building tacit knowing and under-standing practices people adopt in their daily lives. Its basic episteme is inter-subjectivity.

◆ The worldview of people is the ultimate arbiter of what constitutes knowledge and knowing as drawn from people's values and experiences. This axiological understanding is crucial, particularly in a society defined by a multi-perspectival approach. The dominance of objective knowledge no longer holds water as the search for alternative forms of knowledge and knowing gain solid ground across the globe. This shift towards multi-perspectival approaches to knowing is in the service of epistemic justice and resolving super-complex problems. Capabilities of intelligent technologies capable of interpreting huge swathes of subjective data have made it possible to build alternative knowledge and knowing.

◆ To understand people, their lives and values, one has to immerse oneself in the context within which people live and co-create complex knowing drawn tacitly from their lived experiences as people are accorded active agency in the production of new understandings and improved perspectives.

◆ A comprehensive *Code of Ethics* for a broad, holistic therapeutic regime has to be established which, *inter alia*, ensures that health practitioners and spirit medium function strictly within their areas of competence and cross-referral is possible. In pursuance of this holistic approach to well-being, health practitioners ought to have some basic understanding of spiritual interventions even if it becomes an elective subject so that when suggesting referrals to spirit mediums, some basic information on the rationale of referral is forwarded to the spirit mediums.

Restorative Processes

The main reason people consult health facilities and spirit mediums is because there is a measure of discomfort that affect their quality of life which can be divided into reduced state of well-being at various levels: physical, psychological, social, and spiritual. The expected outcome is that of optimum well-being, hence a more compre-hensive approach to restoring optimum well-being is crucial.

Health and spiritual interventions are essentially restorative, that is, it involves recon-struction, rehabilitation, and preservation.

◆ Reconstruction implies that a person's optimum well-being has been adversely affected by some affliction, that is, some quite persistent distress or excruciating pain caused by trauma, physiological and psychological pathologies. In some cases, afflictions can emanate from some mysterious phenomenon that might not fit the known health aetiology. This is the type of affliction that warrants referral to a spirit medium who must reconstruct the therapeutic encounters in such a way as to fit the worldview and culture of the consulting person.

◆ Rehabilitation seeks to restore the improved functionality, quality of life, and optimum well-being of a consulting person who has been harmed one way or the other on a physiological, psychological, and social level. A multi-perspectival approach is essential in restoring a consulting person to optimum well-being and should include clinical and spiritual interventions that are compatible with the spiritual worldview of a consulting person.

◆ Spiritual preservation suggests firstly that spiritual interventions that are inconsistent with the native culture and worldviews of the consulting person seldom have a positive effect on their well-being. In other words, it rarely maintains the consulting person's state of optimum well-being. Secondly, the application of spiritual interventions that represents, in substance and form, intrusions of foreign worldviews and cultures risks damaging the therapeutic rapport necessary for the success of the intervention. It is thus paramount that the native culture and worldview of the consulting person are preserved in all therapeutic encounters to ensure their success potential.

Medicinal Use

Traditional African medicine includes all the knowing, use, and practices of using various plants and trees to cure diseases cast away malevolent spirits whose intent is to harm or cause injuries to others out of hatred or malevolence, spiritually protect homes against malevolent spirits, help those that need to crossover and assume new roles in posthumous life, and reconnect people with their ancestral homes. Traditional African medicine is therefore used for diagnostics, prevention, and treatment of various ailments whether physiological or psychological that seek to compromise optimum well-being of people.

The World Health Organization (WHO) acknowledges and recognises traditional medicine as an integral part of a health regime that signifies a comprehensive approach to health and achieving optimum well-being. Traditional medicine precedes orthodox Western medicine by many centuries and its efficacy in dealing with various ailments has never been contested but a need has arisen that it be tested and integrated into the health regime of each country. The testing of traditional medicine should not be motivated by the need to make it fit the dictates of orthodox Western medicine. Rather, it should serve as part of allopathic medicine and thus as an equally valid regime of health interventions. The aspects of traditional African medicine that require attention are:

◆ Harnessing and integrating it into the allopathic medicine regime.

◆ Researching their side effects and impact when integrated and used with orthodox Western medicine. It is paramount that the effectiveness and safety of traditional African medicine is established through gained insights and tacit knowing. There is also a need to keep a register and database of various traditional medicines, their efficacy in treating specific ailments, quality, and sustainability given use of plants and animals as medicines. This would allow for availability of these traditional medicines in mainstream pharmaceutical stores.

◆ Training and educating spirit mediums and traditional doctors on an integrated approach to health care. Universities have to develop elective courses on traditional medicine in areas such as preventative medicine, curative medicine, palliative care medicine, cleansing medicine, malevolent spirits cast-away medicine, and so on.

◆ An official regulatory body responsible for research, approval, and accreditation of traditional medicine must be established and funded by government.

Social Signalling

Social signalling, in the African worldview, refers to those communicative cues people share in interpersonal relationships, particularly those relating to felt pain and pain-empathising behaviours. It refers to sensory behavioural heuristics people develop over time in social interactions to facilitate non-verbal communication of cues, signs, and gestures relating to the expression of pain and its assuagement through human and medicinal support.

Social signalling in a multi-cultural context can easily lead to communicative cultural bumps and it is important to built a plethora of shared cues drawn from all cultures. A common shared social signalling is crucial in cosmopolitan, global societies in particular as it relates to felt and pain-empathising behaviours. Our concern is with nociceptive pain as a signal to point out the source of pain and its causes so we can determine the healing regime. The source of pain could be physiological, psychological, or emotional.

It is important for a spirit medium to discern sources of pain and discomfort that compelled a person to consult them. For instance, in the case of tactile diagnosis, a spirit medium is able to locate the exact spot or source of pain to administer the correct healing regime. Eidetic spirit mediums visualise the source of pain. The spirit mediums have a responsibility to notice how individuals express pain and those variations are crucial in ensuring that a communication breakdown does not happen between a spirit medium and consulting person. There will always be circumstantial and cultural variability in how pain is expressed and that could make communication difficult between a spirit medium and consulting person, hence the need for spirit mediums to be fully aware of possible cultural bumps.

When pain is viscerally felt and the intensity of the subjective pain is expressed by a consulting person, it is important that a spirit medium measures facial grimaces, distinct bodily movements (Knapp & Hall, 2012), and non-verbal cues and juxtapose that with verbal expressions of pain as that would lead to a more accurate assessment of the source of pain prior to actual diagnostics so we could avoid random probability patterning of pain (stochastic analysis), which could lead to miscommunication between a spirit medium and a consulting person. To develop a deeper understanding of social signalling, it is crucial to analyse its source. Social signalling is a result of a cultural orientation so that an understanding of culture would help us make sense of social signalling and how we could develop a cultural heuristics fit for our globalised, complex society. Culture, according to Danesi and Perron (1999), refers to a way of life that evolved from a system of shared meaning and is passed on from one generation to the other. It is essentially about how humans adapt, survive, and thrive in their chosen habitat on, at least, three levels of human knowing formed through a process of signifying order:

◆ Sensory knowing derives from senses as sources of information that is signified and condensed into digestible and shared signs, cues, texts, gestures, and bodily expressions to convey and facilitate specific messages in a communication en-counter with other human beings in ways that promote understanding and greater harmony. Sensory knowing is a key part of social signalling as a cultural derivative.

◆ Subjective knowing entails understanding things and reality from the perspective of self. It is a self-assessed sense of understanding, which involves the degree to which a person thinks they know about something in a habitat. As in sensory knowing, subjective knowing inheres in individuals such that it is a highly parti-cularised form of understanding and unchecked can easily mutate into solipsism (extreme egocentrism).

◆ Communal knowing is a level of knowing that moderates highly individualised knowing (sensory and subjective knowing), leading to shared forms of under-standing and meanings. It refers to understandings and shared meanings that develop among humans sharing geographic proximity affiliation, having a com-mon interest or similar issues of concern.

The development and growth of common understandings and shared meanings in a social context can occur at a smaller geographic area to which the label 'tribe' may be used. Tribe, in this context, does not assume a pejorative innuendo often associated with a cult. Rather, it takes the form of a culture, a way of life with a strong signifying order. In more complex societies consisting of people with multiple cultural propensities, a super-tribe evolves with its own super-culture. A super-culture is a coalescence of sub-cultures of different tribes sharing a common, broad geographic space and working towards developing a cultural heuristics of common understandings and shared meanings that lead to harmonised signifying order that aggregates into social signalling. Social signalling becomes a strong source of proper communication, planning, and living in complex, cosmopolitan societies, hence it can be considered a product of a developed or developing cul-tural heuristics. It is in this sense that social signalling is considered as crucial in developing a proper communication between a spirit medium and a consulting person who often has a certain level of discomfort (pain, harm) that necessitated the consultation.

In a complex society like ours that is organised to operate in real time and on a global scale, social signalling has to derive from a developed or developing cultural heuristics with the understanding that the broader society with multiple cultural inclinations would consult an African spirit medium. The African spirit medium should be well versed in cultural heuristics so that there are minimal communication-related challenges emerging from social signalling that could easily lead to misdiagnosis.

There is also an important area of psychology that is beginning to declassify mystic and spiritual reality from abnormal psychology, particularly its association with schizotypal personality, schizophrenia and psychotic mental diseases, and considers it a key characteristic of human psycho-spiritual growth or, as other scholars prefer to call it, 'spiritual intelligence' (Bitena & Martinsone, 2021). This scholarly psychology space that dispels previously-held misnomers about psycho-spiritual growth creates opportunities to study areas of spirituality such as cultural heuristics and the significant role that African spirituality plays in shaping globalised cultural heuristics within an understanding that racial and ethnic classifications are nothing more than misleading signifying orders designed to drive a wedge between the least well-off in society, such that the elitist oligarchs that have selfishly accumulated wealth for themselves at the expense of the majority in society can maintain such an economic injustice.

In a purely biological sense, humans defy classification of any sort, whether ethnic or racial. In fact, we emerge from the same chromosomes (Danesi & Perron, 1999). These cheap labels need to be challenged and spirit mediums need to be at the epicentre of dispelling these myths. The greater involvement of spirit mediums in these scholarly endeavours is paramount, because without their contribution in the shaping and development of globalised cultural heuristics, epistemic injustice is likely to continue, leading to a general marginalisation of the Africanist ways of knowing in shared global meanings, leading to the perpetuation and dominance of race and ethnic myths. Spirit mediums should also not use African spirituality as a cult, but rather consider it as an operational construct that seeks to correct a historical mistake committed by myths of coloniality and white supremacy. The endgame is equality and justice in all pursuits of our lives.

Spiritual outcomes as part of practical training

The main, fundamental spiritual outcome that trumps all other considerations is reconnecting a consulting person with their ancestral home, that is, belonging to a specific and correct *isibaya / lesaka*. There is also a need to clarify the **apical ancestor** of this ancestral home / *isibaya* / *lesaka*. It is paramount that a spirit medium ensures that all rituals and rites pertaining to a correct ancestral home have been performed or need to be performed to ensure that the spiritual connectedness of a consulting person is secured. Without this condition then all other expected spiritual outcomes are not possible. The second crucial spiritual outcome relates to the ***cleansing*** of a consulting person, whether this regards death in a family, abortion, miscarriage, divorce, twin death, or any other impurities that might be diagnosed during consultation. All these impurities must be attended to and fixed as a precondition of assisting a consulting person. Cleansing rituals concerning death involve:

◆ A mourning period of 30 days after the burial of a loved one, then a cleansing ritual using either a sheep or goat is performed. Those unable to attend a cleansing ritual at a place of bereavement may use aloe in water to cleanse themselves wherever they might be after the mourning period. The length of the mourning period is impossible to change. It is spiritually decreed. In the case of a deceased father, the paternal uncles must conduct a cleansing ritual to the children of their brother using an additional sheep or goat. This additional ritual is called orphan ritual (*kgutsana*). These rituals can be performed the same day or on different dates, with the cleansing ritual after the conclusion of a mourning period conducted first. When it is a mother that is deceased, the maternal uncles perform such a ritual. Orphan ritual is so important that it can have devastating effects on the orphaned lives. It is performed even when a person is deceased without having performed the orphan ritual. because it could easily cause havoc to the transition of a deceased person to a different space-time zone (land beyond the azure dome).

◆ Cleansing rituals for a deceased husband or wife. In the case of a deceased wife, a period of mourning that ranges from three months but not exceeding a year is set after the funeral and specific apparel may also be imposed or recommended. Once the period of mourning is completed, the wife's in-laws arrange to take her to her family or relative home armed with some money equivalent to half of a cow price called *lehare* in Sesotho. The family of the widow then contributes the remaining half of the money and buy a cow. The half part of the carcass plus cow head and feet accompany the widow back to the in-laws. This process happens over the course of 24 to 48 hours and the widow should arrive at her in-laws in the early hours of the designated day of return. In the case of a widower, a designated rack may be attached to his hand for a designated period, similar to that of a widow. The difference is that upon completion of a mourning period, a widower gets cleansed at his own home. The use of a rack is highly optional as it is a foreign adoption. In the African worldview, mourning occurs within oneself and is shown through respect of certain rites up until the end of it. For instance, the widow or widower cannot arrive home after darkness during that period unless absolutely necessary. Abstinence from all desires is crucial.

- In the case of a first child's death, that the mother going to her family home for cleansing, but subsequent children's death rituals are performed at her home or in-laws.

- Crossover rituals, which are performed in the case of an abortion, a miscarriage, or a deceased who has not crossed over because it was not yet their time to join the ultimate reality. After 72 hours, the deceased child or children should report a safe arrival at the ancestral home. Thereafter, the mourning parent must be cleansed at the parental home, using either a sheep or a goat.

- De-ensorcellment from spirits of the dead or of resurrected, malevolent lost souls to be performed. It is similar to the concept of exorcism.

- In the case of one twin departing earlier than the other, that the deceased twin be buried within 48 to 72 hours in the early morning around 05:00 or 06:00. No ceremony is held, because the other twin is still alive. A day before the funeral, the living twin must be interred in the grave of the departed child, then moved away from where the funeral will be held. This is to perpetuate the life of the living twin.

Spiritual impartation

Transference of one spiritual gift or spiritual mission from a departed soul to a living, spiritually gifted relative, child, or grandchild is a practice common among some African spiritual sects but represents, in form and substance, a highly problematic spiritual proposition. It involves a departed soul that did not complete their spiritual mission identifying a relative, who can complete it so the departed soul can rejoin the junior spirits, the community of the saints (ancestral home).

My main gripe with this proposition is that each one of us is born with our own mission and life purpose (spiritual gift) which defines our inner kingdom, a state of being completely in charge of our lives as guided spiritually. It is this birth-right, this native spiritual gift that needs spiritual nurturing with the guidance of the ancestral home under the aegis of a qualified spirit medium who serves as a spiritual mentor. While spiritual endowments are common in other religions such as Christianity and other spiritual beliefs, it remains an awkward construct in African spirituality.

Prior to providing an African spirituality perspective on spiritual impartation, let us try to unpack it. In ancient African communities, an act of impartation involved sharing resources so that all humans in a community have enough for sustenance and optimum well-being, which birthed the Temperance virtue. It was an act of resource-**sharing** where an individual person or family **received** survival resources from the generously **giving** community members. When applied to belief systems, it refers to three distinguishable types – received, shared and given impartation.

Received impartation, similar to the traditional meaning, refers to one departed soul granting a living being a spiritual gift with a specific mission. Often this granting of a spiritual mission happens when a departed soul either passed on without completing a spiritual mission or had avoided this mission when still alive. The critical question to pose in this kind of spiritual impartation is what happens to the native spiritual gift of a living being, that is, the innate spiritual gift under these circumstances? A reasonable assumption is that we are all born with an innate gift of some sort, whether it is a natural talent of some aspect of mundane life or as a chosen spiritual soul in the form of a spirit medium, prophet, prognosticator, clairvoyant, and so on. Our focus here is on chosen spiritual souls and their innate spiritual gifts and whether transference of spiritual missions is possible within African spirituality. Before we hazard a response to this question, two other types of spiritual impartation add unique complexity to this question.

Shared spiritual impartation refers to a situation where spiritual impartation occurs in a cross-transference way among living spiritual peers, that is, there is a strong element of spiritual confluence among living spiritual peers. Received spiritual impartation occurs between a spiritual mentor and mentee in the form of anointment (use of spiritual oil, incense, or hands blessing on the head). Received spiritual impartation is thus a process of divine election of a spiritual successor. In all these impartation variabilities, the question remains of what happens to a birth-endowed gift, in particular of those chosen to advance spiritual missions of their own? There is an overbearing seduction and immobilisation one experiences stemming from a facile normalisation of Christian orthodox regarding spiritual impartation and its casual superficiality compels a deeper analysis.

Our contemporary society and its global functionality in real time have a reconstructed past that is impossible to understand without deconstructing coloniality and anticipated futures where multi-perspectivalism brings a sort of complexity that makes all sorts of justice in society, including epistemic justice, possible. The traditional Christian presuppositionalism, a notion that Christian faith is the only basis for rational thought and an inerrant divine revelation as well as redemption, represents grounds to expose flaws in other equally legitimate beliefs systems. Deliberate acts of delegitimisation of equally deserving belief systems through efforts of Christian apologetics thriving under an enabling political authority and project of coloniality have had the stakes that enabled them to pulverise and force Christianity to stand on its own logical strength under the weight of a multi-perspectival approach to generating societal mores and an inclusive cultural heuristics drawing from multiple sub-cultures within society.

In this sense, the dominance of originally conceptualised Christian spiritual impartation in discourses of contemporary societies represents a relic of a colonial past. A time has come for Christianity as one of many belief systems in society to stand on its logic and desist from attempting to discredit other legitimate beliefs. Its subsistence on coloniality and erstwhile political authority has expired and its very *raison d'être*, reason for existence, so necessary in this time depends largely on radical Christian scholars who need to reconstruct its logical essence and make its claim as an equally deserving belief system in contemporary societies with the potential to contribute to a complex cultural heuristics. Myopic Christian apologetics do a huge disservice to Christianity as one of many religious beliefs in contemporary societies because it can no longer walk on the saliences of an extirpated coloniality and political authority. As Rossouw (1995:75) suggests, any belief system or theology *"that pretends to be a timeless and closed system [...] unaffected by cultural shifts runs the risk of becoming obsolete"*. The super-culture of contemporary societies is defined through a postmodern culture that defies any rigid orthodoxy and embraces multiple perspectives on any subject, including belief systems. In this sense, spiritual impartation is for all practical purposes a multi-perspectival construct with variation in meanings and content. In African spirituality, impartation of spirits from one person to the other is practised in other aspects of the African spiritual belief but is entirely irrelevant in the case of spirit mediums as each spirit medium practises on the basis of their own innate spiritual gift under the guidance of the ancestral home operating within the aegis of an experienced spiritual mentor.

Other Relevant Rituals

◆ *Soul Retrieval:* Soul loss is a type of loss that occurs when a one's cultural identity is lost and reconceptualised in terms of other foreign cultures or in terms of the rituals of a cult. It is a sophisticated 'forced adoption' where during childbirth, a child is taken away from the mother in a deceitful way and the mother is unaware of the activity itself. The mother is often softened by false praise and pretence that the act is an act of love to both the mother and child. The process of taking away the child's soul and sense of cultural spiritual attachment is through immediate separation of the child from the mother at childbirth. According to Schaffer and Emerson (1964) in the longitudinal study of infants, the first stage of attachment theory is called the pre-attachment stage which occurs between childbirth and the first three months where the child shows no particular attachment to any caregiver. Those seeking to spiritually adopt children know this as most are nurses or doctors trained in these things. Once these foreign rituals have been performed without the mother knowing, then the child's soul is adopted to this cult or culture and no amount of their real *isithakazelo* can retrieve the child's soul. The following steps must be taken to retrieve a soul: identification, retrieval, and healing.

Identification of a lost soul

◆ Identify if the child was born with a spiritual gift. This is done by determining whether the child had a birth caul, a piece of an amniotic cell. This rare kind of birth is called *en caul* birth and involves a child being born inside this amniotic sac, a thin and filmy membrane. It occurs in one in 80 000 babies, which makes it a rare phenomenon. While scientists have not given it any significance, it is a powerful reason for cults and foreign cultures to capture children's souls. A captured soul disconnects one from one's true identity and potentially diminishes one's quality of life and well-being.

♦ The following signs provide the basis for further identifying a lost soul. *Depression* refers to difficulty in functioning optimally in the internal space, mainly because the inner kingdom gets compromised and limits one's resolve to solve one's problems. A strong sense of purposelessness, directionlessness, and worthlessness is diagnosed. A consulting person can always be referred to a health professional for assistance. *Poor adjustment and adaptability* to new challenges. One often struggles to cope with a traumatic event and withdraws from public life (dissociation). One can even adopt unhealthy coping mechanisms like drug or alcohol abuse. *Disconnection* refers to situations where a lost soul is profoundly committed to a particular cult, foreign belief or religion and may have experienced abusive relationships, inconducive work spaces, and lacking passion for life. *Negative thoughts and low energy levels* as exhibited through insomnia, constant fatigue, and backache make one vulnerable. *Self-neglect* means one has lost interest in taking care of one's life, health, or of others. *Difficulty feeling present* means one has lost the ability to negotiate the world on one's own terms. One can shrink in public spaces and avoid being noticed.

Retrieval

1. **A séance for soul retrieval must be led by a highly experienced spirit medium. The credo of equality, love and truth** must be recited and practised during séances and all other spirit mediumship activities.

2. Each spirit medium must indicate if they have spiritual authority to conduct this type of séance or need cleansing prior to the soul retrieval process. It is rare that a spirit medium could recuse themselves from the séance.

3. All spirit mediums must hold their knobkierie and recite their *isithakazelo* to ask for protection and power to overcome the dark forces that hold the soul.

4. All spirit mediums then connect spiritually to find out where the soul is held and follow all efforts to hide the soul until the cult person or leader gives up and brings the soul back. It can take hours for this process to complete and hitting the floor with knobkierie should continue during this process until the soul is retrieved.

5. The closest family member has to embrace and hug the person whose soul has been retrieved and recite *isithakazelo* as a welcome back ritual. Thereafter a sheep is slaughtered so that the person can claim their *isibaya* or follow the guidelines of the ancestors.

Healing

◆ The person whose soul has been retrieved has to spend time with the experienced spirit medium and consult with a health professional such as a psychologist or psychiatric. The main purpose is to help them reunite with their true self and build their inner kingdom.

◆ The person must attend family rituals and ceremonies to connect with their people and follow the advice of an experienced spirit medium and health professional.

◆ *Child Birth.* There are few people allowed to perform midwifery tasks and all those involved in this exercise must undergo a period of abstinence from sex and other indulgences such as alcohol use, witchcraft, and malevolent acts. Midwives are traditionally only women. No one is allowed to see a child after birth until the child completes their first 10 days on earth, not even the child's father (*ho tswa lehlakeng*). The woman who just gave birth waits three to six months before engaging in sexual activity. If the woman just got married, she needs to give birth to her first-born child at her parental home (*ho isa mahlo*). The next children can then be born at the in-laws or their own home. Naming a child occurs 10 days after birth. This often involves waiting for the name from the in-laws if the birth took place at the woman's home as is the case with the first-born child.

The child is always protected against malevolent forces and certain rituals pertaining to an ancestral home are performed, including ensuring that the child belongs to the right *isibiya/lesaka* (*kgwetsa*). A small feast is conducted 10 days after birth to celebrate this birth (*pitiki*). This is followed by introducing the child to the ancestors by showing them the moon often three months after birth (*kuruetsa*), showing the significance of ethno-astronomy in the life of an African. A ritual is also performed to introduce a child to meat and often involves slaughtering a sheep. The child must also be naked when exposed to rain for the first time at around three months old. If a child was born after a dead child, a ritual is performed by maternal uncles that involves slaughtering a sheep, cutting the child's hair, and dressing the child in new clothes.

Orphan ritual occurs at two levels. When it is the mother that passed on, then maternal uncles perform it involving sheep slaughtering, or paternal uncles when it is the father that passed on. This ritual occurs even when a person passed on before the ritual was performed, otherwise it is believed that their journey home will be difficult.

◆ *Marriage Process.* The marriage process involves paying *lobola* (bride price) and must be conducted by the father, uncles from both maternal and paternal side, plus grannies and aunties from both sides, but the actual negotiation is conducted by males. Both mothers of the bride and groom are not involved in the negotiation. Once negotiations are done, the bride's family buys a cow, and the groom brings a sheep to the bride's home. The groom's entourage must slaughter the cow using their own knives and utensils and cut it in half. The bride's entourage does the same with the sheep. Both animals must be slaughtered at the same hole. The half carcasses are exchanged so that each family has half a cow and half a sheep. This process signals the marriage confirmation and if it is not done properly then it must be repeated irrespective of age, even grandparents perform it in their old age. The marriage process and agreement are protected under the customary law in South Africa and is considered a legally binding agreement. The marriage process entails:

- *Stage 1*: A lobola negotiation letter is sent to the bride's family to schedule a negotiation meeting, date, and time. Lobola is an ancient African practice that started off around 300 BCE during the agricultural era, hence it is associated with cows. Cows are traditionally a premium in African tradition.

- *Stage 2*: The representatives of the groom, all family members (family head, uncles, and older brothers, but these days some women, like an aunt, also joins the delegation), arrive at the bride's place for negotiations and offer a bottle of whisky or brandy (traditionally beer was offered in the past) as the basis of starting negotiations (*vul'mlomo*) and the terms and conditions of the lobola (*mahadi*) are set. Lobola is often 12 cows and one extra, because it always has to be odd numbers. The difference is often based on how much each cow costs, beginning with R1 000 and up to R10 000 per cow. The groom's delegation could, as standard practice, demand that the lobola be reduced and even request for minimum payment for marriage to have a legal standing (*loco standi*/*ho phethela hlooho*). The groom's delegation then offers whatever lobola they have and because it is the first time, the amount is not specific but something must be offered as a sign of goodwill. A date for the final payment of lobola is set. The lobola process occurs only twice and only under exceptional circumstances can it go beyond this stipulated number. Lobola is a sign that the groom can afford to raise a family so if he struggles to pay lobola then he is not considered suitable for the bride.

- *Stage 3*: The hand-over ceremony is done where the groom and his representatives offer a sheep and most of the time the bride's family offer a cow (in some cases, sheep). Both are slaughtered at the bride's home as earlier indicated. Later in the same day, in the afternoon, the groom and his friends are invited to the bride's home where they are offered a sheep to slaughter and enjoy whichever way they please (*ho tlotswa mafura*, ordaining of the groom as the legitimate son-in-law). The next day, the bride is taken to the groom's family home where she is shown a sheep (*kwae*) which welcomes her to the groom's family.

◆ In the case of a divorced person, a cleansing must occur in the form of a slaughtered sheep and lobola must now be conducted at the in-laws, not the parental home. One's parents cannot receive lobola twice. Once married, the bride belongs to the in-laws in terms of tradition and must request permission to remarry, not only from the in-laws but also from the departed partner by visiting their grave. When a man wishes to remarry, he informs the in-laws and visits the grave of the departed wife to convey such a desire.

◆ Bigamy and polygamy are warranted under special circumstances if a person wishes to take a second or third wife, or even more. The reasons must be valid and acceptable to the elder wife such as if she cannot give birth to a child or a male child considered the family heir, or any other reasonable grounds such as royalty or tradition. As a rule, the elder wife is the one who chooses the second or other wives. Polyandry (*sethepu*), where a woman marries two or more men, is unheard of in the African worldview and is therefore not our tradition or part of our culture.

◆ Practices such as *seantlo*, taking over the home and wife of one's dead brother, is no longer central to modern African practices.

◆ Children birthed by another man, while the wife is still married to the other, becomes part of the husband's family, but a ritual must be performed involving welcoming the child into the ancestral home / *isibaya* / *lesaka* of the husband.

The Inauguration of an Initiate (bestowing of a spiritual gift)

The apex of spirit mediumship development is when the initiate discovers a sacred space where they will be collecting their spiritual gift. This is also an inauguration ceremony that signals the end of the initiate training as a spiritual medium. From my own experience as a spirit medium, initiates tend to collect their spiritual gifts in sacred places such as mountains, oceans, waterfalls, designated National Parks, and caves, but rarely in rivers, if ever. Two to three days prior to travelling to sacred spaces, the initiate has to spend time with their spiritual mentor(s) to detect impurities that may have encroached in the intervening time between end of mediumship development and inauguration of the initiate. In most cases, initiates have under three months to collect their spiritual gifts at the designated sacred space after completing the mediumship development programme. Irrespective of distance, which can often be more than ten hours of driving, the initiate cannot sleep at any accommodation or place of abode once the inauguration has been performed. It so happens that the only alternative is a power nap at a garage inside the car.

Upon arrival at the home of the newly inaugurated spirit medium, an exchange of strong drinks, both traditional and mainstream and no more than a tot, is shared and accompanied by *isithakazelo*. This starts with the elder of the home and all other home inhabitants related to the spirit medium, then the spirit medium, and lastly the spiritual mentor and their entourage. This is a close-knit celebration that does not involve too many people because they might bring impurities and compromise the inauguration.

A sheep is then shown to the newly inaugurated spirit medium accompanied again by *isithakazelo*. The spiritual mentor and the entourage then leave the home so that the close-knit family can celebrate.

———————————————

9

Evolution of Epistemic Understandings of Spirituality

Introduction

The most complex concept to understand and test, especially its efficacy in enhancing human existence and optimum well-being, is spirituality. Using scientific tools and historical methods of inquiry to better understand and make sense of spirituality represents the most difficult human endeavour ever. The critical question is whether such an endeavour of epistemically understanding spirituality is a necessary exercise worthy of persistent effort so vital in such pursuits. In other words, does science trump spirituality in ways that spirituality must drop a curtsy to what science dictates?

Such deferential respect or obeisance spirituality has to observe in the hallowed parlances of science suggests the superiority of science over spirituality, meaning for spirituality to be taken seriously, it has to succumb to dictates of scientific thought and its methods. The purpose of science is to establish reliable, accurate explanations of natural phenomena and how the natural world evolved to be what it is today. In this sense, science has a history and has built an epistemic capacity that helps humans to understand, interpret, and develop means and technologies that create human conveniences. This epistemic capacity develops and becomes more sophisticated mainly because science proceeds because of constant questioning, revision and total openness to fallibility, that is, the possibility that some scientific conclusions or adduced evidence to support claims could be erroneous and require further refinement as more evidence becomes available.

There are equally multiple versions of science which lead to different understandings of phenomena, and it is crucial to develop an understanding of these versions of science to attempt to find a suitable version that could help make sense of spirituality without forcing it to fit into the tenets of scientific thought and its methods, particularly aspects relating to scholasticism. Situated in a way that does not allow scientific logic to cloud its essence, studies in spirituality could possibly uncover secrets of matter and natural phenomena that could unravel the hidden truths of ultimate reality. This might seem like an insoluble problem, but we must persist in this direction because, maybe in a glide of unspeakable inspiration, the eureka moment could emerge and change the way we understand who we are and the natural world we inhabit. This would help deal effectively with charlatans that use spirituality to their narrow ends.

Many are not aware that rational, scientific thought and its use of advanced observational techniques as well as mathematical measurement started off as priestly castes in Egypt and Babylon. This means that the origins of scientific thought and its methods can be traced to ancient spiritual beliefs and practices of African societies. These technical abilities of advanced observation, mathematical measurement, and theoretical speculation were part of spiritual beliefs and practices in ancient Africa (Strathern, 2001). The refinement of scientific thought and its methods occurred when the ancient Greeks chose to free science and its methods from the constraints of spirituality and religious practices. The Greek philosopher, Thales of Miletus, is considered the first philosopher to venture into developing unrestrained scientific thought (removal from spirituality) and advanced the logic of matching conclusions with credible evidence. This was to represent the onset of building a repertoire of epistemic understandings which evolved into various versions of science (epistemes) and its methods which will be elaborated on in the following sub-sections.

For greater clarity, spirituality in the sense used here refers to the totality of experiences people encounter in the exercise of their spiritual practices as well as the development and growth of their sense of self as succinctly captured through the poetic quote of Avicenna (also known as Ibn Sina in the Arabic language). Avicenna is an ancient Arab philosopher who discovered the first law of motion 600 years before the birth of Isaac Newton, arguing that objects that are in a state of rest or motionless remain so until an external force is applied to them, and a similar case applies when objects run at a constant speed in a straight line. Avicenna also discovered an inexorable link between time and motion arguing that without motion, time has no meaning. In this quote (Strathern, 2001:49), Avicenna shows his hunger for philosophical and scientific approaches to knowledge production by placing at the heart of it a philosophical and scientific understanding of self and its earthly mission or life purpose:

> How I wish I could know who I am, what it is in the world that I seek.

The Epistemic Justificatory Warrant and Spirituality

There are, at least, two scientific perspectives that seek to understand social reality through methods of science – internalism and externalism. These two perspectives of scientific thought provide four epistemic versions of science and their thorough understanding will help locate spirituality in a scientific paradigm that will not constrain its deeper understanding and practices. In other words, how do we make science to come back home where it belongs? It is not a matter of spirituality succumbing to the dictates of science, rather science is seeking expansion to areas it has previously ignored or gave a wide berth to. We believe the exercise will enable science to develop new tools and methods of inquiry appropriate to adequately address esotericism, knowledge production better understood by those who have been initiated into it.

Spiritual knowledge is essentially esoteric and mystic in the sense that access to it involves deep contemplation and self-surrender to mysteries of hidden reality in lieu of intellectual effort. Deep contemplation, in this spiritual context, refers to acts of immersing oneself into a state of heightened awareness about divine matters that are essentially beyond intellectual understanding. In this sense, deep contemplation goes beyond the casual consideration of the divine and involves venturing into its awe and enthrallment which comes about through deep contemplation and deep reflection. This way, spiritual contemplation or reflection begins as a mental state and gradually evolves into a way of life, meaning it assumes the status of a culture with a signifying order. The exercise of deep spiritual contemplation entails an obligatory commitment (Stebbins, 2015), that is, when exercised properly, deep spiritual contemplation is forced upon us by inescapable problem(s) of our lives that demand resolution for us to achieve optimum well-being.

Deep spiritual contemplation is a crucial area of spirituality that begins as an intellectual endeavour as earlier stated and with focused attention transcends the intellect to access the divine and mysterious. Understood this way, deep spiritual contemplation (deep reflection) has cognitive content and divine content with the former capable of scientific gaze in its current *zeitgeist* and the latter seeking new tools of rationality and methods of inquiry. There is some evidence based on a two-year study of a spiritual practice I lead and observing over time séance, other spiritual consultations, and mediumship development that the divine content can be captured through observation and understood, not in its vastness, but in critical snapshots when the practice is in operation. Every moment of the practice brings with it new opportunities to observe and understand critical aspects of divine content. Unlike in other belief systems, African spirituality proceeds on the basis of evidence and there is plenty such data in authentic spiritual practices. The curation of such data for public scrutiny cannot follow the dictates of science, rather it demands new tools of understanding.

The challenge is that for a phenomenon to be considered deep spiritual contemplation and be understood as critical reflection on divine content, it has to meet three criteria:

♦ Highly focused intellectual content. There must be a profound commitment to a mental state purposed to pay special attention to a divine reality and seeking its intervention in resolving an inescapable problem. One good example is through meditation, a focused ancient practice of awakened consciousness achieved by applying focused techniques that ease the mind through assuming a particular bodily posture. It is not a strong factor in African spirituality but is worth probing to determine if it warrants adding to the nomenclature of African spirituality. In African spirituality, there is the concept of "*ho hlapholla*" meaning clarifications that a consulting person make during spiritual diagnostics. This is a good example of intellectual content giving credence to a spiritual message through confirmation of divine content sourced through spiritual diagnostics or séance.

♦ Highly intense, esoteric, and impermeable divine content. Divine content can easily be impervious to logic, rationality, and intellectual capture, hence its access may not be through intellectual pursuit, but rather a search through other means such as séance, spiritual diagnostics, spiritual impartation, spiritual meditation, and conducting of some rituals.

♦ A transition from a mental state into the awe and enthrallment of divinity generally inaccessible to the intellect. The space somewhere between a mental state and divine content has historically been analysed in terms of two main constructs: (1) a mythopoeic intellectual endeavour that involves generating myths, and (2) mythopoetic mental effort which entails creating interpretations of extant myths, the exercise of which can map out power relations in society. The danger in this type of analysis is that myth-generation can easily be made to serve narrow and nefarious intentions as well as assisted-interpretation, that is, meaning generation based on others' perspectives or shenanigans leading to fake news, distortions, menticide, and post-truth discourses. When used within spiritual realms such generation and interpretation of myths become important sources of understanding some divine content because of the intellectual effort.

The clarification and analysis of spirituality as a potential area of scholarly gaze seek to help identify areas of spirituality that can be scholarly examined with currently available tools of rationality and scientific methods of inquiry. This intellectual effort is also attempted to expose the limits of rationality and science in trying to systematically investigate other aspects of spirituality, particularly those that transcend intellectual effort and involve content relating to divinity. In the next sub-sections, the tenets of scientific thought are examined critically to determine the proper location of spirituality as a limited zone of scientific inquiry.

Internalism and Externalism: Justificatory Warrant for Believing

Internalism and externalism are scientific perspectives on epistemic justification for people to believe some propositions and reject others purely based on evidence adduced in a particular way, reason deriving from some cognitive tools, and chosen methods of inquiry. There are two types of epistemic justification. First, the deontological conception of epistemic justification refers largely to adhering to strict rules of conduct or knowledge production, irrespective of whether these efforts will lead to some greater good in society. Knowledge generated this way gains scientific credibility for adherence to set rules of knowledge production and can so be justified epistemically.

Guidance conception of epistemic justification posits that the central role of justification is to guide people in decisions relating to what to believe and what not to believe. In both cases of epistemic justification, there must be sufficient evidence and credible reasons to warrant a belief justifiable.

Internalism is a scientific view that assumes that knowledge can be relied on when it is generated without the influence of people or context. Second knowledge is justifiable on the grounds of its universality, objectivity, and tangibility given its generation in a detached, objective way. Thirdly, given that humans respond mechanically to their environment, they become passive recipients of objective knowledge with no expectation that ordinary humans could influence and shape objectivist knowledge. Fourthly, methods and instruments of inquiry that generate objective knowledge and search for universal laws should, under no circumstances, be influenced by contexts or human subjective knowing. Internalism thus has a strong deontological justificatory warrant given its insistence on rigorous rules of knowledge production.

Two types of epistemic positions emerge from internalism as purist traditions and weak pragmatist epistemic position. The former entirely rejects human and contextual influence on knowledge production as the basis of justifying knowledge as scientific and highly credible while the latter exhibits a low tolerance of contextual influence. These two epistemic positions developed when science was divorced from spirituality from whence it originates.

At this level of scientific inquiry, it is almost impossible to negotiate space for spirituality as a legitimate area of inquiry, particularly the systematic investigation of divine content and the transition from intellectual content to divine content. An area of spirituality that can be inquired under internalism is intellectual content. It would, however, serve no purpose because intellectual content bereft of divine content does not constitute spirituality. Spirituality is a belief system and scientific knowledge is justifiable belief. In this sense, the original relationship between spirituality and scientific thought made sense as both deal with justifiability of a belief. The gap between spirituality and science can be filled when more effort is placed on bringing science and spirituality on equal justificatory warrants as true beliefs. The congruence of the reliable process of belief formation between spirituality and science is a central issue in efforts towards equal justificatory warrant of both forms of belief.

Scientific thought thrives on building the internal evidence that justifies objective knowledge sourced through methods of inquiry considered as fundamental in providing credibility to a belief so that its truthfulness can be warranted. Internalism thus rejects the notion that people have voluntary control over their beliefs which could justify the construction of truth values that give legitimacy to their beliefs. These assigned truth values to beliefs are too arbitrary to be trusted via the exercise of internalism and warrant rejection.

Internalism can be understood at three levels. It appeals to the Cartesian project initiated by Socrates, who argued that it is not enough to believe something to be true. There must be a good reason and credible evidence to warrant such a view. The process of belief formation must be based on reason and evidence. This is the essence of rational thought that demands good reasons for a belief to be considered as true and is the defining feature of internalism. Beliefs need to be tested and justified at a rational and evidential level. As stated earlier, internalism also subsists on a deontological character of justification that suggests that one must perform an intellectual obligation to ensure that good reason and credible evidence exists to support the truthfulness of one's belief. Conclusions of a true belief need to be based on credible evidence and good reason to fit into the internalism process of belief formation and the performance of an intellectual duty that ensures the existence of credible evidence and sound reason to support a belief.

All these intellectual exercises emanate from internal mental processes of critical reflection on evidence and reason to determine their merit or worth in supporting a belief claim. Epistemic purists and weak pragmatists are two areas of internalist justificatory warrant (credible evidence sourced through rigours of postpositivist scientific methods and logical disputations). Framing spirituality with strong moral and axiological content within these epistemic positions would mean subjecting spirituality to the dictates of scientism, an excessive belief in the justificatory warrant of traditional scientific tools and techniques, and completely discarding alternative justificatory warrants. This would not provide opportunities for traditional science to open new vistas of research areas such as in spirituality. It cannot be considered as warranted that new avenues of scientific inquiry should not open new possibilities for science to grow its instrument and tools. Purists would want all areas of scientific inquiry even new ones to submit to extant instruments and tools of science while weak pragmatists mouth polemics about exploring new possibilities of developing new scientific tools and instruments unaccompanied by actual action.

Externalism, on the other hand, accepts the possibility that a belief is true without submitting a good reason or credible evidence for it. The process of belief formation is based on guidance often from a signified other, that is, on an external source that is considered reliable, credible, and commands huge integrity, at least, from the perspective of the believer. Justification of a belief truth value is thus externalised meaning it requires external confirmation.

The most important aspect of externalism is that individuals construct beliefs so that individuals become active agents in the construction of these beliefs even when external confirmation is sought but not always necessary. There is a stronger prudential justificatory warrant (moral ethics) in externalism and some moderate epistemic justification, that is, reliance on sound reason and credible evidence in justifying beliefs as true.

However, our endeavours here are on epistemic justificatory warrant and its role in processes of belief formation with regard to spirituality, that is, whether sound reason and credible evidence can be adduced to justify belief claims of spirituality. In other words, whether instruments and tools of qualitative research can be used to generate merited evidence to support belief claims of spirituality. It is, at this level, that processes of belief formation between science and spirituality can assume the status of being equal and spirituality can be considered a legitimate scientific area. The question is whether such a scientific legitimisation process is necessary as spirituality is quite capable of standing on its own logic and merit. Spirituality has its own checks and balances that can stand on its own terms. Spirituality also created science. Consider for a second that the periodic table, the basic tenet of chemistry, came to the Russian chemist, Dmitri Mendeleyev, in the form of a dream (Strathern, 2001:7), a mystical experience considered heretical in the scientific realm. Scientific thought is erroneously considered to have been started by Thales of Miletus in Greece, yet the origins of advanced thinking, advanced systematic observations, and using mathematical models for measurement

> had been the domain of priestly castes in both Babylon and Egypt. These techni-
> cal abilities and any theoretical speculation they provoked, were part of religious
> practice. (Strathern 2001:10)

This happened a millennium prior to Thales's forages into scientific thought. At the time, the Greek religion was primitive and relied on *"ill-behaved gods roistering and philandering on Mount Olympus"* (Strathern, 2001:10). The contribution of Thales on scientific thought was to extricate it from religion and spirituality so it could be guided by *"reason and the actuality of the world it confronted"* (Strathern, 2001:10). This was an onset of the process of belief formation based on reason and evidence adduced in the real world. The divine was of no relevance to science and its endeavours which marked a perennial schism between science and spirituality. Efforts to locate spirituality within the ambit of science, particularly on the epistemic positions emanating from externalism, suggest a move towards bringing science and spirituality into a congruent process of belief formation which many scholars of science consider as retrogression or regression. Science has not evolved to examine ultimate reality and its almost inaccessible divine content by instruments of science.

Yet, in ancient times, religions such as Zoroastrianism, which shaped Abrahamic religions of Judaism, Christianity and Islam, and Pythagoras number religion from which most of the parables in the New Testament originated, ensured the spread and growth of science and religion. Pythagoras, in turn, gained significant knowledge of numbers in his 22 years of study in Egypt which he later used to shape the Christian religion. Most of the sources of parables in the New Testament as sourced from Pythagoras can be traced back to ancient Africa and in particular Egypt not as the current country but as a reference Greeks gave to the entire African continent. The purist traditions of science (objectivist internalism and subjective internalism) in their current form seek to subject spirituality to their dictates. This is an undesirable situation and must be rejected outright but traditional science must not be entirely discarded in pursuit to understand spirituality but must be encouraged to find new tools of investigating reality. Social idealism under subjectivist externalism as an area of science still must develop strong tools of data collection, analysis, and leading to new understandings of divine content. It holds promise for understanding spirituality through instruments of science.

What then is social idealism?

Tronn Overend (2008) argues that it proceeds, based on prescriptive ethics, and thus essentially rejects objectivity. Overend further argues, from an immanent perspective, that the logical, methodological, ethical, and ontological grounds of social idealism are problematic and rest on some ontological and inevitable subjective mistakes. The essence of social idealism is consciousness and mind as the origin of the material world and suggests that knowing and knowledge can only derive from consciousness and mind. It can be considered as extreme subjectivity but that is too simplistic. In its ontological stance, social idealism argues that all material world and entities consist of mind and spirit, hence its appeal in studying and understanding African spirituality.

Max Weber, a German historian and political economist, asserts that it is not unusual that the rise of a capitalist society was enabled by a Protestant ethic, made possible as early as 1529 by the Diet of Speyer, who voted to end the Christian teachings of Martin Luther within Germany, and to promote John Calvin's Protestant work ethic that saw nothing wrong with the profit motif of capitalism and thus explicitly advanced the capitalist spirit. This explains, to an important degree, how Protestant Christianity set parameters for the origins and growth of modern capitalism across the globe (Barbalet, 2008).

Unlike the Roman Catholic church that sought to obstruct economic development, the Christian Protestant ethic decreed that obedience to God included the demand to work diligently, energetically, and in an enterprising way in one's occupation in the service of capitalism (Shea, 2015). In other words, making profit for others was considered God's calling. There is an egregious blasphemy right there. The Protestant ethic and capitalist spirit developed features of Western culture; particularly its Christian underpinnings that created cultural conditions that are conducive to perpetuate modern capitalism. As Weber surmises, the Protestant ethic and spirit of capitalism urged "*social actors to work hard, remain frugal and to make money for its own sake*" (McKinnon, 2010:109), leading to these Western cultural conditions spreading Protestantism in Western Europe and eventually became part of the colonial project to conquer and defeat Africa for its resources upon which capitalism rested.

It is, therefore, the Protestant work ethic that compelled multitudes of people in the secular world to work diligently, to open their own enterprises and trade to accumulate wealth for its sake. The crucial force behind the emergence of capitalism and puritan work ethic is Christian Protestant ethic. The puritan work ethic asserts that work in a capitalist system has moral benefit and is both a virtue as it is a value that strengthens one's character, abilities, and individual prosperity. The key values promoted by a Protestant work ethic are frugality, discipline, diligence, and respect for authority.

It is important to also note that Weber (1904) suggests that not only Protestant ethic promoted capitalism, but also Calvinist doctrines of asceticism and predestination. Asceticism is a lifestyle whose features includes abstinence from sensual pleasures to pursue spiritual goals and is linked to capitalism because of its stance on frugality as a crucial value. Predestination is a doctrine which posits that work and all other events on earth have been willed through the might of God. In a capitalist sense, supported by a highly problematic Protestant ethic, people need to work in a system that promotes avarice and poverty on grounds that it is the will of God, not my God fortunately, not an African God of ubuNtu. Instead of John Wesley, the man behind the Methodist church, as an example, challenging and contributing towards the elimination of the capitalist society, he enabled and legitimised it by cushioning the poor against an abhorent system of worker exploitation. Wesley, part of the denominational churches of mainline Protestant churches such as Lutheran, Presbyterian and Anglican, introduced a Methodist loan fund for those left behind in Britain's industrial society (the poor) and saw it as assisting the *"needy brethren"*. Not even John Wesley ever challenged the underlying Protestant ethic as inherently malevolent. The Protestant ethic literally promoted a capitalist system that generated an oligarchy as modern gods of the world.

Social idealism, in the African spirituality context, is relevant in that it goes into the internal psychology of people (mind) to understand spiritual growth and positioning based on observable behaviour and experiences. The mind, a space of consciousness, is understood from the perspective of higher-order thought theories as a critical and special inner faculty that enables awareness of the ideas and thoughts that shape one's behaviour towards otherness (humans and nature). The essential thesis of social idealism ethic, unlike the Protestant ethic, is the promotion of social and economic justice and outright rejection of avarice, inequality, and excesses of wealth.

The ontological stance of social idealism is the assertion that the human mind (consciousness) is the source of all reality. Awareness of thoughts and ideas that influence the behaviour of people is the ontological priority of social idealism. In this sense, the human mind asserts its will on the environment in such a way that nature and existence depend largely on subjective awareness and experiences. Thoughts and ideas, in African spirituality, are grounded in ubuNtu philosophy, which underpins our sense of living, existence, and approach to nature and other humans. Unlike in extreme subjectivism, social idealism in African spirituality is premised on the moral essence of ubuNtu which is the source of everything else in the world, including the spiritual aspect. Given its ontological stance, social idealism is open to all research methodologies that quest truth, including those from the natural and behavioural sciences, art, philosophy and theology.

The emphasis is on what works at a particular point in time and under which circumstances, as long as the intent is to exert the human mind on understanding and generating reality within the ubuNtu philosophical outlook. This could be considered as the prescriptive ethic of social idealism in the African spirituality perspective. African spirituality ethic is inherently prescriptive on its credo of truth, love, and equality emanating from its philosophy of ubuNtu.

Ontological error and subjective mistakes as other scholars prefer to refer to social idealism depend on the criteria used to make such a determination. When objectivity is the underlying criterion of judgement then it is inevitable that many scholars would see social idealism as essentially erroneous because the only reality that exists to them is that of the postpositivist traditions. This view that an objectivist reality as an ontological stance is the only show in town must be rejected without rejecting the merit of naturalism as a legitimate area of ontology existing in the myriad of other ontological stances, which is an expanded view of reality understood from multiple perspectives rather than on a narrow, myopic objectivist stance. We do not question the merit of an objectivist ontological stance but frown at its insistence that it is the only legitimate ontological stance which must universally be accepted as the only path to truth. It has its place, its recognition, its value in our society but so are other ontological stances including social idealism and its understanding within African spirituality.

Table 9.1 Epistemic positions and their potential as justificatory warrants for spiritual knowing and knowledge (Adapted from Pitso, 2021)

Objective Internalism		Subjectivist Internalism	
Epistemic stance:	scientific purism	Epistemic stance:	weak pragmatism
Scientific vision:	traditional academic values, elitist	Scientific vision:	modified traditional academic values that include low external influence (social, political, economic)
External influence:	zero to lowest	External influence:	low to moderate
Objectivist Externalism		Subjectivist Externalism	
Epistemic stance:	strong pragmatism	Epistemic stance:	social idealism
Scientific vision:	market-related values	Scientific vision:	social justice and ubuNtu values
External influence:	moderate to high	External influence:	extremely high

10

Narrativisation of African Spirituality: Towards its Canonicity

Introduction

Prior to Roman and colonial conquest of Africa, there was a cultural canon that drove the African society. While we acknowledge differences among these African societies, the concept of ubuNtu has always been the main centripetal force that pulled these societies together.

The signs, symbols, and codes of ubuNtu remain largely intact despite sustained attack from highly individualised capitalist societal values also promoted by belief systems that centre on individual heroes such as Moses, Jesus and Muhammad (PBUH). ubuNtu values of collectivism, absence of poverty, love, truth, equality, and their frowning at avarice are central tenets of African spirituality. The individualised signs, symbols, and codes that characterise capitalist societies tend to be pervasive even in the Abrahamic religions and serve fundamentally as critical resources that marginalise African spirituality. Given that these signs, symbols, and codes have been promoted since the colonialisation of Africa to the present day via media, religious sermons, education, and well-curated narratives, it is not unreasonable to discern these signs, symbols, and codes as the basis of understanding how their dominance in modern societies tended to marginalise and attempt to extirpate African spirituality.

The victim narrative of Jesus, a key tenet of Christian belief system, as the basis of believing in Jesus as a saviour makes for such a weak argument that it is difficult to understand how people buy into it and firmly believe it. The only plausible explanation is that the marketing infrastructure of Christianity and sustained mental assault on African psyche have had an impact that led Africans to believe in this victim narrative rather than a good, logical argument. This effort on extirpation of African spirituality symbology and semiosis, the process of condensation and displacement deriving from signification of signs, symbols, and codes, has been on-going for years but has failed to entirely wipe out African spirituality. African spirituality resilience and resistance has ensured that its practices remain relevant and continue to thrive even under these hostile conditions. African spirituality is not entirely strong on semiotic representation.

Semiotic representation is fundamental to learning of any sort, particularly in attempts to make a generally weak concept or belief accessible to immediate perception or intuitive experience (Duval, Klamma & Wolpers, 2007). Furthermore, semiotic representation makes it possible for ideas of a particular belief or concept to express that concept or belief and become instrumental in making the converts communicate and articulate ideas of such a belief. It is at this moment, when a convert becomes othered self as a result of believing in the foreign symbols, signs, and language of a foreign belief or concept such that the entire identity of a convert is reconceptualised in terms of a foreign belief or concept. Not only that but a convert becomes the mouthpiece of a foreign belief or concept. To develop a better understanding of how narrativisation works to promote and extirpate other beliefs via signification of particular signs, symbols, and codes, one of which is language, it is important to understand these basic concepts:

◆ **Signs** – language, pictorial data, diagrams and tables.

◆ **Symbol** – a representation of an object, process, phenomenon or function. For instance, a red cross can represent the entire phenomenon of health care.

◆ **Code** – shared understandings and cultural conventions used as a means to communicate a particular meaning.

◆ **Narrativity** – an attitude deriving from the signification of signs, symbols, and codes which also involves displacing other signs, symbols, codes, unshared understandings, and intuitive experiences. It involves the manner of experiencing a concept as either evoking positive or negative attitudes. Hence, narrativisation in semiotics refers to imposing narrativity on a new or unknown concept. In this sense, narrativity is based on an entrenched belief or concept which then gets defended via imposing an entrenched belief narrative to a new or alternative belief or concept in ways that lead to distortions or half-truths. There is no demand of logic or irrefutable evidence in this kind of situation. The objective is to protect the entrenched belief or concept at whatever cost, even truth and honesty.

◆ **Narrativisation** – the structuring of the flow of a narrative using *contextualisation*, *inter-subjective positioning* and *semiotic borders*. It can also refer to imposing a narrative on new or unwelcomed concepts. Instead of accommodating newness, the concept is either out rightly rejected or assimilated, that is, it is incorporated and made to look like acceptable signs, symbols, or codes leading to imposition. However, narrativisation is capable of sharing a narrative based on logic and evidence. It can transmit empowering narratives whose purpose is to restore one's identity and integrity. This is the sense of its use in this chapter.

◆ **Narration** – a contextualised, situated, and contingent process of sense-making.

◆ **Border crossing** – disruption of taken-for-granted signs, symbols and codes so as to embed displaced signs, symbols and codes. It is related strongly to imposing narrativity on a new or unwelcomed concept also known as cheap labelling.

◆ **The narrative process** – a subjective articulation of signs and codes in a contingent social context using semiotic borders. It involves knowing which signs and codes to use in a specific situation when addressing friends, colleagues, congregants, bosses, wives, children, and so on.

◆ **Semiotic borders** – knowing signs and codes of a particular discourse as well as their usage to achieve certain ends.

Framework for Canonising African Spirituality

Efforts to reclaim African spirituality canon and make it fashionable again would require that we restore its signs and codes at the heart of dominant discourses of a capitalist society that now operates in real time and on a global scale. While not a normal practice of African spirituality, restoring the signs, symbols, and language of Africans should be a buffer against the onslaught of marketing puffery of other beliefs. This calls for understanding how narrativisation works. It also compels a deeper understanding of working against a privileged, elitist discourse such as those of Abrahamic religions which have had devastating effects on the survival of African spirituality.

In this book, we move on the multi-perspectival approach, meaning we recognise the right of every belief system to exist and convince people based on its superior logic, not attempt to extirpate equally deserving alternative belief systems. We have no gripe with Abrahamic or any other belief systems as they have a place in the universal cultural heuristics we seek to advance as the main source of driving modern societies. We reject outright their attempt to exist based on extirpating African spirituality. This means that no single discourse is given precedence over the other, that is, currently popular discourses are results of huge backing infrastructure in the form of buildings, dominant signs and codes in media and religious gatherings as well as huge swathes of books written on it and the effective use of inerrancy as the fundamental basis of the Bible, Holy Quran and Torah, despite scant evidence to support these claims.

Narrativisation must be understood as applied in terms of distinct, specific circumstances to achieve certain ends, which have traditionally included extirpating African spirituality. It is in this sense that African spirituality must advance its own narrativisation without aping traditional discourses of Abrahamic religions with strong semiotic borders, although Christianity had been forced to embrace African spirituality thus relaxing its semiotic borders to accommodate it or risk losing support among Africans. The composition of a narrative structure is thus crucial and should begin with narrative consequence then use of backward mapping. This approach would enable modifications and reconstruction of narratives to meet demands of acceptability under specific prevailing circumstances. There will be a lot, considering the following levels of narrativisation in its construction and reconstruction.

Levels of Narrativisation Useful in Constructing and Reconstructing a Framework for African Spirituality Canonicity

It is important to understand that in each narrative representation, the narrative attributes need to be extensively imposed on the narrative representation in ways that progressively shape the account of the African spirituality discourse into a culturally acceptable discourse to achieve desirable outcomes. At the initial level of narrative representation is the *shared cultural convention* (Perry, 2000:166), where people have certain embedded and entrenched discourses of belief manipulated into their psyche over many years which affect their behaviour and communication patterns. In this sense, these are partially predetermined because it is known which discourses influence their behaviour and speech. Expectations of a narrative, as part of cultural awareness, have to provide evidence and demonstrate that they have been able to resolve others' problems once African spirituality has been embraced. This is the only way of achieving a shared cultural convention where more people incline positively towards African spirituality and can attest to its effectiveness in resolving real, practical problems right here on earth, not in some pie in the sky. The idea that one's earthly problems will be resolved once one is dead is not only silly but represents the most egregious illogicality ever advanced in the world. It is so ridiculous that it is difficult to understand how people can be so gullible as to accept such silliness.

In my spirit mediumship development of initiates, I seek permission to videotape these sessions to use them as evidence of the effectiveness of African spirituality. I also encourage those that receive African spirituality intervention to send me WhatsApp messages and audio clips as testimonies. This way, the shared cultural convention in the form of shared African values and virtues such as life sanctity, respect for elders, collective success (*letsema*), Temperance, Fortitude, Prudence and Justice increases, and semiotic borders of other belief systems begin to grumble. In this sense, a universal cultural heuristics becomes the main focus of shared cultural values and virtues.

Since this approach to understanding African spirituality has gained credibility, there have been increased consultation demands, mainly from highly educated Africans. It is crucial that this form of narrativisation is replicated. I have been working with undergraduate students, postgraduate students, students studying for medical degrees (MBChB), and professionals from all walks of life. These are very influential people whose increased number is likely to lead to a better understanding of African cultural values and their need to influence the universal cultural heuristics. In addition to their intrinsic benefits, cultural values become the crucial basis for Africans to re-reconceptualise their identities in terms of their culture and spirituality, thus defeating othered self, an *infra dignitatum*. Furthermore, African culture is quite tolerant of other belief systems and therefore has quite flexible semiotic borders. This could explain why it was relatively easy to abuse and attempt to extirpate it. The shared African spirituality cultural conventions would require these highly influential and educated people to make it transparent and popular once again. It is a sure way of confronting silences about African spirituality. This thing of reducing African spirituality and displaying its signs and symbols only on Heritage Day must end.

Another important aspect of narrativisation is **authorial conception** (Perry, 2000: 167), the careful selection of textual and spoken contents necessary to drive an African spirituality narration. This may include cases and events that showcase African spirituality as functional and effective. One of the critical events of the year that needs annual celebrations and increased number of attendees is 1 August/1 September when Africans celebrate their new year and organisations of *letsema/ilima* for the entire month where we encourage people to empower those less privileged to improve their conditions. *Letsema/ilima* events must be a constant activity that occurs throughout the year and is published on various media platforms to heighten its real significance away from its abuse by political parties that have failed our societies. At the heart of *letsema/ilima* events must be the land issue and how it can be reclaimed. *Letsema/ilima* activities must enjoy media coverage throughout the year so that the values of Africa are shared and embraced.

All organisations or entities that fight for land restitution must be joined in this struggle and their events supported. Other events that can be organised involve *letsholo* (campaigns). There is a need to organise and make pervasive various campaigns that target schools, universities, any other events of social, cultural gatherings where African spirituality is advanced via superior logic but also the need to respect other belief systems. Other specialised events such as educating people about their *isithakazelo/sereto/ho thella* (clan-praises) and clan histories need to be conducted on a regular basis. Once one has undergone spirit mediumship development and have gained basic principles and understandings of African spirituality, one can start engaging in these cultural events and conceptualise them as an authority in the field. Spirit mediums and influential people have to be seen launching such public activities that promote African spirituality.

The third aspect of narrativisation is *visual narrative conventions* (Perry, 2000:167) with a strong accentuation on imagery. Traditional dress code and attire should not be a once-a-year activity occurring during Heritage month, but Africans must be encouraged to dress in their traditional gear and traditional style clothes. Every garment must have a strong traditional theme as a way of dealing with silences meted out by Western civilisation and colonialisation. Those that history demonstrates are from royal blood must wear appropriate traditional gear of kings, *amambatha* (leopard/cheetah), all the time, including in the workplace to reassert their identity. School uniforms should begin to reassert African identity and culture rather than perpetuate colonial mentality, and this includes police, nurses' and paramedics' attires. The use of traditional cloth hanging on one's shoulder should become a normal practice. The most ridiculous aspect of modern society is that one wearing church or Muslim attire are seen as unproblematic, but those wearing African attire are regarded as weird. This is an extraordinary level of psychological capture.

Narrative production interactivity (Perry, 2000:167) refers to consistent debates and discussions around African spirituality and culture that must be organised and ensue incessantly where people become increasingly aware of their own identity, African belief system, and ways of knowing and doing including foods, mores, clothes, and stories that are distinctively African. Photography, playwrights, and film must be geared towards advancing African spirituality and both linear and non-linear narratives must be used optimally to promote African spirituality. However, the promotion of African spirituality via interactive narratives should bear in mind the multi-perspectival nature of belief systems and should thus not occur in ways that undermine or seek to extirpate other belief systems. African spirituality must stand on its own superior logic. When mythical stories relating to African spirituality are told then efforts should be made that cultural verisimilitude is achieved, the degree to which a work of fiction or myth reflects real life or approximate the truthfulness of a belief system. Otherwise, verifiability must remain central to the narration of African spirituality as it is essentially evidence-led.

A crucial aspect of narrativisation particularly relevant when increasing the number of African spirituality narrators is the role of *ikhehla/gogo* (spiritual mentors). *Ikhehla/gogo* have the responsibility to help create these African narratives and uncover imposed narrativity on them. The Abrahamic belief systems are particularly inclined to impose their narrativity on other equally deserving belief systems using concepts such as inerrancy to attempt to deify their belief systems. Spiritual mentors direct the construction of African spirituality narratives and become responsible for their promotion and articulation so that they can gain ground and compete for space with other belief systems' narratives and myths.

Directorial construction (Perry, 2000:168) as the competence of *ikhehla/gogo* occurs at different levels. *Narrative diachronicity* (Bruner, 2019:6) refers to the understanding of concepts as used, interpreted, and understood over time in a particular context. For instance, the concepts of *lapeng/indawo yokuhlala* (abode) and *hae/ikhaya* (home) assume entirely different meanings in African spirituality. *Lapeng* is where we were born, grew up, and learned critical values. It is always a parental home. *Hae* is the spiritual home, the source of our inspiration and a sacred place where rituals are performed. It can either be our paternal grandparents' home or parental home and its sanctity must always be preserved. The responsibility of the spiritual mentor is to develop an understanding of how African spirituality concepts have been understood over a sustained period of time and identify efforts to give these concepts negative meanings and connotations for them to be rejected and foreign ones imposed. It is part of the semiotic borders that attempt to eviscerate people of these African spirituality concepts and replace them with their own preferred meanings, a process often sustained over time. It becomes critical that spiritual mentors glean correct meanings of these African spirituality concepts and restore their actual meanings and understandings.

African spirituality has been labelled sorcery or evil worship over many years and ancestral worship has been considered a heresy. Yet, all these meanings are incorrect. African spirituality has been deliberately misrepresented to advance foreign belief systems. There is no worship in African spirituality and ancestors serve as intermediaries between the world of the living and ultimate reality. These were obvious distortions. It is important to note that deliberate action has been taken since 1793 when Christian missionaries first set foot in Xhosaland, and 1833 when other Christian missionaries came to Lesotho to extirpate or provide a negative connotation to African spirituality concepts as part of a bigger agenda to wipe African spirituality from the worldly space and to promote Christianity as the only legitimate belief system. This explains the huge infrastructure and resources committed to promoting Christianity, huge physical buildings of churches, huge swathes of priests, and lay preachers who are mostly captured imperialist apologists, and myth perpetrators who so believe in their own righteousness that it is almost impossible to make them aware that they are part of a grand agenda of mass deception and a menticide project. These are the people who have managed to change meanings of African spirituality concepts, leaving them open to obsolescence or pejorative connotation. It is only the resilience of African spirituality that has ensured the survival of the meanings of these concepts. A spiritual mentor has the responsibility to reverse these imposed meanings and to promote the actual meaning of these concepts as central to the lives of Africans.

Particularity (Bruner, 2019:6) in narrativisation refers to cases of individuals that have re-reconceptualised their identities according to African spirituality thus restoring their dignity and sense of pride. Spiritual mentors ought to identify these people and share their experiences with those who will be helping others to reclaim their culture and beliefs. These cases serve as testimonies and evidence of the benefits of reclaiming one's true identity and culture. Furthermore, the distinct features of African spirituality such as ubuNtu, Temperance, Fortitude, Prudence, and Justice need to be highlighted in every conversation to increase the visibility of African spirituality as an attempt is made to reverse the devastation of menticide and propaganda of Abrahamic religions. This should not be confused with demanding the extirpation of these beliefs as we believe firmly in their right to exist and survive on their own superior logic, not at the expense of an equally legitimate African spirituality. There has to be mutual respect and a strong sense of equality among all belief systems. Their distinctiveness should not be treated as grounds of disadvantage, but rather a source of promoting spiritual diversity and a multi-perspectival approach to beliefs. Those that seek to promote African spirituality as a distinct belief must do so on terms that show deep respect for other belief systems in the spirit of ubuNtu.

Intentional re-alignment involves the spiritual mentor understanding that over time Africans have lived and survived within certain settings that were strongly mediated via capitalist and colonial intent, including religious intent such as Protestant ethic. These compelled ways of knowing and doing led to people reconceptualising their lives around these ideologies and foreign cultures which normalised over time. The responsibility of the spiritual mentor is to develop mentees that are capable of being sensitive to where Africans are now in terms of commitment. Most Africans are deeply committed to the ways of capitalism and foreign belief systems, particularly Abrahamic religions. They are mostly in situations where they do not know that they do not know and, even worse, do not know what they do not know. In most cases, the capitalist system and Abrahamic religion are their only reality and offsetting that means treading with prudence, because one could meet up with huge resistance which could then be detrimental to our project of conscientising and nudging Africans towards re-reconceptualising their identities around African spirituality.

As earlier stated in the book, every commitment has a taken-for-granted belief. which leads to intentions and actions. Critical to designing a narrative around African spirituality is a gentle sharing of knowledge and benefits of African spirituality, as well as the accompanying evidence when these captured Africans begin to embrace their own belief. There are therefore reasonable grounds to gently disrupt extant beliefs based on Abrahamic religious assumptions and conjectures, as well as showing the benefits of reclaiming one's Africanness, meaning re-aligning Africans with their beliefs so that their intentions and actions can so be re-aligned.

At the heart of menticide and cognitive capture is the successful conversion of Abrahamic religions' books, the Bible, Holy Quran, and Torah to English and later to vernacular languages. This convertion of books to other languages made them crucial sources of meaning-making or extracting meaning about notions of a Supreme Being, afterlife, and the meaning of life within Abrahamic religions parameters. This is one of the powerful ways Abrahamic religions gained traction in African societies and converted most Africans to these religions, while attempting to extirpate African spirituality. The second powerful instrument of capture was to create an impression that these Abrahamic beliefs are inerrant and unproblematic, leading to their literal interpretation, which lacks rigour.

The third is the fact that African spirituality relied heavily on oral communication and thus lacked written texts. At the heart of interpretation is the availability of texts, because it freezes reality for posterity, while oral narratives are vulnerable to obsolescence. When spiritual mentors develop mentees to drive African spirituality narratives, there is a need to focus on *hermeneutic composability* (Bruner, 2019:7) and training Africans to understand that there is a huge difference between what the text expresses and its exact meaning. In trying to compose an interpretation, people need to understand the nature of the text, its context of writing, the intentions of the author, and whether any benefit could be derived from the text, particularly as Africans function in a materially different world than the one where the text was written. It is important for Africans to understand that the texts and embedded narratives in them were not intended for them. They were simply not an audience of interest to the authors of these religious texts.

The nature of a text is particularly important when composing an interpretation, because there are at least four levels of interpretation. Literal interpretation refers to the meaning of text as it is originally conceptualised, its denotation. Allegorical interpretation whose hidden truth lies in uncovering them from mostly fictional, mythical stories. Moral/tropological interpretation deals with issues of justice, right and wrong. Most Abrahamic religions treat people as children (born-again) because their level of moral development is that of a child of 11 years where complex issues are simplified as right and wrong, heaven and hell, true or false yet the highest point of moral development is justice (Kohlberg, 1981). Hence, African spirituality insists that its highest virtue is justice and adults must grapple with moral issues at that level. Narratives have to revolve around justice and its principles, not function at immature levels of obedience, punishment, rewards, blind following of authority, and unexamined social contract (see Table 10.1 below). Another interpretation involves the afterlife, the final stage of corporeal reality where an ascent to an ontology beyond the azure dome becomes a source of fear to whip people under control and capture their minds. Anagogical interpretation deals with these matters of afterlife and incorporeal reality and has been abused by some belief systems to control and manipulate people into submission. There is no greater malevolence than to use afterlife reality as the basis of control and manipulation as that generates fear and blocks people's deeper understandings.

Table 10.1   The Kholberg's moral development table

Level	Age range	Brief description
Obedience/punishment (Heaven/hell)	Infancy	Effective use of threats and possible harm to gain obedience.
Self-interest (behave to gain rewards)	Pre-school	Behaviour is regulated via accruing greater benefits for oneself.
Conformity and peer pressure (seek recognition and acknowledgement)	Primary to early secondary school age	Seeking approval and friendly relations with others is crucial and maintained at all cost.
Authority and social order	Adolescent and high school age	Obeys fixed rules and follows social order.
Social contract	Late adolescent and teenage years	Mutual benefits and reciprocity.
Justice and its universal principles	Adulthood	Morality is about belonging to the ubuNtu cycle and advancing restorative justice.

In a capitalist society such as the current one dominating the global world and characterised by domination and unfair wealth redistribution, where humans are capable of living their lives, while other fellow humans languish in poverty, justice becomes highly contested. Composing narratives that facilitate conversations and debates about fairness, equality, and love (ubuNtu) will also be highly contestable yet necessary. Spiritual mentors and mentees that advance African spirituality must be mindful of these challenges. Adults function at the highest level of moral development and there is no honour in behaving like a child. This is *infra dignitatum* and emphasis must be made to Africans that ubuNtu embodies this highest virtue of African spirituality.

Interpretation has a history in jurisprudence and even Biblical exegesis, but has mostly focused on context rather than text which has often questioned its objectivity and achievement of veracity. African oral traditions, mythical stories, and fables have often reduced interpretation to these contexts rather than text, except on ubuNtu with a strong motif of observing external behaviour for signs of internal psychology (mindset) and its relation to principles of ubuNtu as based on justice. In this book, the interpretation takes one step further and includes universal cultural heuristics that goes beyond just ubuNtu values but embraces multiple values from various beliefs and cultures.

Referentiality (Bruner, 2019:13), in the African spirituality context, includes reference to ubuNtu philosophy, the four virtues of African spirituality, folklore, myths, clan-praises, and the history of a clan and an African nation. Both these non-fiction and fictional narratives must be told in a manner that promotes African spirituality and demonstrates its power and effectiveness in ordering lives for the better. These efforts on canonising African spirituality are understood as changing African mindsets, the outcome of which is to allow them the opportunity to re-reconceptualise their identities in terms of their own cultures and beliefs.

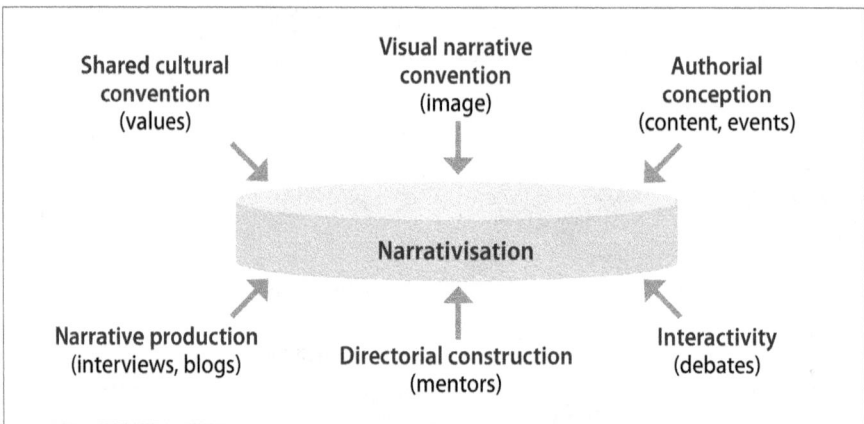

Diagram 10.1 The Framework for Canonising African Spirituality

The essential purpose of canonising African spirituality is to restore its doctrinal essence and its influence on Africans so that they can reclaim their heritage. Furthermore, canonisation of African spirituality seeks to expand its geographic usage way beyond Africa as an integral part of universal cultural heuristics. It is not intended to extirpate or undermine other belief systems.

At the beginning of this book, Christianity comes under intense scrutiny: first, its inerrancy is contestable. Second, the impression that it is beyond disputation cannot go unchallenged, because Christianity is at the heart of menticide which sought to extirpate African spirituality and replace it with its own doctrine. However, its inalienable right to exist as one of many belief systems is incontestable. Third, the deliberate effort to hide the role of Africa in shaping Christianity and Western civilisation needs to be illuminated. Fourth, the dominance of Christianity in Africa as the only doctrine needs to be moderated and questioned in this era.

The canonicity of African spirituality thus proceeds since restoring its doctrine and expanding its geographic usage.

———————————————

11

Inconclusive *Post Scriptum*: Confronting Hard Truths

Reconstructing a belief system is quite a daunting task that must not be treated callously, especially regarding the existing pantheon of other entrenched legitimised belief systems in the world. It is a work in progress whose conclusions should not be treated flippantly. Instead, a more rigorous effort must be applied to bring forth the essence of African spirituality and its value in shaping a universal cultural heuristics in a highly complex and diverse global society. We know the following about African spirituality:

♦ It essentially rejects an anthropocentric view of reality and human power over the universe. Humankind is hardly a cynosure or crown of creation as many belief systems tend to surmise. Mankind is not separate and superior to nature but is integral to it in ways that a disturbance in nature has dire consequences for humans. Climate change, the result of the misconception that humans are superior to nature and the direct outcome of incessant avaricious systems of resource accumulation, provides irrefutable evidence of this. African spirituality posits the view that the fortunes of humans and nature are inevitably intertwined and deep reverence for other fellow humans and nature is the surest path to ultimate reality. It frowns at the detrimental misuse and abuse of natural resources to feed avarice and unquenchable greed. Humans are equal and natural resources as well as wealth accumulation draw from the efforts of the collective human hand. Thus, it must be equally and evenly distributed in ways that ensure the sustainability of natural resources. The persistent flippancy with which nature is treated in our current wealth accumulation systems risks the livelihood of future generations. The time has come to arrest these insatiable human urges before we all fall into a vortex of nothingness. An effort at rejecting political ideologies and replacing them with universal cultural heuristics has to start **NOW** before it is too late. While we acknowledge the immense contribution of modernity on human advancement, its devastating effects on the environment remains an albatross on the neck of humanity and its future survival. We believe firmly that a universal cultural heuristics would compel humanity to adopt values that decimate avarice and penury as it preserves the environment for posterity.

♦ There is nothing more malevolent and outrageously inhuman than poverty in the presence of abundance. It reduces all of us to inhuman and inhumane beings unworthy of our presumed superiority. Those seeking the unfettered accumulation of wealth even when it leads many to poverty are not only demented but need mental health attention. There is something inherently wrong with their mindset. A curb on individual wealth accumulation has also become necessary to manage the Gini coefficient, the deviation of income or consumption from a perfectly equal distribution leading to a profound and uneven distribution of wealth among individuals and households.

♦ It assumes a One Creator Supreme Being who created a dynamic universe and had remained remote from human affairs and concerns. Instead, a spiritual protocol is in place that involves ancestors as intermediaries between the Supreme

Being and humankind to ensure individuals belong and exercise their affairs via ancestral homes (*isibaya*). Any deviation from this protocol creates all sorts of mundane problems for humans. It is also blasphemous to bridge this set of sacred protocols and communicate directly to the Supreme Being, hence **the concept of prayer is alien to African spirituality**. African spirituality has adapted the Lord's Prayer only for **reverence and veneration** to the Supreme Being and is in no way intended as a direct communication line to the Supreme Being. Furthermore, the Lord's Prayer was intended as an outline, a framework, thus an imperfect instrument open to further refinement. Plus, if it comes from the creative genius of Jesus, real or mythical, as the gospels would have us believe, then the Lord's Prayer is not a Christian prayer. Jesus, mythical or real, knew nothing about Christianity, a phenomenon that occurred two decades after Jesus left this world, noted by Christian scholars. Prayer in African spirituality requires extraordinary circumstances such as dire drought to be resided by highly respected elders of the community in a special, sacred mountain, and a play organised by virgin girls of the community (*lesokoana*, an African oar game). African spirituality is based on the quest for personal inner kingdom as functioning within a cycle of ubuNtu, rather than an imaginary place somewhere in outer space, hence its general rejection of routinised prayer. The Christian prayer tends to promote dependence and learned helplessness, hence its modification in African spirituality.

African spirituality does not seek salvation outside self, but rather seeks a humane environment in which social justice, economic freedom, and collective dignity are present. It has a close resemblance with the dictum of the Gospel of Thomas, which is based on some semblance of scientific discovery and the search for inner kingdom as central tenets of human life. It draws from immanence, the idea that our spirituality is drawn from our treatment of other humans and nature, because the greater good is our collective goal which indicates our **divine spark** that link us with ultimate reality.

♦ The universe, in African spirituality, includes the human world, the physical world, and asomatous beings (spirits) with benevolent and malevolent intent. The highest form of asomatous beings is the Supreme Being, who is considered as Omniscient (all-knowing), Omnipotent (all-powerful), and Omnibenevolent (all-good). Living humans have no direct access to this Supreme Being, except through ancestral homes, asomatous beings who traversed this mundane world, and because of their benevolent conduct and functioning within a cycle of ubuNtu occupy the incorporeal space of junior spirits (community of saints), who serve as intermediaries between humans and the Supreme Being. Because attempting direct communication with the Supreme Being is considered as blasphemy, the Lord's Prayer in African spirituality is intended to serve only two purposes: demonstration of reverence to the Supreme Being and our undying commitment to the Supreme Being's ways of life, understood as functioning within a cycle of ubuNtu. In this cycle of ubuNtu, all humans are equal, have access to sufficient resources to meet the needs of the Temperance virtue, show love to all creation, and remain steadfastly truthful from which our credo of truth, love and equality derives. Poverty and inequality are heresies in African spirituality, and systems of the world that result in and perpetuate poverty and inequality are considered as malevolent and belonging to capricious and alienated humans that pursue self-interest, avarice, and act outside a cycle of ubuNtu. These avaricious humans mutate into malevolent spirits upon their death and get cast away to celestial hades, a place somewhere around the sun until rituals of forgiveness and restorative justice are conducted by living relatives summoned via dreams, spiritual diagnostics, or séance to perform such atonement rituals. This exercise of atonement is possible, because in African spirituality nothing is ever permanently lost (Paris, 1993). This is consistent with our second reason for adopting the Lord's Prayer which is its emphasis on forgiveness, a crucial aspect in defining all life as sacred and revering the highest virtue of African spirituality – Justice. Those located in celestial hades must ascend to the higher spiritual echelon (community of saints) once the spiritual cleansing and forgiveness rituals have been performed.

◆ Free will, the exercise of arbitrary discretion in decision-making and behaviours is a gift granted to humans so they can account for their deeds and take full responsibility. It is at the centre of African spirituality because without it, freedom and choice, so necessary in the proper exercise of African spirituality, become impossible to the extent that accountability and atonement become vague concepts. There would be no need for restorative justice and atonement when humans cannot be free to choose their courses of action and conduct. Debates on free will in areas such as philosophy and psychology have shifted to consider free will elusive and illusory because modern, contemporary societies have developed sophisticated instruments of manipulation that give people the veneer of being free to choose, yet these choices are already made for them through conditioning, media control, and marketing. Free will suggests that one has no constraints placed before them and no form of manipulation or coercion that influences choices on certain courses of action have been applied. In African spirituality, people are free to the extent that they function optimally in a cycle of ubuNtu and the critical question is whether this spiritual conditionality is not a form of constraints which might impact the concept of free will negatively. Doesn't this spiritual conditionality impede freedom of choice? To respond adequately to this question, it is important to consider causation and whether it constitutes a constraint. Some actions are caused by good intentions that enhance our freedom and ability to make better choices. In situations where we choose freely, these choices and actions derive from intrinsic motives of general good, love of others, equality, and truth. In such cases, the causes and intents of people are driven by benevolence, which influences these freely chosen courses of action in ways that make these choices serve the greater good, thus enhancing and spreading freedoms from hunger, hate, avarice, and egocentrism. Free will exercised under conditions of serving the greater good cannot be seen as constraints, but rather as the enhancement of broader meanings of freedom and choice. Free will exercised within a cycle of ubuNtu is thus individual freedom and choice that enhance greater freedoms in society.

◆ African spirituality is essentially based on freedom and dignity for all humans, which give them meaning and power. In this African spirituality sense, collective freedom and contribution to it trump individual freedom. Collective dignity makes better sense than to strive for individual dignity. I have dignity and freedom on the basis that others too have the same, or both concepts cease to exist in African spirituality as meaningful constructs worthy of human attention. In this sense, poverty and inequality in any society represent the supreme antithesis of freedom and dignity. Both poverty and inequality are direct consequences of entrenching economic and political systems based on avarice and a higher Gini index. The Gini index measures how outcomes of an economic activity accumulate to a few individuals in society forming an oligarchy of extremely rich individuals and a poor majority, resulting in greater inequality in society. Greater inequality and a state of penury usurp our collective freedom and dignity because they compromise our fundamental virtue of Temperance upon which the other three virtues of African spirituality hinge. The greatest struggle facing humanity in the 21st century is to create conditions of equality and fairer redistribution of collectively produced resources so we could be temperamentally virtuous and start a journey of achieving all forms of justice, including economic and social justice. This is the real meaning of dignity and freedom defined in the context of the cycle of ubuNtu. In this ubuNtu context, dignity is about human worth measured in terms of the totality of collective human worth. This is the ancient meaning of dignity that has not survived the modern era and is at the heart of our effort to reconstruct African spirituality and reclaim and make this meaning of dignity fashionable in the world that worships individualism and avarice. There are remnants of this ancient dignity in modern life, but we need it to be a way of life, a plinth of 21st-century life. A universal cultural heuristics can make this possible.

Modern society has evolved through political ideology with cultural understanding mostly occupying a backseat. Many scholars have studied ideological effects on human mindsets, particularly its mechanisms of persuasion, control and manipulation that compel societies to function in ways that support the minority oligarchy. Modern societies have been designed in ways that accumulate wealth to a super-rich minority with most politicians serving the interests of the oligarchy.

There is a necessity to refocus studies on cultural understanding and the development of a universal cultural heuristics that supports the elimination of inequality, poverty, and injustices of various types including epistemic injustice, a key source of driving white supremacist agendas. Society must enter a post-ideological period, which bequeathed us wars, skewed resource distributions, and supremacist ideologies. A post-ideological period must be marked by creating universal cultural heuristics that should shape our society and nudge it into spaces of equality, love, and justice. Universal cultural heuristics involves a sample of a wide diversity of cultural precepts from which we could select those that shape our political, social, economic, and psychological spaces. The basic principles that should guide our actions must be geared towards creating conditions for equality, including resource-sufficiency for all not a minority, in society should form the basis for universal cultural heuristics. In other words, cultural essentials with strong universal values should serve as the bedrock for the creation of universal cultural heuristics with a strong sense of equality, love, dignity for all, freedom for all, various sorts of justice, and truth.

This is where African spirituality will play a major role in the shaping of a universal cultural heuristics as a key driver of societies, instead of political ideologies that have proved generally disastrous in shaping human affairs and directing property relations in a manner that places social and economic justice at the heart of these endeavours. A key part of reconstructing African spirituality was precisely because the shift away from political ideology towards universal cultural heuristics as the key source of shaping globalised societies is evolving and becoming central in defining societies. As humans increasingly interact and collaborate with intelligent technologies, the power relations increasingly shift towards culture as key in modelling societies as political ideologies become relics of the erstwhile societies of the 20th century.

In this 20th-century period, even issues of culture and morality were analysed in terms of political ideology. For instance, Marxism-Leninism, a political ideology, analysed and understood culture and morality as a class issue in society (Khan, 1999) with the rich seen as more cultured than those living in penury, which is absolute nonsense. Human behaviours were determined through various historical periods and the dominance of a particular political ideology which, in turn, shaped culture and morality in society. Ideology seeks political and economic power either exercised to serve minority oligarchy or the greater good. However, the dominance of political and economic power that serves an oligarchy and leaves many in poverty has turned our society into the most unequal of human relations. Even those ideologies that claim to pursue the greater good have proved inadequate in resolving inequality and poverty in society. The trap of ideology can no longer be sustained by a good argument as its disastrous outcomes in society are glaringly obvious. The time has come to rest this undesirable, anachronistic relic of our sad past and focus on using universal cultural heuristics as the basis of conducting our human affairs.

Universal cultural heuristics does not seek homogeneity, rather it seeks to find the best cultural ideas that could eliminate poverty and inequality and set humans on the path towards understanding that selfish accumulation of resources in a system that leads to deprivation cannot be justified in any meaningful way. There is no honour in celebrating riches when others lack basic resources to meet all the requirements of the Temperance virtue. Our society has made money and wealth the ultimate reality, that is, once one can accumulate huge resources to oneself then happiness is an obvious outcome. Yet rich people are mostly unhappy, gripped by fear, and fail to understand that the ultimate pursuit is to find inner kingdom in which equality, love, and truth are the key pillars of a good life and a path to ultimate reality.

There is no greater satisfaction than to strive for collective dignity and happiness. Therein lies true freedom. True freedom is an aggregate of greater social, cultural and economic equality, including epistemic equality, a societal state in which all forms of knowledge and knowing are acknowledged as necessary in the progress of human societies. True freedom is not possible without the fairer exercise of and access to goods, wealth, and land. A sick society is measured by its inability to ensure that all its people have reasonable access to land, can accumulate wealth in ways that do not disadvantage others to do same, and can create goods in ways that make their redistribution fairer.

More than 500 years ago, humans developed an economic system supported by political power that deified private ownership of wealth generated by a majority in society and created, over time, skewed property relations that benefit an oligarchy and keep the rest of society in a state of survivalist mode. The driving motive of this capitalist economic system is profit, that is, the production of goods and services occur on the logic of surplus generated within pressures of market forces. Producers of goods and services in a market-driven economy seek utility through increasing surplus, a precondition for private wealth accumulation. This system of private wealth accumulation is at the heart of creating greater inequality in society and a prime suspect in generating generational penury. It is this illogicality of this economic system that needs to be entirely pulverised and those ideologies that drive state ownership of the means of production are no better given the propensity of uncultured humans to seek political power and use it to serve self-interest under the guise of serving public good. In this sense, all political ideologies end in the generation of an oligarchy and inequality, hence the need to shift from ideologies to a universal cultural heuristics as a key source of driving human relations, including resource accumulation.

Extant political ideologies have driven a narrative of transparency and full accountability but have always delivered, in the words of Okafor, Smith and Ujah (2014:3), "*a trans-lucid accounting milieu*", where corruption and unethical conduct are revered and celebrated. Index measures of accountability for political ideology show an utter failure of ideology to serve the best interest of society. Human hope can no longer depend on a system of political ideas and practices that have delivered kleptocracy, kakistocracy, nepotism, and a minority of super-rich oligarchs whose claim to public glory and accumulated wealth emanate from what a popular aphorism terms "*behind every fortune there is a crime*", implying that under an economic setup supported through political ideology, getting rich is impossible without committing some well-concealed crime. That is how the system is designed. Pursuance of ethical conduct and cultural morality means accepting to function in a lower class than an oligarchy in society who appears immune to these precepts. This is what needs to change. That change should involve abandoning political ideologies in preference of universal cultural heuristics as the dominant driver of society. Universal cultural heuristics places premium on the spiritual conduct of humans for spirituality builds in people ethical conduct and high morality which leads to a culture of equality, love, and truth where transparency and accountability are revered. Political ideologies have delivered practices that ensure the exploitation of public resources and wealth, collectively generated, to favour minority interests of the oligarchy (Okafor et al., 2014).

Within the African spirituality context, this means that natural resources deriving from land are designed to serve nefarious acts of avaricious lots, malevolent souls at the expense of the majority of people thus the majority of people lacks access to the very embodiment of their spirituality, meaning inaccessibility to land, an unalienable right that must be universally protected. African spirituality cannot serve **any other gods** including capital demigods and has to rage against all human systems designed to take their embodiment which is land. In essence, this is a complete takeover of their very being even beyond the corporeal because land is immanently linked to our ultimate reality. We see God in land. We see life in land. Land is everything in African spirituality, that is why transnational oligarchy, our modern criminal syndicate masquerading as true gentle humans supported by various political ideologies, can never allow the majority of people to own land, in particular Africans, where land is a spiritual matter for them. There is no greater crime than unresolved land issues in Africa.

The oligarchy know this, hence they manipulate political processes to install their own stooges, who will serve their narrow interests rather than the interests of the majority of people in society. Democratic processes are a sham because of the ease with which the oligarchy can manipulate their outcomes to favour their narrow interests. If we establish a universal cultural heuristics in society, then the narrow interests of an oligarchy would take a backseat. These leeches will not stop the march of history to an equal society.

I give no honour or respect to those who decide, mostly by force or shenanigans, to amass wealth for themselves when others become poor. It entrenches the animal culture of "*survival of the fittest*" in humans with superior intellectual capacity and inhumane disposition. No other earthly gods should rule over others on the basis of skewed wealth distribution, because the accumulation of such wealth involves the entire global society. This is inherently unjust and contrary to acceptable humane conduct, which the universal cultural heuristics seeks to achieve. Some argue that this is an impossible mission, but I disagree. It is a simple mindset change. Once we show deep, collective disdain for economic oligarchic tendencies and frown more profoundly on those with such intent or have already selfishly amassed such wealth, then we could see progress. It is society that legitimises such behaviour and we can, once again, delegitimise it so we can reverse it.

Science, in particular sociology and psychology, have shown that once behaviour has been assigned as deviant and society reacts as a collective to it in a negative way then such behaviour either becomes exceedingly moderated and in the long term significantly modified or reduced (Obradovic, 2019; Vijayalakshmi, 2019). A deviant conduct breaches commonly accepted principles of society leading to negative consequences for perpetrators.

Once individual wealth accumulation exceeds a certain set societal limit and leads to other individuals becoming poor, thus compromising their Temperance virtue, then such an individual must be treated as deviant and rejected by society. There are several behavioural modification techniques developed over time in psychology which can prove effective in reducing oligarchic tendencies in society. This is a valuing exercise and for as long as the oligarchy is given a positive and even envious valuing then such individuals would never modify their behaviour. In such instances, society, not the avaricious individuals, is to be blamed.

Society conditions these avaricious individuals by giving them undeserved credit and respect, treating them as demigods for participating in wealth processes whose accumulation is collective but distribution is skewed towards the few individuals in society. This societal approach to avaricious conduct leads to societal ills such as property crimes, drug crimes, and other felonies with a high recidivism rate. Property crimes have an average of 67% recidivism rate meaning for as long as property relations remain skewed towards the few and the majority of people in society lack this basic right and access to property including land, then this particular society will be impossible to justify. Property including land is a critical and fundamental aspect of the Temperance virtue and for society to experience a paragon of high morality then all conditions of Temperance must be met unconditionally, meaning property relations, access, and ownership must be distributed equally.

The drug recidivism rate is closely linked to property crimes at two levels, calibrating to almost 63%. First, drug crimes relate to opulence where too much wealth makes people search for happiness in drugs, completely unaware that striving for a society where wealth is evenly spread to all people in society would lead to collective happiness and there will be no need to seek it in drugs. Second, those living in highly deprived conditions with a lack of basic resources and inaccessible property including land are more likely to resort to drugs.

Other felonies associated with economically-related crimes have a recidivism rate of 74%. It is clear from the US study conducted in this epitome of capitalism, a system of economic activity that produces an oligarchy and justifies that a great many people in society should be poor for the few to be super rich, that economic freedom results in a lower recidivism rate (Hall, Wooten & Lundgren, 2011). This study shows that a one percentage increase in economic freedom in a society has a direct, positive correlation with a decreased recidivism rate. In a similar study, Ashby and Sobel's (2008) research on income inequality and economic freedom indicates that increased income equality is positively associated with economic freedom and reduced criminal activity.

The greatest source of societal ills, including crime, is a lack of economic freedom for the great number of people in society. This is because the Temperance virtue, as a fundamental tenet of high morality in society, has to undergird the motion of every society so that economic systems designed to benefit the few are rejected and condemned forever. This way, other virtues, including the supreme virtue of Justice, would thrive and societies will be better off for it. Once these virtues order societies through their variants in universal cultural heuristics then better, more advanced societies are more likely to emerge and our better, more spiritual selves are likely to form.

These are issues that warrant further critical engagement, and their conclusion could take our global society to the next level of advancement. What is certain and conclusive is the longitudinal study that tracked a sampled group of youth up until their old age. The study was led by Dr. Robert Waldinger, a notable psychiatrist, and took 75 years. It took the West 75 years of intensive study to learn what gets inculcated to Africans from childhood as encapsulated in our ubuNtu philosophy. Interest in this topic is gaining significant traction in the West and psychologists are at the forefront of advancing it. In a powerful conversation penned for the respected *Guardian* newspaper in the UK on 15 April 2022, Brad Chilcott critiques the celebration of the gory and macabre during Easter by Christian religious groups and implore them to rather join the struggle to end exploitation of people for gain in power, profit and avarice, even within their own ranks. Brad Chilcott further shares advice he received from his psychologist, who made him aware that altruism is based on a strong self-interested intent, because those seen as altruistic seek instead public fame as philanthropists of note, hence the accompanying public exposure of such deeds.

Those contributing selflessly to such altruistic endeavours would eschew public exposure and remain anonymous. The psychologist further insisted that well-being and health are strongly linked with people who have joined the struggle to seek social justice, economic equality, and collective dignity for all. These views from a psychologist and the three findings below from the Waldinger study are consistent with the African Temperance virtue, and show that Western science and societies are catching up with basic tenets of African spirituality:

1. Our well-being and health benefit greatly from strong social bonds.

2. Strong social connectedness is essential for a good life, not avarice.

3. Good relationships are essential for our physical and mental health.

There may well be a reversal at hand here. After many years of attempting to extirpate African spirituality, the West is gradually coming to terms with a special kind of consciousness. A consciousness that recognises many years of systematic and systemic African cultural devastation that nearly robbed humanity of its last hope of creating conditions where humane values drive global societies.

There are several factors that allow a strong possibility of creating universal cultural heuristics that could shape our collective destiny. First, most cultures are dynamic and are therefore open to continual growth and development. We, as African scholars, have made it clear that African spirituality is one of many belief systems in the world noticing cultural variations even within African spirituality itself. In recognition of all these cultures of the world, there is a common threat we must collectively pursue that other scholars call "*the psychology of oneness*" as succinctly captured in the concept of universal cultural heuristics. Culture has agentic power. hence it can find creative and alternative solutions to problems besieging global societies (Falola, 2003).

At this point, the greatest threats to dominance of humane values in global societies are avarice and selfish elites. These are the people Greeks call **idiots**. Idiots are not necessarily stupid but are driven by narrow private interests and tend to be highly intelligent and creative which they use to achieve narrow interests. These are the people that need to be defeated if universal cultural heuristics is to pursue collective dignity for all and equality of resource distribution in ways that ensure that all humans live way beyond the poverty line is adopted. Some scholars prefer the concept 'commensuration' than 'equality' given that commensuration means similar measurable standards whereas equality refers to the same in all respects and is thus unattainable. The key advantage of commensuration is that it eliminates heteroge-neity of values and can thus be a powerful instrument in selecting universal cultural heuristics as a key driver of global societies. It turns human values more stable as it significantly reduces *akrasia*, acting contrary to one's deeply held moral values and one's better judgement.

Avaricious people or idiots tend to be driven by a deeply held **avaricious passion** (impetuosity) to accumulate wealth for themselves by all means necessary and tend to be **rationally weakened** by the deep desire to be socially recognised as opulent. It is, in this sense, that stripping these idiots of social status and marginalising them would go a long way towards moving global societies towards the greater good and equality measured by means of commensuration that recognises that all people live way beyond the poverty line and towards collective dignity. There is a level of admission here that given the human condition then equality, in its purest form, is unattainable but all humans can live a comfortable life way beyond the poverty line when universal cultural heuristics is used to shape societies rather than political ideologies that have proved disastrous. The greatest threat to humanity is *akrasia* (avaricious passion, rationally weakened individuals) and societal propensity to defer such agentic power to the political and economic elites.

Avaricious passion refers to an obsessive-compulsive urge to pursue unbridled wealth accumulation with no regard to its impact on the greater good and general well-being of society. Rational appeals to the greater good or general well-being in wealth redistribution falls on deaf ears. It is the values of these idiotic elites that are imposed on society, turning societies into savages in the **Age of Rationality** that stretches into the 21st century. The Age of Rationality involves humanity's use of reason, logic, and creative problem-solving to deal with our challenges. However, without universal values that are collectively shared then the use of rationality in ordering human affairs is futile. Rationality significantly reduces reliance on religion as the sole arbiter of human values, instead recognising the true value of drawing universal cultural values from the multitude of cultures across the globe.

In addition, these universal cultural values, once agreed upon, function within the framework of heuristics meaning these values anchor societies and necessary adjustments are regularly made to ensure that values of fairness, equality, and collective dignity prevail as they influence human behaviour. It is this agentic power enabled by culture that needs to be harnessed to develop a highly representative universal cultural heuristic.

Culture is also dynamic meaning it is susceptible to external influences and pressures, making it highly malleable to malicious intent if not constantly monitored to preserve its humane values. It is quite possible that the elites would use every possible power avenue to preserve their selfishness and narrowness. In our most recent years, the concept of **affiliative truth** in our societies has become prevalent and is an effective form of influencing public opinion and social behaviour. It refers to *"ways of knowing, capable of mobilising audiences"* (Kalpakos, 2019:1). Knowing implies a highly subjective awareness and understanding of something and can be highly solipsistic when serving narrow interests.

How then does affiliative truth get to shape public opinion and social behaviour on a global scale?

Part of the response to this question is the idea of how *"cocreated fictions"* get generated and are used to influence public opinion and social behaviour. The content of the desired narrative is well curated, that is, carefully selected and thoughtfully designed to have the expected effect on public opinion and social behaviour. This is done in ways that create perceptions that the elites live good and virtuous lives and that all can achieve such life with sacrifice and indefatigable effort. This is obviously an erroneous presentation of information, because elitist oligarchs are direct beneficiaries of a highly problematic resource accumulation and distribution framework. In this framework, wealth accumulation requires the effort of every human in society, but benefits accrue to the few, well-connected individuals who are often exploiting political power to gain greater advantage and amass huge wealth, while there is some trickle-down effect to the majority of the society that builds that wealth. To be fair to capitalism and the theory that guides it, let us summarise its basic logic.

First, society needs resources of all sorts in good condition to create conveniences for humans. This has been the flagship of capitalism. It has created complex systems of delivering these resources to society with most of the risks taken by private owners and not consumers. In the name of fairness, this seems like a reasonable proposition. However, a capitalist system thrives on three basic elements since, at least, the 20th century, although vestiges of these elements can be traced to ancient times.

The first is **division of labour**. Capitalism makes specialisation possible, meaning individual people become experts in one area of product or service development leading to huge resources accumulation of the highest quality. In the early 20th century, however, specialisation was meant for the few who could simplify tasks to a point where uneducated, cheap labour can successfully complete these tasks in ways that generate top-level products or services. The costs of production were significantly reduced leading to high profits. With mechanisation or automation came significant reduction in using human muscle, a course that is likely to be exacerbated by digitisation and intelligent technologies in the next 40 years. The capitalist system is increasingly getting rid of human muscle in product development and wealth is increasing exponentially. Its system is now capable of functioning on a global scale and in real time.

Another key aspect of capitalism is its impersonal exchange based on pricing. Pricing factors out human emotions thus making it a highly objective endeavour. Benefits accrue to individuals patterning property relations in highly unequal ways but society benefits from a wide range of choices on products and services that are reasonably priced, making access to the majority of people in society possible. While capitalism is based on the private ownership of resources, there are variations such as oligarchic capitalism which entirely rejects state intervention in economic activity, thereby creating conditions where society benefits from trickle-down effects such as job creation. It is this extreme capitalist paradigm that has been shaping societal values across the globe.

State-guided capitalism refers to an economic system in which a mixed economic activity thrives, because it allows the private sector and the state to participate in business and commercial activities that lead to profit. The basic principles of capitalism such as labour division and exploitation, profit motive, and private ownership remain intact with such modifications that allow state participation in the economy and certain levels of ownership such as state-owned enterprises (SOEs). As a mixed economy, it has features of both the capitalist and socialist state. State-guided capitalism is different from state capitalism in that state capitalism involves using all the tenets of capitalism to run an economic system where the means of production are owned by the state and all commercial and business-generating entities are nationalised. The difference also relates to state intervention in economic activity with state-guided capitalism having a slightly lesser state intervention than in state capitalism where such state intervention is heightened. There are other types of capitalism such as big-firm capitalism where multinational corporations run the economic activity on a global scale and entrepreneurial capitalism in which private capital is used to invest in private start-ups and new ventures for profit.

This brief description of capitalism reflects the central problem in African spirituality which is that the exercise of an economic activity rests on the unbridled exploitation of humans and nature, the very foundation of African spirituality. Private ownership occurs in ways that direct nature's resources towards the few elites / oligarchs whether in their personal capacity or as public servants. This approach is unsustainable, and its logical end is a crisis that will lead to a revolution as Karl Marx warned. The exploitation of humans in economic activity, although now threatened by digitisation and complete automation, meant that humans do not participate in these economic activities voluntarily and with all the freedoms that go with that. This means that work is not related to spirituality and the achievement of the Temperance virtue. Rather, it serves to benefit mostly avaricious individuals turning the majority in society into perennial glorified modern slaves whose material conditions have slightly improved to keep society stable, a requirement for oligarchies to retain their power. The oligarchies have no interest in sharing their resources and only allow fewer individuals to occupy the upper middle-class status, meaning becoming better-off slaves of the oligarchy.

It is this patterning of work to serve narrowness that African spirituality contests. This work patterning in terms of private ownership and human exploitation is mainly responsible for the co-creation of fictions that perpetuate the myth that under any type of capitalist economic activity some form of equality or elimination of poverty from the face of this earth is possible. It is fictitious to assume that any capitalist arrangement of the economy can end human exploitation and eliminate poverty. The major challenge is that in selling this 'truth' to society, its affiliative nature makes the very society that reels under this capitalist imbroglios, active participants that justify a capitalist state of affairs. This is the scale of psychological damage to society that capitalism of all sorts has meted out.

The oligarchy knows that to sustain and perpetuate their self-interest in the current economic activity, strong social bonds and connectedness with the masses in society is crucial to prevent a revolution, so affiliative truths are hatched by big marketing and PR companies to generate artificial bonds of solidarity between the oligarchy and society. When society falls into the trap of believing this elitist truth then society voluntarily participates in co-creating the very myths and fictions that condemn it to perpetual exploitation and abject and glorified poverty (middle class: owe a lot and own few assets). The marketing companies exploit the very basic need that humans have, that of affiliation, connectedness, and sense of belonging. By investing in aspirational narratives, that is, narratives deliberately designed to evoke a common world vision framed within the dictates of capitalism, the marketing and PR companies compel society to embrace and protect the very system that disadvantages it. The marketing and PR companies know that our brains are wired to understand and interrogate the world in terms of stories, so they use these stories as effective tools of managing societal expectations. The most powerful technique used in aspirational narratives is to position society or the audience as a protagonist in the story. This is the most powerful way of capture because the veneer of being in charge and in control will also be too tempting to ignore for many who are gullible enough to fall into these traps. It is important to note that all narratives have a common basic structure which is that of a protagonist attempting to achieve a meaningful goal. The marketers know this and make society believe that the capitalist goal of being super-rich is attainable and all can achieve it.

A simple statistical measure called Gini coefficient which measures income distribution and income inequality in society shows that the capitalist mirage is a myth and is impossibly unattainable by the entire society because its design is to benefit an elitist oligarchy, the few super-rich individuals. Efforts on affiliative truth, as the key driver of society, are that the capitalist value system is attempting to trump all other cultural values and impose its own. This is why we warn that using political ideologies is a hackneyed concept and must be eliminated so we can set up universal cultural heuristics as the main driver of societies. We must always be on high alert for the intrusiveness of invasive values of self-interest, avarice, and idiocy, the very tenets of capitalism, because they enter our souls insidiously and ravage our psyches as they reduce us to modern savages. Our psyche contains the motive force, the ultimate driver of our actions and behaviours. Whoever successfully influences our psyches very much controls our actions and behaviours. The marketing and PR companies know this. Our universal cultural heuristics is aimed at working our collective psyche so we can exhibit actions and behaviours that serve the greater good, entrench selflessness, and preserve our collective dignity as humans.

However, it is important not to conceptualise universal cultural heuristics within the post-truth nomenclature, because that would dignify and justify an essentially dishonest enterprise. Truth, within post-truth discourses, is a matter of who asserts their claim more effectively, making effective assertion of a claim a measure of truthfulness. In other words, a claim is true if the majority of people in society believe in it, that is, the claim has been *"asserted effectively"* (Kalpakos, 2019:3). This explains why such huge resources are invested in marketing and PR companies under a capitalist economic system. When verifying claims, their substance takes a backseat as only claims that support the altering of our collective psyche to believe in the goodness of a capitalist economic system count. Emotions, the visceral kind, and managed experience are key to ensuring affiliative truth and its curating to benefit capitalism. In this scenario, the relationship between a truth claim and verifiable facts has become strained and rendered redundant. A truth claim has a strong link with visceral experiences of the people as the target audience. Affiliative truth is therefore based on *argumentum ad populum* (majority fallacy) that affirms that something is true purely on the basis that it has the approval of the majority (beware the tyranny of the majority, to paraphrase Lord Acton [Acton, 1902]).

This approval of the majoritarian claim is today generated via big data analytics to give it the veneer of science. Big data analytics refer to the use of highly advanced analytical tools to glean insights and findings from large, diverse datasets from different sources to justify or provide grounds for the believability of truth claims on the strength of the size of data. While there are various kinds of big data analytics, the prescriptive and predictive type seem to be preferred in affiliative truth-making.

Another huge development in generating affiliative truth in this century is the effective use of social media, which paradigmatically shifted society from information to the visceral experience age. We now live in the Experience Age where 92% of young people and a substantial number of adults access mixed reality almost on a daily basis (Hu-au & Lee, 2018). A mixed reality, according to Hu-au and Lee (2018), consists of reality as understood traditionally (the **real world** we access via our sensory perception), **augmented reality** defined as an integration of the **digital / virtual reality**, and the real-world reality as well as the **virtual reality** as created through technology-mediated experiences. Technology-mediated reality allows humans to traverse neon geometric spaces, communicate virtually with others using various social media platforms, video games, virtual simulations and search for our technology-enhanced selves (*homo deus*, the ultimate, perfect, apical human being). The mixed reality creates conditions where owners of these immersive platforms enable interactions and communication beyond geographic limitations and collect, interpret, and sell data generated in these platforms to marketing and PR companies. These generated data become crucial infrastructure for the creation of preferred affiliative truth, one that serves the sustenance of a capitalist economic system that disadvantages the majority of people in society.

Capitalism values individualism and wants society to see it as a virtuous goal to pursue yet it is a collectivist culture we need to embrace on a global scale. A collectivist culture promotes selflessness, equality, serving societal interests, forging collective dignity, and banishing poverty of all kinds. Individualistic cultures promote self-reliance, independence, and autonomy thus making it easy to pursue self-enrichment as a key source of self-reliance even when that includes harming others. North America and western Europe's cultures are highly individualistic, hence they are strong defenders of a capitalist economic system and its societal ordering which essentially promote individualism. This explains why a universal cultural heuristics based on collectivism should be the key driver of societies. Universal cultural heuristics should out of necessity attempt to be evidence-led so it can cushion against passing emotional and visceral appeal as truth which could not meet the demands of verifiability.

While universal cultural heuristics involves a certain degree of belief, care should be undertaken that this is supplemented by facts and strong evidence. African spirituality is essentially evidence-led and therefore seeks verifiable facts and quests for truth. Some confusion exists that link post-truth with lies or even with *"routinisation of blatant lies"* (Billgin, 2017:55). Post-truth is a mental state that creates its own effects. These post-truth effects create and sustain a social world, organised around a worldview which produces its own culture that influences how society lives. In this case, societal lives have to create a perception that the oligarchy wants and protects its own narrow interests. This idea of weaving a belief within a culture to advance an ideological agenda is not new. Christian missionisation has been at the forefront of it, hence Christianity was able to spread all over the world. Christianity is not necessarily a big fat lie as that would be too simplistic and such labelling could deter our intellectual effort to understand its essence and challenge it intellectually and logically. The success of Christianity and its global spread is based on mastery of affiliative truth and how to embed it within a culture. Christianity has successfully created and sustained a social world in which people are prepared to live and defend it with every iota of their strength. In this social world of Christendom, truth is what is in the Bible, which is not necessarily composed of entirely verifiable facts. Biblical truth becomes true through its own effects. Truth, in this sense, is a central feature of how people conduct their lives, understand reality, and make sense of posthumous life. In this social world, how truth is judged excludes **verifiability** as a key value of judgement (Harsin, 2018). The key element of verifiability is replication, the idea that anyone can repeat the process of truth-claim to verify its credibility. The main difference between truth understood within a particular worldview such as that of Christianity and truth as a universal construct is that truth claims must be open for verification by anyone, not just a particular sect or grouping.

Another condition of a truth-claim as a universal construct is that new evidence should be able to assist us to abandon truth-claims whose salience has been challenged by this new information so that there is a continual verification process of the truth. Truth that becomes true by means of its own effects (affiliative) in a particular world cannot withstand the rigour of verifiability and the strength of new evidence.

Let us now analyse how truth becomes true through its own effects, which is only possible when applied within a particular social world. This is how the Christian missionisation worked to render Christianity popular throughout the world. Christian missionisation embedded Christianity within cultures of people to alter their beliefs through menticide, indoctrination, and successfully implanting Christianity into human cultures. Culture exhibits the following characteristics that enabled Christian spread in Africa (Eller, 2010:33):

◆ **Culture creates a total design for living.** It serves as a blueprint to conduct our lives, determine what counts as truth and the afterlife. It covers all aspects of life and regulates our behaviours. Christian missionaries knew the benefits of turning Christianity into a culture because it would take total control of all aspects of our living. To reverse this centuries-old Christian reality, there is a need to reclaim our cultures and eliminate Christian imprints in it. This aspect of culture as the very design for our living compelled our people to reconceptualise their identities in terms of Christian religion including adopting Biblical names and using its narratives as sources of wisdom. This identity reconceptualisation, adoption of Biblical names and narratives are the surest signs of a captured nation. Suddenly, we have no stories of our own to tell, our traditional names full of meanings no longer carry any cultural weight, and our lives become Christian lives. This is total capture and truth, in Christian cycles, is what the Bible tells despite its errors of facts and evidence adduced in books such as *Christian Delusion* indicating its falsehood and mythically-derived narratives.

◆ **Culture as an inerrant legacy.** Once it is perceived and understood as absolute and perfect, culture becomes almost impossible to break. When adherence to culture becomes the only reality, any efforts to challenge the merits and core of that culture meets with the toughest of resistance.

Christian missionaries knew that if they could succeed in breaking Africans culturally and embed Christian doctrine within them, then those seeking to reclaim and restore African culture would be resisted by Africans themselves. It would be seen as an act of taking away their life essence rather than as a restoration and reclamation project designed to reclaim its collective dignity and freedom from capture. Christianity positioned as a culture assumes status of a false consciousness. A false consciousness is an inherited and learned cognitive status that makes it difficult for people to recognise their own oppression and mental capture. People captured in this false consciousness are incapable of collective effort and action that could better their lot, reclaim their collective dignity, and fight for fairer redistribution of resources that banish poverty. False consciousness creates an illusion that things will get better without collective effort and victims often embrace values and beliefs of those that oppress them. Christianity is a huge resource accumulation project, drawing such resources even from the poorest of the poor and selling mostly the nonsense that rewards will come in the afterlife. Christianity is not set up to benefit and empower people, rather it seeks to control and manipulate them into believing that the afterlife is better than current corporeal life. False consciousness is understood therefore as deriving from defective reasoning and faulty social cognition that comes about through a process of acculturation and assimilation to a different, dominant culture. In this case, Christianity acculturation and general abandonment of one's own culture. Thompson (2014: 449) argues that

> [false consciousness] is a state of accepting the value patterns and cognitive styles of thinking generated by others, particularly by forms of institutional norms and cultural patterns of activity that can deform critical-cognitive capacities.

This way, the creative genius and cognitive capabilities of critical thinking and reflection get stunted as the values and thinking of manipulators take precedence and people believe that manipulators have their best interest at heart. At this point, false consciousness is at its most powerful, when it requires no effort to defend itself as the victims become the primary defence against their own interests, better known as self-sabotage.

Given its strong link with social power, false consciousness creates conditions in which people in society submit to the interests of elites who deliberately and consistently use it to distract people from questioning the status quo that disadvantages them. Christianity is seen as a socio-cultural force within administrative-capitalist societies that generate a pathology of highly subjective and dubious moral and cognitive reasoning that position humans in such societies as active agents in their own oppression and capture. In such situations of a capitalist order, the elites perpetuate without hindrance and Christianity is the greatest enabler of this oppressive and offensive state of affairs. In this sense, while Christianity enables oppression and mental capture in a capitalist order, it is itself captured to serve these narrow interests of the elites. As Christianity inveigles society to its own mores, it too becomes inveigled in capitalists' narrow agendas that serve the elite oligarchy. **The entrapper becomes entrapped**. Christianity in capitalist societies, in particular in African societies, has a strong legacy as a weapon of mass deception and is implicated in spreading the pathology of defective reasoning that 'kills' creativity and critical thinking among Africans and all those believing in it. This kind of pathology comes from a situation where people are unable to cognitively track the objective social reality around them. Instead, they get routinised into believing in values and actions that benefit the elite as they disadvantage them. People become active participants in their own humiliation and oppression. Defective reasoning is thus the real legacy of Christianity. There are ways of correcting these intellectual defects generated over time by Christian missionaries and they involve reading well-researched books such as *Christian Delusion* (Loftus, 2010), *Christianity: An Ancient Egyptian Religion* (Osman, 2005), and *Why I am not a Christian* (Russell, 1927). Ahmed Osman's book argues that the Roman version of Christianity that the Roman Catholic Church promoted was manufactured by the Roman Empire to maintain political power. In the 17th century around 1611, a King James Bible version was introduced as a legitimate Bible in England after undergoing revision by 47 scholars and was declared an official document sanctioned by the political power in England.

There is nothing inerrant about the Bible. It is a human-made creation intended to sustain political and church power. The Bishops' 15th-century Bible, while popular among the clergy, could not receive official acceptance of the then political head, Elizabeth I. Further proof that Christianity without political power has no salience. It cannot stand on its own superior logic and cannot escape its own legacy as a stolen Egyptian cult (Osman, 2005). We urge people to conduct their own research and come to their true consciousness. Functioning within affiliative truth created by any religion fosters false consciousness and makes people act against their own interests. More painfully, it fosters defective reasoning that leads people into a state of mental capture, a woeful descent to nothingness. Nothingness, according to Bang (2016), refers to the presence of cultural absence among people which comes about because people have been made to assimilate cultures of others and abandon their own. Culture, when used as a tool for assimilation and acculturation, becomes a weapon of mass mental destruction and this is the only legacy of Christianity with some degree of credibility. It is a legacy that went way beyond a belief system and became a worldview with embodied realities that dictate the terms of living for its adherence.

◆ **Culture as a worldview with embodied realities**. The world consists of multiple cultures with their embodied realities and worldviews. This recognition of culture as multifaceted suggests that there is a need for mutual respect among varied cultures and treatment of all cultures as equal and legitimate. There is no reasonable basis for one culture to dominate others or have the urge to do so. Worldviews come about as a result of sustained exposure to objective reality, which compels designing our lives around these realities. It is obvious that when deliberate efforts are made to dislodge people from their inherent cultures through acculturation and assimilation then the realities of those people, their sense of being, and life are significantly distorted to a point of creating a warped reality.

Reality warping is the power to change the reality of others, including their belief systems, spirituality and worldview to impose the preferred reality and destroy in the process, the omnificence (unrestrained power to create) of those whose reality has been warped successfully. Xenopsychic reality warping is particularly effective in manipulating others' thoughts and understandings into accepting realities, worldviews, belief systems, and lives created by others. This is how Christianity spread in Africa via xenopsychic reality warping using multiple communication tools such as conquest persuasion, menticide, and sustained reality warping techniques. Examples of reality warping includes decimating our culture of ubuNtu that seeks a peaceful, equal society, destroying the collective dignity of African people, and extirpating our immanent belief that the Supreme Being resides in how we treat others as well as nature.

Concepts of a pie in the sky such as heaven, a superhero such as Jesus, and the sadomasochistic derivation of hero-worship in the form of crucifixion are foreign in the African worldview. These foreign concepts represent key aspects of distorting the African worldview. The glorification of the macabre and grotesque in Christian horror movies such as *The Passion of the Christ* shows how Christianity is willing to trade on "*torture porn*" (sadistic violence) to strengthen its generally weak intellectual case. It knows it cannot withstand the muster of logical rigour and thus uses torture porn to whip emotions and attract empathy, a critical diversion from our inquiring minds and a strong element in African ethos called ubuNtu. Hence, empathy became a crucial marketing tool for Christianity in Africa and how Africans were convinced to accept a foreign concept of a hero saving them when Africa is about "*vuka osenzele*", an empowering self-determination philosophy that promotes omnificence and self-reliance rather than learned helplessness that serves Christian doctrine well. In sacred architecture of the 17th century in Europe, the "*danse macabre*" theme sought to represent artistically a human dealing with death, lame attempts to resist it, the grim procession to the ultimate end to this dance, and the final curtain. This is the storyline of Jesus as narrated in synoptic Gospels, unashamedly trading on the macabre and grotesque as well as plagiarising the sacred architectural theme.

Given that the popular King James version of the Bible was written in this 17th-century period, it is not unreasonable to suggest the plausibility of this plagiarism claim. It is not clear how this warped reality helps Africans other than as a means of mental capture and creating conditions to rape our natural resources leaving us helpless and poor in our milieux of plenty. In this sense, the rationale for reconstructing African spirituality is precisely to eliminate this warped reality (post-truth puffery) and accurately bring back the essence of who we really are and our general quest for a peaceful, complex world ordered in the form of a universal cultural heuristics, where powerful global cultural voices that empower and make all of us great are signified. African spirituality seeks to contribute to those voices. The days of dominant, narrow voices that dignify mental capture and avarice are gone. We live in a world that recognises multi-perspectival approaches such as universal cultural heuristics to deal with the inherent complexities of our times.

♦ **Culture as an adaptive system**. In our times, the world has moved swiftly to act in a unified form on a global scale and in real time, particularly at an economic, political, and social level albeit via digital connections that enable online trading, communications, and social engagement through social media. The greatest enabler of this worldwide phenomenon is embracing complexity as the key driver of this phenomenon. However, it is important to note that there are two dominant worldviews that seek to drive the global society. The first and simplistic worldview is premised on the mechanical rationality. In this rather simplistic world, efficiency, control, predictability, and measurability create the certainty that is required for stability and order so many crave and desire. The economic field prefers this kind of worldview to thrive but also survives on innovation, that is, a disruptive worldview that introduces new or substantially improved products or services. The present can be analysed using big data analytics and the future can be accurately predicted in this worldview, but it lacks the following:

◆ Learning that encourages creativity and imagination.

◆ Variation is frowned on because it creates instability and disturbs the order.

◆ Adaptation to materially new conditions and changes in the environment.

◆ Innovativeness that produces new or substantially improved products that upset the stability in well-established traditional markets.

Mechanical rationality has become a way of life for many and resonates with many belief systems, because it routinises life and becomes a dogma-driven societal phenomenon. Mechanical logics is at the heart of what we challenge in this book in terms of entrenched ideologies and faulty belief systems that advance idiocy and avarice. We suggest universal cultural heuristics because it caters for complexity as the key driver of global society as enabled by digital systems. Complexity enables the generation of new perspectives and practices that create conditions for multi-perspectival approaches to all human endeavours. The systems of stability tend to gravitate towards equilibrium and that of complexity tend to actualise into adaptive yet dynamic conditions of existence. This is the paradigmatic shift that suits the fostering of a universal cultural heuristics. Universal cultural heuristics should thrive under these conditions of dynamism and adaptation and create an environment where the creative genius of all humanity is unleashed. The following characteristics of complex adaptive systems as the key driver of global societies need further research within the context of universal cultural heuristics.

◆ **Complexity**. The dominance of one belief system over all other belief systems, in this century of digital and variety systems, is hackneyed and outmoded. The flourishing of all belief systems of the world in particular those that have been marginalised would enrich our existence and create conditions of dynamism and adaptability **from which we can develop a universal cultural heuristics.**

◆ **Self-organisation.** The nature of these systems to interact constantly without allowing one system to dominate, the dominance of their feedback loops and fluctuations plus their dynamism that compel humans to adapt to these materially different conditions resonate with ideals of universal cultural heuristics. Furthermore, the evolution of these interacting, dynamic systems veer closer to a constant state of flux rather than towards equilibrium.

◆ **Emergence.** As systems interact and constantly create a dynamic environment, new perspectives, new ways of understanding, and new practices emerge. It is a space full of innovation, potential, and opportunity for humans to pursue higher ideals and better designs of self and the world. The greatest gift we can give to ourselves is to operate within this dynamic and innovative ambience because our spiritual self is better harnessed and developed under these fluid and uncertain conditions. Our spiritual power develops more optimally under these dynamic, unpredictable, and uncertain spaces. This is because these unstable conditions allow for the emergence of new perspectives, new practices, and continual possibilities of spiritual and cultural growth.

◆ **Resilience**. The capability of a belief system to react to its internal malfeasance and unforeseen often self-inflicted negativity and reorganise to present its better side is a crucial aspect of its adaptability capabilities. Adverse effects on a belief system creates conditions for a belief system to adapt and restore its healthy functioning in society. Greene (2002) identifies key aspects that define resilience more exhaustively:

  – It entails *bio-psycho-social and spiritual aspects*. While resilience assumes a strong spiritual connotation in this book, it is related to human behaviour. Mental health (the biological) such as genetic vulnerability to certain diseases tend to be some afflictions that beset spirit mediums but through spiritual resilience such afflictions tend to be overcome as long as all the rituals are in order. Neurochemistry relating to mental state also tends to afflict spirit mediums especially if rituals have not been properly done but through spiritual resilience, most spirit mediums overcome these challenges. It is seldom that spirit mediums can have drug problems. Psychologically, spiritual resilience refers to the ability of spirit mediums to achieve high self-esteem and self-actualisation. Given that African spirituality is evidence-led, this builds the confidence of spirit mediums to convey the spiritual messages with high degrees of confidence. Socially, spirit mediums have an above average lifestyle because they need to build confidence in people that their lives will be better because the spirit medium lives a comfortable life. We do not celebrate poverty as spirit mediums as that is unAfrican. Our spiritual resilience helps us deal with socio-economic matters quite successfully including those of our consultants.

  – *Adaptability*. Spirit mediums adjust to challenges and complexity more satisfactorily, because the essence of their work involves complex problems, hence their critical thinking abilities have to be quite poignant.

◆ **Observer dependency**. The capability of a belief system to allow people to be persuaded by evidence and superior logic should be the main tenet of all belief systems. Things should be understood from the perspective of the believer not the other way round. This way, the dignity of the person rules supreme not that of a belief system. This also allows a belief system to grow and self-correct. No belief system is perfect, hence the need to keep them in a state of constant dynamism and adaptability or risk irrelevance in this century. African spirituality places the search for inner kingdom at the heart of its belief, so the perspective of the believer trumps all other considerations.

◆ **Path dependency.** The tendency of a belief system to steadfastly rely on its traditions, doctrines, and past successes serving as a deterrent to explore new paths of possibilities and growth to stay relevant under materially different conditions. The 21st-century global society, while besieged by dark forces of avarice and idiocy using post-truth nomenclature, has chosen superior logic and evidence-led propositions and beliefs as instruments of persuasion. Belief systems that continue to myopically depend on past traditions and successes are more likely to become irrelevant and extinct over the course of the next five decades. There is increasing evidence that society that sticks to its cultures become more successful than those that have adopted foreign beliefs. We suggest that a more universal cultural heuristics would most likely generate general wealth, well-being, and happiness across the entire globe because it draws from multiple cultural sources. This would entail exploring new pathways and breaking up with our past and our deeply held familiar pathways.

◆ **Chaos.** In belief systems that thrive on predictability and stability brought about by traditions, rituals, and routines harnessed over years, the randomness and unpredictability of behaviours of believers that wish to break with the past are undesirables the belief system would seek to squash. Our view is that the discomforts that come with these unpredictable behaviours create opportunities for a belief system to self-correct and become relevant in the lives of 21st-century people. Chaos is therefore a good thing for any system, including a belief system, because it creates conditions of discomfort in an era where we must become comfortable with the uncomfortable and uncomfortable with the comfortable. The era of static systems is gone, and we now live in a dynamic environment that requires appropriate adaptability to emerging realities and the proposition to develop and grow a universal cultural heuristics stemming from this new reality, which compels recognition of a complex world. A singular belief system can no longer function optimally in a system of the world that thrives on multiplicity of diverse perspectives. Chaos, in this sense, refers to the disturbances and disruptions that occur in traditional perspectives and practices leading to discomforts that are vital to take humanity forward through enabling innovation and creativity. While the world proceeded based on strategic plans up until the onset of the 21st century, and indeed its relics remain intact in our society, 21st-century societies thrive on heuristics that unlocks creative intelligence of humanity. Heuristics thrive when conditions of conduct are flexible, dynamic, and in constant flow to allow for adaptability through integration of data-gleaned information and quick experiential learning into our practices. As many scholars of organisational behaviour suggest, this new reality of complexity and the chaos it generated has become our new version of our universal pattern of growth and development and an antidote against the relics of our modern past. We need access to humanity's creative intelligence to which belief systems have played a major role in blocking. The innate intrinsic creativity we are born with and stunted by economic and religious puffery needs to be restored as this, in essence, is akin to challenging our very human essence and connectedness with the ultimate reality. Without our innate intrinsic creativity, we are as good as animals that survive on instinct. We are no nearer to our full potential and any culture or belief system that stunt such a Deity-given or natural talent, as atheists would prefer to call it, deserve our collective contempt and activism to get rid of such ungodly or unnatural tendencies and doctrines. A universal cultural heuristics has to replace narrow-minded, poorly conceptualised, and anachronistic religious and belief systems that are unable to adapt to new global conditions. The use of heuristics as a singular is deliberate and intended to emphasise how an adaptive system driven by complexity needs a unified functioning of a complex system.

◆ **Irreducibility.** That which is complex cannot easily become predictable or reach a state of equilibrium, maximum constraint the outcome of which is stability. Any belief system that becomes unpredictable and allows for a dynamic flow of ideas and multiple perspectives is most likely to survive this century as long as it also forms an integral part of a universal cultural heuristics where its claims of superiority are tested via evidence and superior logic rather than naive faith. A universal cultural heuristics thrives on multiple belief systems to sustain itself therefore it would be difficult to reduce it to one or few dominant cultures as that would compromise its very essence.

In addition to these aspects of resilience, there is another aspect of resilience worthy of our analysis. For African spirituality to reclaim its status and resume its influence, the concept of 'forgotten' as an absence needs attention. It would be simplistic to assume that forgotten is only about absence, as presence is an equally valid attribute in forgotten. Presence depends on *remembering, recognition* and *reflection* (the 3Rs of presence).

Remembering or recalling depends on the repetition of the same information at regular intervals, hence Christianity leveraged this advantage by entrenching a tedious routine of attending church and its associative activities at regular intervals to maintain the flow of Christian doctrinal information. This was not a sufficient condition for its survival in the discursive space, because its belief system contains no superior logic and its case as a belief system is quite weak, and irrefutable evidence has been provided to attest to its inferior logic. A discursive space refers to three concepts: spatiality, materiality, and agency (Baker, J., 2017; Baker, M., 2002; Maciag, 2018; Meyer & Woodhorpe, 2008). *Spatiality* is about occupancy of a discursive space, a space of knowledge or information existence, flow, and acquisition. *Materiality* refers to the establishment of relevance or the significance of a discourse in this discursive space. *Agency* is about taking a specific course of action to produce a particular effect. Christian missionaries used this strategy of a discursive space to entrench Christianity in Africa.

They ensured that Christianity occupied the larger portion of that discursive space through fighting for its relevance and significance, hence its perennial struggle with science and scholars of atheism. Christianity had the overt intention of producing certain favourable outcomes by discrediting its perceived threats such as science, atheism and, in the case of Africa, African spirituality, a strong source of Africa's solidarity. This was intended to ensure the survival and thriving of Christianity on a global scale. It had to be the only show to be remembered, a privileged presence like no other. This was an almost successful project of cultural extirpation particularly in Africa. It also explains the encroaching of Christian intelligent design in the school curriculum of the US. This shows the success of mastering presence as a construct of remembering so as to claim a right to exist in a discursive space even when grounds of doing so are extremely weak.

Recognition is the other tool of convenience for claiming a discursive space through presence. Signification even when subjective is crucial in identification of what is considered important in ordering one's life, and Christianity ensured that it is recognisable throughout the world and fought to entrench its generally weak knowledge form and its flow in the global discursive space. There had to be some kind of a discursive structure to sustain Christianity in the global discursive space and it came in the form of a promise and identification with sadistic violence to elicit empathetic feelings with the writers of Christian narratives, purported as the true account of Jesus's life. The promise of heaven – an effective, illusory escapism – represented a welcome respite from the mundane suffering, so it appealed to base emotions rather than intellect. Intellect would expose heaven as a thought-control mechanism and a typical escapism technique, which could collapse Christian doctrine and expose it for what it is – a scam of the highest order that has robbed this world of its creative genius. A scam claims to serve your interest, but you always lose. Imagine how many talented creative geniuses got buried through this scam. Humanity is poorer for it.

The last aspect of the 3Rs of presence is *reflection*. Reflection implies the possibilities of changing direction and gaining new insight or perspective. This is the most undesirable R of presence in Christianity because reflective people take time, energy, and effort to think deeply about things and where evidence is stacked against something, these people have no difficulty to ascend to a superior logic or evidence-based proposition. In *Christian Delusion*, the superiority of the Christian faith is pulverised by facts and superior logic, hence fewer if any Christians would dare use it for reflection. Reflection is a key aspect of resilience because it includes the possibility of changing direction, owning a new perspective, even abandoning old perspectives and insights whose logic has proved spurious. It creates possibilities to be better and ascend one's higher design in the discovery and exercise of one's God-given gift – the gift of creative genius, perspicacity, and superior intellect. For instance, a reflection on Christianity would reveal that it is a belief system based on three very logically weak tenets or pillars – a promise, an empathetic feeling, and fear. There is a promise of not only heaven but also of all one's mundane problems resolved if one accepts Jesus as one's saviour. Heaven is some kind of a fairy home that one can occupy upon death if one has accepted Jesus.

Who needs a pie in the sky, really?

Those whose intellectual capabilities have been stunted by a disempowering belief system and whose creative genius has been rendered dormant by the very system are strong candidates for believing that heaven awaits. Given that there is no evidence to support the existence of planet heaven after many years of gaining planetary and astronomical knowledge, believers can only proceed on the basis of wishful thinking, nicely framed as faith or blind belief.

Another pillar of Christianity is empathetic feel. The story of Jesus, particularly the crucifixion which is based on sadistic violence, seeks to whip emotions to their apex, which is the level of empathy that can easily expose one to gullibility. We need to identify with Jesus' pain on the cross and his failure to carry his own cross, which an African had no problem carrying to show empathy. However, to stretch empathy to a point where people should believe that Jesus did all these things, including his failure to carry the cross to save us, sounds extremely ridiculous. None is supported by evidence adduced in the very synoptic Gospels that describe the journey of Jesus. An African saved Jesus by carrying his cross; who saved who exactly? How does a story get so easily distorted? Africa saved Jesus, real or mythical, twice. In his childhood years and during his crucifixion. How can a guy we saved, save us? It is illogicality of the highest order.

The evidence of Jesus' failure is right in our face and well-narrated in the synoptic Gospels and requires no mental effort. The stronger of the two between Jesus and the African man is this African man; what else do we need to figure ou?. This requires little mental effort, not empathetic feel. Empathetic feel, while at the heart of African spirituality, is being used here as a manipulation tool and this could explain why so many Africans fell for the trick of Christianity. Christianity has a place in our complex societies, but needs to up its logical game. It has scholars who can do that once its inerrancy is abandoned and its fallibility recognised as a source of research and further discoveries. This intellectual path is sure to contribute positively towards increasing the Christian salience.

Our inherent kindness and empathetic feel were poorly reciprocated by our guests and remain to this day an albatross around our neck. One does not abuse the courtesy of one's host and claim to be civilised. This is barbarism of the highest order drawn, I surmise, from 900 years of the Dark Ages in Europe. It has become generational and there is a need for intervention. The entry of universal cultural heuristics in the grand global discursive space is crucial. We need to expose a privileged, constructed presence of violence and its acceptability as inevitable for what it is, a glorification of sadistic violence intended to map power relations in a particularly skewed way.

We also need to deal with a binary between the privileged and dignified presence of violence and war in our society and the absence of peace and the myth that violence and war represent some kind of irrefutable fact or a sense of truth. There is no dignity in any kind of violence or war, and efforts to justify such represents a relic of the Dark Ages. Weapons of negotiation, dialogue and invitational persuasion need to be normal tools of conflict resolution in a civilised society.

Persuasion in itself is a form of gratuitous violence although there is a benign form of persuasion called invitational persuasion. In this kind of persuasion, people get invited into a dialogue, conversation, and negotiation as equals with no intent to conquer or convert others as that represents gratuitous violence. Another form of violence on our psyche is described in detail in Lawrence Kohlberg's Moral Development Theory. In the study of moral development, Lawrence Kohlberg's Moral Development Theory, while critiqued for its developmental or stage theory and cultural bias with emphasis on individualistic rather than collective cultures with emphasis on societal values, provides invaluable insight on how humans develop their morality. It also explains how adults get fixated at a level of fear (obedience and punishment) and thus prosecute their lives in the domain of children.

Kohlberg posits six stages of which the first three stages describe an idiot: an immoral, self-centred individual whose behaviour is motivated by obedience, punishment and self-interest. Kohlberg considers these initial stages of moral reasoning as childish and unworthy of adult conduct yet many adults get fixated in these initial stages, while some proceed to the conventional stages of conformity and respect for authority. Adults focus a lot on obeying rules, being nice, and respecting authority in this conventional phase. According to the theory, all adults in society must engage and constantly critique the social contract between society and government to determine whether it proceeds on the basis of human rights and justice, the highest virtue of African spirituality. Christianity values obedience (entry point to heaven), punishment (entry point to hell), self-interest (incorporeal preservation; better afterlife), and conformity (following tedious church doctrine). In other words, it prefers **treating adults as children**.

Adults should engage, debate and maintain principles of justice even in circumstances where they conflict with church doctrine, rules and laws. It is difficult to respect people who accept to be treated like children for it is impossible for them to self-actualise and unleash their creative genius so essential in prosecuting adult life and venerating God-given gifts. The universal cultural heuristics would need to enter the global discursive space where global cultural knowledge exists, flows, and can be acquired. This way, it would begin to produce particular desirable ends that will lead the world towards greater good, equality, justice, and love, where poverty is banished, and respect for nature is paramount and sacrosanct. This way, it is likely to gain relevance and significance that would lead to change in global behaviour. Our responsibility is to hold in readiness a universal cultural heuristics which should be the outcome of rigorous debate and discussions of all nations of the world. This is the rationale that compels the reconstruction of African spirituality so it could make contributions to this universal cultural heuristics and creates its own space in the global cultural discursive space.

African spirituality has always been there but marginalised from dominant global discourses of culture. This is what we seek to centre on the global discursive space as we negotiate universal cultural heuristics as the dominant idea that drives global society. Political ideology is so last century, its persistence in this century is embarrassing. This is the fundamental reason why reconstructing and reclaiming African spirituality is so crucial. African spirituality was never absent, it has always existed, years before Abrahamic religions, and its flow within Africans was never abated despite deliberate efforts to silence it. It continues to be acquired and practised without hindrance even by those claiming to be Christians or Muslims. The hypocrisy of these Abrahamic religion converts is nauseating. **The most dangerous person in the world is one who is in the grip of folly, believing erroneously in the supremacy and inerrancy of such folly.** These people rob humanity of their God-given creative genius which could make the world a slightly better place. Many go gently into their graves without reaching the highest echelons of their intellectual capacity because they have been fed folly dressed as religion. This is the tragic end of a life that never really started, some kind of hubris of the intellectually defeated who sing the song of the earthly masters masquerading as God-sanctioned truth conveyors.

What would be the point of God giving us creative genius and intellectual capacity to solve our own problems when, in turn, the same God demands obedience and stunting of the most beautiful gifts of all – creative genius and intellectual capacity. Our divine role is to use these super powers of creative genius and intellectual capacities to leave the world in a better condition than what we were exposed to otherwise our lives become meaningless. The true meaning of life is to find one's life purpose or mission and use the tools of creative genius and intellectual capacity to help make the world a slightly better place. Any belief system that attempts to derail one from these lofty ideals of creative genius and intellectual capacity to solve complex worldly problems is unworthy of our attention. Its intention is to stunt one from realising one's full potential and this is blasphemy to the One who endowed one with these gifts.

African spirituality is about celebrating these gifts, hence its close association with science and evidence-led beliefs. There is nothing greater than the search for truth and engaging issues intellectually and rationally. Any system that seeks to stunt these lofty goals cannot claim to represent the Supreme Being. The tendency also to reduce the Supreme Being to human attributes such as a gendered, murderous, vengeful, punishing, and low-esteemed Being is blasphemy of the worst kind. My Supreme Being and that of Africa is non-gendered, non-sexist, non-racist, all-loving, merciful, and forgiving all the time, irrespective of our wicked ways, and expects no human accolades or prayer in return. Only a low-esteemed Supreme Being needs a prayer to enhance its own status. Laws of nature created by the Supreme Being and discovered by science cannot be altered by a prayer to suit praying individuals. This is laziness of a special kind. We have it in ourselves to do things for ourselves and our Supreme Being dispenses no favours based on a prayer.

Individuals must appreciate the intellectual tools and creative genius bestowed on individuals to resolve their own problems. This is the essence of living. We must also show deep respect and profound appreciation for the gift of life irrespective if such honour to traverse this world came about even through unsavoury acts of rape. Once we are here, we need to appreciate the privilege of living and live to our full potential instead of being trapped by regrets, self-pity, and despondence. The world needs to know one was here long after one is gone. One's footprints must exhale loudly and serve as the reminder that one once walked these spaces on one's own terms and left indelible African marks in the sand of worldly time. As an African, one's role in changing the lives of others for the best, building institutions that transform lives, living a humble life, and preserving nature are sacrosanct. This is the true meaning of African spirituality that we all, across the globe, must embrace and revere. For Africans, the world is for sharing, not domination. The Western paradigm of individualism, even in research, has bequeathed us an unjust, cruel world.

———————————————————

References

123Helpme (2022). Similarities between Biblical stories and Greek mythology. https://bit.ly/3JV98lp [Accessed 2021/11/18].

Acton, L. (1902). The tyranny of majority. https://www.acton.org/ [Accessed 2022/05/12].

Adofo, D. (2016). *Ancestral voices: Spirit is eternal*. Createspace.

Alain (Emile Chartier). (n.d.). AZ Quotes. [Online]. https://www.azquotes.com/author/20987-Emile_Chartier [Accessed 2023/03/31].

Ambady, N. & Rosenthal, R. (1993). "Half a minute: Predicting teacher evaluations from thin slices of non-verbal behavior and physical attractiveness". *Journal of Personality and Social Psychology*, 64(3): 431-441. https://doi.org/10.1037/0022-3514.64.3.431

Ameh, A. (2021). *Land in African ontology*. https://bit.ly/3Z73Hpc [Accessed 2020/02/20].

Arabian (n.d.) Arabian / Quotes. *Goodreads*. [Online]. https://www.goodreads.com/author/quotes/1573855.Arabian

Ashby, N.J. & Sobel, R.S. (2008). "Income inequality and economic freedom in the U.S. states". *Public Choice*, 134:329-346. https://doi.org/10.1007/s11127-007-9230-5

Asmal, K., Asmal, L. & Roberts, R. (1997). *Reconciliation through truth: A reckoning of apartheid's criminal governance*. London: Palgrave MacMillan.

Babinski, T. (2010). The cosmology of the Bible. In: J. Loftus (ed.). *The Christian delusion: Why faith fails*, 109-147. New York, NY: Prometheus Books.

Baker, J. (2017). *The agency of absence: Contextual understanding*. Oxford: Oxford University Press.

Baker, M. (2002). Argumentative interactions, discursive operations and learning to model in science. In: P. Brna, M. Baker, K. Stenning & A. Tiberghien (eds.). *The role of communication in learning to model*, 303-324. New York, NY: Psychology Press.

Bang, J. (2016). *Nothingness: Philosophical insights into psychology*. New York, NY: Routledge. https://doi.org/10.4324/9781315125381-1

Barbalet, J. (2008). *Weber, passion and profits: The Protestant ethic and the spirit of capitalism in context*. Cambridge: Cambridge University Press. https://doi.org/10.1017/CBO9780511488757

Baumeister, R. (1988). "Masochism as escape from self". *Journal of Sex Research*, 25(1):28-59. https://doi.org/10.1080/00224498809551444

Bernal, M. (1987). *Black Athena: The Afroasiatic roots of classical civilisation, vol. 1. The fabrication of ancient Greece, 1785-1985*. New Brunswick, NJ: Rutgers University Press.

Biko, S. (1987). *I write what I like: Selected writings*. Oxford: Heinemann. https://pdfroom.com/books/i-write-what-i-like/NpgpZBkx5jr

Billgin, P. (2017). "Resisting post-truth politics, or primer: or how not to think about human mobility and global environment". *Global Policy*, 8(1):55-59. https://doi.org/10.1111/1758-5899.12411

Bitena, D. & Martinsone, K. (2021). *Mystical experience has stronger relationships with spiritual intelligence than schizotypal personality traits and psychic symptoms*. Riga: Riga Stradins University Press.

Bradshaw, M. & Ellison, C.G. (2010). "Financial hardship and psychological distress". *Social Science and Medicine*, 7(1):196-204. https://doi.org/10.1016/j.socscimed.2010.03.015

Bruner, J. (1991). "The narrative construction of reality". *Critical Inquiry*, 18(1):1-21. https://doi.org/10.1086/448619

Caldwell, C. (2017). "Understanding kindness: A moral duty of human resource leader". *The Journal of Values-based Leadership*, 10(2):1-19. https://doi.org/10.22543/0733.102.1188

Carleton, N. (2016). "Fear of the unknown: One fear to rule them all". *Journal of Anxiety Disorder*, 41:5-21. https://doi.org/10.1016/j.janxdis.2016.03.011

Carrie, R. (2012). *Proving history: Bayer's theorem and the quest for historical Jesus*. New York, NY: Prometheus Books.

Chomsky, N. (2022). The Best Quotations. [Online]. https://best-quotations.com/authquotes.php?auth=1341

Connell, R. (2007). Southern *Theory: The global dynamics of knowledge in social science*. New York, NY: Routledge. https://doi.org/10.22459/AHR.44.2008.04

Crump, D. (2010). "What does intent mean?" *Hofstra Law Review*, 38(1059):1060-1081.

Csikszentmihalyi, M. (1997). *Finding flow: The psychology of engagement with everyday life*. New York, NY: Basic Books.

Danesi, M. & Perron, P. (1999). *Analyzing culture: An introduction and handbook*. Bloomington, MN: Indiana University Press.

Dasré, A. & Hertrich, V. (2020). "Addressing religious practices in sub-Saharan Africa: Insights from longitudinal study in Mali". *African Population Studies*, 34(1):5013-5033. https://doi.org/10.11564/34-1-1345

Deguchi, A., Hirai, C., Matsuoka, H., Nakano, T., Oshima, K., Tai, M. & Tani, S. (2020). What is Society 5.0? In: Hitachi-UTokyo Laboratory. *Society 5.0: A people-centric super-smart society*, 1-23. Singapore: Springer Nature Singapore. https://link.springer.com/chapter/10.1007/978-981-15-2989-4_1

Duval, E., Klamma, R. & Wolpers, M (eds.) (2007). *Creating new learning experiences on a global scale*. Proceedings of the Second European Conference on Technology and Enhanced Learning, Crete Greece, 17-20 September. https://doi.org/10.1007/978-3-540-75195-3

Eller, D. (2010). The cultures of Christianities. In: J. Loftus (ed.). *The Christian delusion: Why faith fails*, 30-61. New York, NY: Prometheus Books.

Erasmus, D. [1876] (2012). *In praise of folly*. London: Reeves & Turner.

Falola, T. (2003). *The power of African cultures*. New York, NY: University of Rochester Press. https://doi.org/10.17/9781580466189

Franz, E. & Gillet, G. (2011). "John Hughlings Jackson's neuroscience: A unifying cognitive neuroscience". *Brain*, 34:3114-3124. https://doi.org/10.1093/brain/awr218

Goldman, A. (2006). *Stimulating minds: The philosophy, psychology and neuroscience of mindreading*. Oxford: Oxford University Press. https://doi.org/10.1093/0195138929.001.0001

Goldman, A. (2013). *Theory of mind*. Oxford: Oxford University Press.

Goleman, D. (1995). *Emotional intelligence*. New York, NY: Bantam Books.

Greene, R. (2002). *Resilience: Theory and research in social work practice*. Washington, DC: NASW Press.

Hall, T., Wooten, N. & Lundgren, M. (2011). "Post incarceration policies and prisoner reentry: Implications for policies and programs aimed at reducing recidivism and poverty". *Journal of Poverty*, 20(1):56-72. https://doi.org/10.1080/10875549.2015.1094761

Harsin, J. (2018). Post-truth and critical communication studies. *Oxford Research Encyclopedias*. https://doi.org/10.1093/acrefore/9780190228613.013.757

Hatch, E. (1895). *The influence of Greek mythology on Christianity*. New York, NY: Harper.

Hodge, D. (2011). "Evidence-based spiritual practice: Using research to inform the selection of spiritual interventions". *Journal of Religion and Spirituality in Social Work*, 30(4):325-339. https://doi.org/10.1080/15426432.2011.619896

Holm, A. (1963). *I am David*. Copenhagen: Gyldendaal.

Hu-au, E. & Lee, J. (2018). "Virtual reality in education: A tool for learning in the experience age". *International Journal of Innovation in Education*, 4(4):215-255. https://doi.org/10.1504/IJIIE.2017.091481

Iliffe, J. (2007). *Africans: The history of a continent* (2nd Edition). Cambridge: Cambridge University Press. https://doi.org/10.1017/CBO9780511800375

Jaladoni, M. (2015). *Filipino temperance: Towards a contextualised yet critical social virtue ethics*. Boston, MA: Boston University College Libraries.

James, G. (1954). *Stolen legacy: Greek philosophy is stolen Egyptian philosophy*. Global Grey ebooks.

Joseph, G. (2011). *The crest of the peacock: Non-European roots of mathematics* (3rd Edition). Princeton, NJ: Princeton University Press. https://doi.org/10.1515/9781400836369

Josephides, L. (1999). "Disengagement and Desire: The tactics of everyday life". *American Ethnologist*, 26(1):139-159. https://doi.org/10.1525/ae.1999.26.1.139

Kalpakos, I. (2019). *The political theory of post-truth*. New York, NY: Palgrave Pivot. https://doi.org/10.1007/978-3-319-97713-3

Kaufman, S. (2018). *What does it mean to be self-actualized in the 21st century?* Scientific American. https://bit.ly/2JTgnLs [Accessed 2020/03/02].

Kentake, M. (2020). Kemetic (ancient-Egyptian) mystical wisdom. https://kentakepage.com [Accessed 2021/09/03].

Khan, M. (1999). Theoretical frameworks in political ecology and participatory nature/forest conservation: The necessity for a heterodox approach and a critical moment. *Journal of Political Ecology*, 5:1-13.

Knapp, M. & Hall, K. (2012). *Non-verbal communication in human interaction*. https://www.researchgate.net [Accessed 2022/09/03].

Kneale, M. (2014). *An atheist's history of belief*. Cape Town, South Africa: Penguin.

Kohlberg, L. (1981). The philosophy of moral development. *British Journal of Psychology*, 1:1-7.

Lammers, J. & Imhof, R. (2015). "Power and sadomasochism: Understanding the antecedents of a knotty relationship". *Social Psychological and Personality Science*, 1:1-7. https://doi.org/10.1177/1948550615604452

Le Roux, M. (2007). "The survival of the Greek gods in early Christianity". *Journal for Semitics*, 16(2):483-497.

Loftus, J. (ed.) (2010). *The Christian delusion: Why faith fails*. New York, NY: Prometheus Books.

Maciag, R. (2018). Discursive space and its consequences for understanding knowledge and information. *Philosophies*, 3(4):34-40. https://doi.org/10.3390/philosophies3040034

Marques, L. (n.d.). Luis Marques/Quotes. *Goodreads*. [Online]. https://www.goodreads.com/author/quotes/1423217.Luis_Marques

Mawere, M. (2010). "Indigenous knowledge systems' potential for establishing a moral, virtuous society: Lessons selected from IKSs from Zimbabwe and Mozambique". *Journal of Sustainable Development in Africa*, 12(7):209-221. https://doi.org/10.2307/j.ctvk3gm3j.13/02/2020

Mbiti, J.S. (1969). *African religions and philosophy*. London: Heinemann.

Mbiti, J.S. (1977). *Introduction to African religion*. Nairobi: Henneman.

McKinnon, R. (2010). *Money and capital in economic development*. Washington, DC: Brookings Institution Press.

Meerlo, J. (2006). *The rape of the mind*. Columbia, NY: University of Columbia Press.

Mercier, B., Kramer, S. & Shariff, A. (2018). "Belief in God: Why people believe and why they don't". *Current Directions in Psychological Science*, 27(4):1-6. https://doi.org/10.1177/0963721418754491

Meyer, M. & Woodhorpe, K. (2008). "Dialogue between museums and cemeteries". *Sociological Research Online*, 3(5):1-7. https://doi.org/10.5153/sro.1780

Miller, D. (1992). "The Icarus paradox: How exceptional companies bring about their own downfall". *Business Horizons*, 35(1): 24-35. https://doi.org/10.1016/0007-6813(92)90112-M

Obradovic, S. (2019). "Publication pressures create knowledge silos". *Nature Human Behaviour*, 3:1-5. https://doi.org/10.1038/s41562-019-0674-7

O'Connor, S. & Robertson, H. (2012). "African influence on Italian culture". In: J. Spicer (ed.). *Revealing the African presence in Renaissance Europe*. Baltimore, MD: The Walters Art Museum.

Odora-Hoppers, C. & Richards, H. (2011). *Rethinking thinking: Modernity's "other" and the transformation of the university*. Pretoria, South Africa: Unisa Press.

Okafor, C., Smith, I. & Ujah, N. (2014). "Kleptocracy, nepotism and kakistocracy. The impact of corruption in sub-Saharan African countries". *International Journal of Economics and Accounting*, 5(2):97-115. https://doi.org/10.1504/IJEA.2014.063736

Osman, A. (2005). *Christianity: An ancient Egyptian religion*. Simon and Schuster.

Osterholm, M. (2010). Beliefs: A theoretically unnecessary construct? In: V. Durand-Guerrier, S. Soury-Lavergne & F. Arzarello (eds.). *Proceedings of the Sixth Congress of the European Society for Research in Mathematics Education. January 28th - February 1st 2009, Lyon, France*, 154-163. Lyon: Institut National de Recherche Pédagogique.

Overend, T. (2008). *Social idealism and the problem of objectivity* (2nd Edition). Brisbane: University of Queensland.

Paris, P. (1993). "The spirituality of African peoples". *Journal of Black Theology in South Africa*, 7(2):114-324.

Parker, J. & Rathbone, R. (2007). *African history: A very short introduction*. Oxford: Oxford University Press. https://doi.org/10.1093/actrade/9780192802484.001.0001

Parry, J. (2014). I choose happiness. https://jackieparry.com/2014/12/01/i-choose-happiness/ [Accessed 2022/06/07].

Perry, M. (2000). "Connected and culturally embedded beliefs". *Teaching and Teacher Education*, 24:140-153.

Pew Forum Research (2010). https://www.pewresearch.org [Accessed 2021/03/17].

Pierini, A. (2014). Incarnation and incorporeality. https://www.academia.edu [Accessed 2022/04/23].

Pitso, T. (2020). *Privileged: Identity, history, culture and heritage in the age of deep learning*. South Africa: Teboho Pitso.

Pitso, T. (2021). *Contextualised critical reflections on academic development practices: Towards professional learning*. Stellenbosch, South Africa: African Sun Media. https://doi.org/10.18820/9781991201218

Radcliffe, S. (ed.) (2017). Honoré de Balzac 1799-1850: French novelist. *Oxford essential quotations* (5th Edition). [Online].

Oxford: Oxford University Press. https://bit.ly/3JXPyoJ

Ratner, P. (2018). Ten common traits of self-actualized people. https://bigthink.com/neuropsych/10-characteristics-of-self-actualized-people [Accessed 24/6/2022].

Rossouw, D.V. (ed.) (1995). *At the crossroads: Perspectives on religious, educational and Biblical studies in a new educational system.* Pretoria, South Africa: Arcadia.

Russell, B. (1927). Why I am not a Christian: An examination of the God-idea and Christianity. https://bit.ly/3G9Xke0

Schaffer, R. & Emerson, P. (1964). *Attachment theory.* Springfield, MO: Missouri State University.

Seybold, M. (2016). The apocryphal Twain: "The two most important days of your life…", 6 December. *The Center for Mark Twain Studies.* [Online]. https://bit.ly/42UmoQ6

Shakespeare, William (n.d.). *Sonnett 116: Let me not to the marriage of true minds.* Poetry Foundation. [Online]. https://bit.ly/40QMaCN

Shea, B. (2015). "Capitalism and the new economic model: Implicit and explicit attitudes of protesters and bankers". *Social Movement Studies,* 14(3):311-330. https://doi.org/10.1080/14742837.2014.938732

Skjaervo, P.O. (2012). *The Spirit of Zoroastrianism.* New Haven, CT: Yale University Press.

Snedegar, K. (1998). "First fruits celebrations among the Nguni peoples of Southern Africa: An ethnoastronomical interpretation". *Journal of the History of Astronomy,* 29(23):1-7. https://doi.org/10.1177/002182869802902304

Stebbins, B. (2014). "Contemplation as leisure and non-leisure". *Leisure Reflections,* 11:1-3. https://doi.org/10.1057/9781137399731_2

Stencel, S. (2010). *Tolerance and tension: Islam and Christianity in sub-Saharan Africa.* New York, NY: Pew Research Center. https://pewrsr.ch/3GDWSVV

Strathern, P. (2001). *Mendeleyev's dream: The quest for elements.* San Francisco, CA: Gardener's Books

Thompson, M.J. (2014). "False consciousness reconsidered: A theory of defective social cognition". *Critical Sociology,* 41(3):449-461. https://doi.org/10.1177/0896920514528817

Tobin, P. (2010). The Bible and modern scholarship. In: J. Loftus (ed.). *The Christian delusion: Why faith fails,* 148-181. New York, NY: Prometheus Books.

Van Sertima, I. (1983). *The lost sciences of Africa.* Indexed African Journals Online. http//www.affrefovjo.net

Vijayalakshmi, N. (2019). "Behaviour modification techniques: An awareness study". *Shanlax International Journal of Education,* 7(2):20-24. https://doi.org/10.34293/education.v7i2.333

Weber, M. (1904). *The Protestant ethic and the spirit of capitalism.* London: Penguin.

Woodard, C. (2004). "The construct of courage: Categorization and measurement". *Consulting Psychology Journal Practice and Research,* 59(2):135-147.

Woolf, Virginia [1929] (1935). *A room of one's own,* 4. London: Hogarth Press.

www.ingramcontent.com/pod-product-compliance
Lightning Source LLC
Chambersburg PA
CBHW050744100426

42739CB00016BA/3438